# PROFILES IN COWARDICE IN THE TRUMP ERA

from the author of
*Profiles in Courage in the Trump Era*

# KENNETH FOARD MCCALLION

Also by Kenneth Foard McCallion:

*Shorham and the Rise and Fall of the Nuclear Power Industry*

*The Essential Guide to Donald Trump*

*Treason & Betrayal: The Rise and Fall of Individual-1*

*COVID-19: The Virus That Changed America and the World*

# PROFILES IN COWARDICE IN THE TRUMP ERA

Bryant Park Press
An imprint of HHI Media,Inc.

from the author of
*Profiles in Courage in the Trump Era*

# KENNETH FOARD MCCALLION

Bryant Park Press
An imprint of HHI Media, Inc.

Copyright © 2021 by Kenneth Foard McCallion
Published by Bryant Park Press

All rights reserved, including the rights to reproduce this book or portions thereof in any form whatsoever.

For information about permissions,
email permissions@hhimedia.net
or submit request by facsimile to +1646-366-1384

www.hhimedia.net

www.kennethmccallionauthor.com

Jacket and Book Design by Christopher Klaich

Manufactured in the United States of America

ISBN: 978-1-7371492-1-7

# ACKNOWLEDGMENTS

This book would not have been possible without the assistance of Aaron Jerome and Anna Freymann, who did much of the painstaking research, fact-checking, and countless edits. A special thanks to my editor, Alexandra Uth, who has made me a better writer and to Christopher Klaich for his excellent design work.

# TABLE OF CONTENTS

## VICE PRESIDENT MIKE PENCE ....................................................... 1

## TRUMP'S SENATE ENABLERS ..................................................... 11
Mitch McConnell – Kentucky ............................................................... 14
Josh Hawley – Missouri ......................................................................... 20
Ted Cruz – Texas .................................................................................... 22
Lindsey Graham – South Carolina ...................................................... 25
Lamar Alexander – Tennessee ............................................................. 27
Robert "Rob" Portman – Ohio ............................................................. 28
Ron Johnson – Wisconsin ..................................................................... 30

## TRUMP'S HOUSE OF REPRESENTATIVES ENABLERS ............. 33
Kevin McCarthy – California ............................................................... 36
The House Sedition Caucus .................................................................. 38
The House QAnon Caucus .................................................................... 41
Lauren Boebert – Colorado ................................................................... 44

## TRUMP'S "HERD IMMUNITY" GANG ........................................... 47
Paul Alexander ....................................................................................... 48
Michael Caputo ...................................................................................... 50
Scott Atlas ............................................................................................... 53
Dr. Deborah Birx ................................................................................... 54
Ronny Jackson ....................................................................................... 57

## TRUMP'S CABINET ............................................................................ 59
Attorney General William P. Barr ....................................................... 60
Michael R. Pompeo ................................................................................ 73

EPA Administrator Scott Pruitt ..................................................................75
HUD Secretary Dr. Ben Carson ..................................................................78
Commerce Secretary Wilber Ross ..............................................................80
Interior Secretary Ryan Zinke ....................................................................84
Education Secretary Betsy DeVos ..............................................................88
Transportation Secretary Elaine Chao ......................................................91

## TRUMP'S SENIOR ADVISORS .................................................. 95
Kellyanne Conway .......................................................................................96
Stephen K. Bannon ....................................................................................101
Stephen Miller ............................................................................................108
Peter Navarro .............................................................................................111

## ALL THE PRESIDENT'S LIARS ............................................... 115
Sean Spicer .................................................................................................116
Sarah Sanders .............................................................................................121
Kayleigh McEnany ....................................................................................125

## TRUMP'S LAWYERS ............................................................... 131
Rudolph Giuliani .......................................................................................132
Sidney Powell ............................................................................................143
L. Lin Woods .............................................................................................146

## TRUMP'S FELONS ................................................................... 149
Roger Stone ...............................................................................................150
Paul Manafort ............................................................................................155
Michael J. Flynn ........................................................................................160
Rick Gates ..................................................................................................162
George Papadopoulos ...............................................................................162
George Nader .............................................................................................162
Alex van der Zwaan ...................................................................................163
Michael D. Cohen .....................................................................................163

## TRUMP'S CORPORATE BOOSTERS ...................................... 165
Cambridge Analytica ................................................................................166

My Pillow, Inc. ................................................................................ 168
Goya Foods, Inc. ............................................................................. 170
**CONCLUSION** ................................................................... 173
**ENDNOTES**.......................................................................... 175

# PREFACE

In my companion book, *Profiles in Courage in the Trump Era*, I discussed some of the most notable examples of men and women in government who displayed the courage to do what was right and what was in the best interests of the country despite the extraordinary pressures brought to bear on them by former President Trump and others to do otherwise.

This book is the reverse side of the coin. It is about those men and women who lost their moral bearings in the maelstrom of the Trump administration and put their own self-interests and that of a rogue president over the higher duties to the U.S. Constitution, their oaths of office, their fellow citizens and their country. This book will hopefully help to keep their names in the country's consciousness, so that their infamy can serve as an example for generations to come. Joining the ranks of America's first great traitor Benedict Arnold, these men and women who betrayed their country and put our constitutional republic in peril will always be remembered for their slavish service to their own self-interests and that of a would-be authoritarian megalomaniac who nearly succeeded in irredeemably eroding the pillars of our democratic system.

Greenwich, Connecticut                                    Kenneth F. McCallion

June 15, 2021

*Those who can make you believe absurdities, can make you commit atrocities*

**– Voltaire**

*So maybe it is for the best that they stand up and be counted. Maybe it is best for Americans to know who will 'support and defend the Constitution of the United States against all enemies, foreign and domestic'—and who will not. By all means, let's engrave their names into a marble slab—a roll call of those who failed the most important test of self-government in our lifetimes. There are a lot of monuments honoring bravery. Let's have one dedicated to abject cowardice.*

**– Michael Gersen, *The Washington Post*** [1]

# VICE PRESIDENT MIKE PENCE

After his near-death experience at the hands of a pro-Trump mob that stormed the U.S. Capitol on January 6, 2021 and was seeking to hang him, Vice President Mike Pence would be the last person you would expect to take the lead in perpetuating the dangerously false myth that the 2020 election was stolen by President Joe Biden and his Democratic allies. And yet, on March 3, 2021, Pence broke his silence by writing an op-ed piece for the *Daily Signal*. The piece opposed HR 1, the voting rights bill backed by House Democrats, which proposed what Republicans believed was the radical and dangerous concept that American voters should be encouraged to vote and that the procedures should make it as easy as possible to do so.

Pence's op-ed started out by stating: "After an election marked by significant voting irregularities and numerous instances of officials setting aside state election law, I share the concerns of millions of Americans about the integrity of the 2020 election."[1] This remarkable (and totally false) reference to "significant voting irregularities" put Pence exactly where he decided he wanted to be if he expected to have any future in the Republican Party, which was now the 100% anti-democratic party seeking to cling to what remaining power it could through voter suppression efforts. Simply stated, Pence and the entire Republican Party leadership realized that the only way their party could avoid becoming a permanent minority party of right-wing conspiracy theorists, white nationalists, and xenophobic populists was if the states sharply restricted voting rights. This meant requiring photo ID, signature verifications, restrictions on mail-in and absentee voting, and other Jim Crow-type laws that discouraged or prevented voters who aren't white from exercising their voting franchise. In order to justify these restrictions, they first had to promulgate and perpetuate Trump's Big Lie, which was that the 2020 election was rigged and stolen from Trump through massive election fraud.

Across the country, Republican state legislators proposed hundreds of bills to do things such as scale back voting by mail, despite no evidence of substantial fraud with regard to mail-in voting or any other form of voting, and these voter suppression efforts became the number one priority for Republican-controlled legislatures in several key swing states.[2]

If former Vice President Pence had just restrained himself from jumping on the election fraud and companion voter suppression Republican bandwagon after Trump lost the 2020 election, he would have gone down in history as one of the preeminent examples of profiles in courage during the Trump era. After all, he had resisted extreme pressure from Trump to invalidate enough state electoral slates to swing the election results away from Biden and to Trump on January 6, 2021. But Pence, to his credit, performed his constitutional responsibility on January 6 by correctly certifying the actual election result, not the fictitious one that Trump was angling for. Pence then paid the price for it by being vilified by Trump and being hunted down inside the Capitol on January 6 by a mob shouting, "Hang Mike Pence!"[3]

Before the fleeting courage he displayed during the counting of the electoral votes in Congress on January 6, there had been nothing particularly extraordinary about Mike Pence's tenure as vice president. He displayed a seemingly limitless ability to quietly sit on the sidelines as President Trump wildly careened from one crisis to another, usually of his own making. Pence remained silent even as his boss insisted on picking fights with our country's friends in NATO and elsewhere around the globe while, at the same time, cozying up to President Vladimir Putin of Russia, Supreme Leader Kim Jong-un of North Korea, and other despots that he clearly admired and wished to emulate. Pence's dedication to the president seemed limitless, and no controversy—not the *Access Hollywood* tape, the Ukraine scandal, nor the St. John's church photo op with an upside-down Bible—ever caused Pence to break with Trump or even try to put a little daylight between them.

For four long years, Pence watched this disastrous combination of White House soap opera and reality TV show with perfect equanimity. No matter how outrageous the president's words or actions, he stood by his man with a smile permanently affixed to his face and never a single hair on his perfectly coiffed head out of place. His legendary equanimity was forever memorialized when a large fly landed on his head for a full two minutes during a televised debate with now Vice President Kamala Harris. Pence never flinched, causing the fly to eventually give up from boredom, flying off in search of a more interesting venue.

Pence came direct from central casting for his role as vice president, displaying all of the qualities that we would expect of someone playing the part of second fiddle to the leader of the free world. He was disciplined, always on message, and loyal to a fault. But then, through no fault of his own, all of the goodwill that he built up with the president and his supporters over a long and stressful four years was put into jeopardy on one fateful day: January 6, 2021.

The vice president, as we all know by now, does not generally have any real responsibilities other than to stay alive and be available to step up in the event that the president dies or is disabled. Thus, the vice president is literally "only one heartbeat away from the presidency." However, the office has been less generously described by John Nance "Cactus Jack" Garner, Franklin D. Roosevelt's running mate in 1932, as "not worth a bucket of warm spit."

While Garner's description is memorable, it is not entirely accurate. The vice president also serves as president of the Senate, which requires him or her to do two things. First of all, he or she has to break any tie vote in the Senate with the deciding vote. Secondly, every four years, on the sixth day of January of the year following a presidential election, the vice president must preside over a pro forma certification of the Electoral College vote and formally announce who will be the next president to be sworn in on January 20.

As you may guess, this is a job any sixth-grader could handle, since it only requires the ability to add up the number of state electors for one of the candidates (in this case, President Trump), add up the number of electors for the opposing candidate (in this case, Joe Biden), and then declare the one with 270 or more electoral votes to be the winner of the presidential election. Sounds simple, right? The answer is "yes"—usually. But the 2020 election in the Trump era was anything but usual. After losing to Biden, Trump clung to the fantasy that he could retain power and continue to occupy the White House by alleging, without any basis in fact, that there had been widespread voter fraud and that the election had been stolen from him.

Trump's scheme to overturn the 2020 election results failed to win the support of Republican state election officials and governors in key states. Even the Republican-controlled legislatures would not help him in dumping the Biden electoral slates and replacing them with Trump electors. President Trump was quickly running out of time and options. The 60 or so election challenges brought by Rudy Giuliani and the rest of his legal gang-that-couldn't-shoot-straight failed miserably in one after another state and federal court. These election challenges failed even in courts where Republican elected or appointed judges presided. These state and federal judges almost uniformly refused to reverse the election results in states where Biden had won narrow victories. This was not especially surprising, since judges are sworn to make decisions based upon the facts presented and the applicable law, and the Trump campaign and pro-Trump lawyers failed miserably in presenting any evidence of widespread fraud in support of their specious claims of voting irregularities. As long as they were not biased and uninfluenced by political consideration, even these Republican appointed or elected judges could not rule in favor of the Trump team while, at the same time, upholding the rule of law and their oaths to act impartially.

This left Trump with only one last line of defense before he had to suffer the shame and ignominy of vacating the White House. The label that Trump always liked to pin on any adversary or critic was "Loser," and he could not bear the thought that such a label would finally, at long last, be applied to him as well. Only Vice President Mike Pence and the Republican members of Congress who were willing to usurp the Constitution and overturn the election results could snatch victory from the jaws of defeat. All Pence had to do was violate his oath of office and do something that the Constitution did not permit him to do, which was to discard the Biden slates of electors submitted to Congress by Arizona and Pennsylvania and perhaps other states. Then Pence, as the president of the Senate, would recognize Trump's bogus slates of electors for those states and declare Donald J. Trump as the once and future president of the United States. That, anyway, was the plan. This was Vice President Pence's ultimate loyalty test: either back Trump and overturn the election results or incur the wrath of Trump and his increasingly agitated supporters by ratifying the victory of Joe Biden as required by the Constitution and federal law. Trump felt he could count on Pence this one last time and with good reason: Pence had done his bidding up to that point, so why would he dare cross Trump this time?

The first signs of trouble for Trump from his erstwhile loyal factotum and vice president came when a federal lawsuit was filed against Pence in late December 2020 by Republican congressman Louie Gohmert and 11 other Arizona Republicans who would have become presidential electors had Trump actually won that state. The plaintiffs sought to give the vice president the power to reject state-certified presidential electors in favor of "competing slates of electors" so that Biden's victory over Trump could be overturned.[4] The U.S. Department of Justice represented Pence in this case, and in arguing for its dismissal stated that the lawsuit was a "walking legal contradiction" because it sought to grant powers to the vice president not found in the Constitution while, at the same time, suing the vice president.[5] Within a week, the lawsuit was dismissed in the U.S. District Court for the Eastern District of Texas, and the appeal was rejected by the United States Court of Appeals for the Fifth Circuit panel. Both courts held that the plaintiffs lacked standing to sue Pence.[6] Gohmert then appealed to the Supreme Court, which on January 7 summarily denied his petition.[7]

In the days preceding the Joint Session of Congress that the vice president would be presiding over on January 6, Trump ratcheted up the pressure on Pence to go along with the plot to overturn the election results and prevent the Biden-Harris team from being certified. Trump publicly stated that he expected Pence to use his position to overturn the election results in swing states and declare Trump-Pence the winners of the election.[8] Pence told Trump that the relevant portions of the Constitution and federal law did not give him that power.[9] Trump ignored him, publicly insisting: "The Vice President and I are in total agreement that the Vice President has the power to act."[10]

Before the start of the Joint Session, however, Pence stated in a letter to Congress that the Constitution prevented him from deciding which electoral votes should be counted and which should not, writing that "vesting the Vice President with unilateral authority to decide presidential contests would be entirely antithetical to" the system of checks and balances between branches of the government designed by the framers of the Constitution.[11] He concluded: "The Presidency belongs to the American people, and to them alone."[12]

Trump must have thought he was bluffing, and that when push came to shove, Pence would fold like a rusty lawn chair and go along with the program carefully orchestrated by Trump loyalists in the Senate and in the House. After all, Pence had gone along with Trump on everything up until then. Trump would tell his vice president to jump, and Pence would ask, "How high?" This was just one more bridge for them to cross together. Much to Trump's dismay, however, this one was a bridge too far for Pence.

On the morning of January 6, the day on which a joint session of Congress met to count and certify the results of the electoral college for the 2020 presidential election, Trump held a rally near the White House at which he urged his assembled army of supporters to march on the Capitol, repeatedly expressing the expectation that Pence would "do the right thing."[13] His MAGA troops then marched to the Capitol at the president's direction and stormed it. Some rioters were overheard saying they wanted to seize Pence and lynch him, with many others loudly shouting that he should be executed.[14]

The bloodthirsty mob of rioters searching the U.S. Capitol for Pence missed him by only a matter of seconds. *The Washington Post* reported on January 15 that Pence came "dangerously close" to the rioters during their occupation of the Capitol. He was not evacuated from the Senate chambers until fourteen minutes after the initial breach of the Capitol was reported. He and his family were eventually ushered from the Senate chambers into a second-floor hideaway, but only in the nick of time.[15] One minute later, the mob rushed onto a stair landing only 100 feet away, from which they could have seen him enter the room if they had arrived a minute earlier.[16] Pence later approved the deployment of the National Guard after Trump delayed taking that action and after frantic calls to the White House informing Trump's staff that many of the members of Congress were trapped in various rooms and could not leave until relief forces arrived.[17]

This January 6 insurrection at the Capitol, and the plot to prevent the certification of the election results that day, were without precedent in American history. The closest equivalent was the 1860 presidential election, after which seven Southern states seceded because they objected to the election of President Abraham Lincoln. After Lincoln's inauguration, four more states joined the newly formed Confederate States of America, and two others partially seceded. And yet none of the seceding states or their elected representative in Congress claimed that Lincoln's victory was illegitimate or stolen. Nor did anyone ever argue that Lincoln's predecessor, the pro-slavery James Buchanan, should remain in office after the election. Until Trump, there had never been a sitting president who encouraged his supporters to forcibly stop the certification of a presidential election so he could stay in office.

Fortuitously, neither the vice president nor any of the members of Congress were seized by the mob, and none were physically injured. While still holed up in a secure room in the Capitol, Pence defiantly tweeted that "the violence and destruction taking place at the US Capitol Must Stop and it Must Stop Now. Anyone involved must respect Law Enforcement officers and immediately leave the building."[18] Trump was in his radio silence mode at that point, waiting to see which way the pendulum would swing. If the insurrection succeeded, he would be the beneficiary of it. If it failed, he would deny responsibility.

While his vice president was still in peril of being captured and killed by the pro-Trump mob ransacking the Capitol, Trump unleashed a torrent of invective, attacking Pence for not doing his utmost to illegally overturn the results of the election. "Mike Pence didn't have the courage to do what should have been done to protect our Country and our Constitution, giving States a chance to certify a corrected set of facts, not the fraudulent or inaccurate ones which they were asked to previously certify. USA demands the truth!" Trump tweeted.[19] L. Lin Wood, a Georgia lawyer associated with Trump, was more explicit as to what should happen to the vice president, calling for Pence to be "executed" by "firing squad."[20] A gallows and a noose was actually erected just outside the Capitol.

In spite of the mortal danger that Pence was in, Trump never contacted him during the siege of the Capitol to inquire as to his well-being or that of his family members who were with him.[21] It appeared to knowledgeable observers that Pence was being set up as a scapegoat for Trump's failure to overturn the results of the election.[22] Pence was understandably angry with Trump, but still held his tongue.[23] What he did do was more important than what he said, anyway. After the Capitol was cleared and Congress reconvened on the evening of January 6, Pence declared Biden and Harris the winners after Republican objections were voted down.[24] He also bluntly told the rioters: "You did not win."[25]

Trump probably wishes in retrospect that he had chosen a vice president even more compliant than Mike Pence. It is likely that he will forever blame Pence for letting him down. Just when the Trump-incited insurrection was on the brink of success and needed him the most, Pence hesitated to jump on board, using the excuse that what Trump was asking for was not permitted by the Constitution.

For the rest of us, however, Pence's decision to do his constitutional duty on January 6, 2021 was a historic moment of truth for the country. When Vice President Pence certified the actual 2020 election results (rather than the phony ones that Trump was looking for), all Americans grounded in reality and in favor of the continuation of our noble democratic experiment breathed a collective sigh of relief.

Vice President Pence and second lady Karen Pence then stood by at the inaugural ceremony for President-elect Joe Biden on January 20, from which outgoing President Trump was noticeably absent. Although these were courageous acts, Pence incurred the wrath of both Trump and his diehard base. As Trump re-emerged as the odds-on favorite to be the 2024 Republican presidential nominee, there was talk circulating that Trump would dump Pence as his vice-presidential candidate, since Pence had shown himself to be disloyal to Trump by refusing to violate his oath of office and constitutional responsibilities.

Pence squandered his opportunity to be remembered for all time as a great American hero, however, by cravenly falling back into lockstep with the other Republican Trumpists who felt it was necessary for their own political survival to reaffirm their allegiance to the Big Lie that there was rampant election fraud in the country and that sharply restrictive voting laws needed to be urgently enacted to combat this fictitious scourge upon our nation.

# TRUMP'S SENATE ENABLERS

*Some Republicans have been forced to face their biggest fear: reality.*

– Stephen Colbert – December 15, 2020

Republican Senate Majority Leader Mitch McConnell belatedly acknowledged President-elect Joe Biden's electoral victory on Tuesday, December 15, 2020—42 days after the election and 36 days after even Fox News, the Trump administration's unofficial news network, had declared Biden the winner of the 2020 presidential election.[1] The Fox News announcement came after the Associated Press, CNN, and MSNBC had already made the call, and only an hour after Trump falsely tweeted that he had won the 2020 election by "A LOT."[2]

Notwithstanding McConnell's belated acceptance of reality, Senate Republicans—with the few limited exceptions noted in the companion book *Profiles in Courage in the Trump Era*—completely sacrificed their honor, decency, and legislative independence during Trump's entire presidential term. This craven obsequiousness to the Great Orange One in the White House was somewhat surprising, since at least some of the Senate Republicans had reasonably distinguished records prior to the Trump era. Others had run against Trump in the 2016 presidential primary, such as Marco Rubio, Ted Cruz, and Lindsey Graham, and had accurately portrayed him as the despicable human being he was. Lindsay Graham perhaps summed up the prevailing establishment Republican view of candidate Trump, describing him as "a race-baiting, xenophobic, religious bigot,"[3] adding, "He doesn't represent my party. He doesn't represent the values that the men and women who wear the uniform are fighting for. He's the ISIL man of the year."[4] Graham also prophetically warned in 2016: "If we nominate Trump, we will get destroyed. . . . and we will deserve it."[5]

Similarly, Ted Cruz called Trump a "serial philanderer," while Trump insulted "Lyin' Ted" Cruz's faith, his family, his wife, and suggested that Cruz's father was connected with Lee Harvey Oswald, the man who assassinated President John F. Kennedy.[6] Trump floated a birther rumor about Cruz's supposed birth in Canada, thus making him ineligible to serve as the U.S. president.[7]

Trump continually belittled Florida Senator Marco Rubio during the 2016 primary, referring to him as "Little Marco,"[8] with Rubio responding in kind with a series of personal attacks, including "Donald is not going to make America great, he's going to make America orange!"[9]

Nevertheless, as soon as Trump became the Republican presidential nominee in the summer of 2016, all three of these senators and the rest of their Republican colleagues in the Senate fell into line, groveling before him as if he were some kind of modern-day Napoleon, rather than just some glib reality TV star and phony billionaire. It was politically expedient for them to remain silent and to refuse to condemn Trump's habitual lying and his coddling of dictators overseas and racist criminals at home, as well as his disdain for democracy and the rule of law. They supported him when he tried to gut the defense budget in order to divert funds for a worthless border wall that the country didn't need. They supported him when he was caught attempting to blackmail Ukraine's president into helping him dig up political dirt on Joe Biden that could be used against him in the 2020 campaign. They supported him when his response to the greatest public health calamity in a century was to say, "It's going to disappear."[10] Finally, and unforgivably, they supported him when he promoted the dangerous fiction that he had actually won the 2020 election and refused to condemn him when he unleashed a mob of insurrectionists on the capital in an attempt to subvert the will of the American people.

Eight Senate Republicans joined with 139 House Republicans in voting *not* to certify the election results in at least one state, even after a pro-Trump mob sacked the U.S. Capitol on January 6, 2021 with the goal of usurping the election for Trump. Although Mitch McConnell and some other Republican senators actually voted—at the eleventh hour—to certify Joe Biden as the 2020 election victor, their votes were too little, too late to salvage their reputations as cowardly Trump enablers for the entire four years of his presidency.

Democracy did not prevail that fateful day just because Mitch McConnell and a few other Trump apologists in the Senate finally put a stop to the Republican madness. The cold harsh fact is that our democracy barely survived. It is now time for a full reckoning, and responsibility must be squarely placed where it belongs: with Trump and his anti-democratic Republican cronies.

## Mitch McConnell – Kentucky

When you make a deal with the devil, the devil will eventually have his due. Mitch McConnell made his deal with Trump early on in the administration when he tacitly agreed to go along with whatever senseless and harmful policy emanated from the White House. McConnell was perfectly happy as long as Trump gave him a free hand to pursue his three most cherished goals: to control the senate as majority leader, to continue to pass massive tax cuts for the rich; and to confirm conservative judges that would control the Supreme Court and federal judiciary for at least one or two generations. This was, however, a Faustian bargain. The price, as McConnell finally realized on January 6, 2021, was the near destruction of our constitutional democracy and the rule of law.

Notwithstanding the national near-death experience he facilitated, McConnell will surely go down in history as one of the Republican Party's most successful leaders in the filling of federal judgeships and Supreme Court openings with conservative judges and Federalist Society faithful. He also did an outstanding job in achieving the perennial priority of the Republican Party: tax breaks for the super-rich. During the Trump era, the rich and uber-rich never did better, and there was little or no concern in Republican establishment circles for the dangerously accelerating income and wealth gap in the country.

But these accomplishments came at an extraordinarily high price. It resulted in the degradation and transformation of the once proud and principled Republican Party into the Party of Trump. In the end, it stood for nothing more than the holding of raw political power. Remember the days when Republicans would wring their hands over deficit spending and were the chief proponents of free trade? No longer. As "Never Trumper" Republican Steve Schmidt aptly put it: "The Republican party of Teddy Roosevelt and John McCain and Ronald Reagan and George W. Bush is dead. It's over. It doesn't exist anymore. It has been taken over, lock, stock, and barrel [by Trump]."[11]

The Republican Party under McConnell's leadership was once staunchly anti-Communist and deeply suspicious of the Soviet Union and its successor, the Russian Federation. However, under Trump, McConnell had no problem with his party taking a 180 degree turn and blindly following the lead of an avowed Russia-phile. For some odd reason, Trump could never bring himself to criticize Russia, the country's longstanding geopolitical adversary, or to acknowledge that it interfered with the 2016 election. McConnell was even willing to live with the well-deserved nickname of Moscow Mitch in order to remain in the good graces of the White House, as he opposed any serious effort to investigate the depths of Russian interference in this country's electoral processes. McConnell also presided over what had previously been known as a free trade party, but under Trump, was now advocating aggressive protectionism, xenophobia and tariffs.

In the 2020 elections, the Republican Party did not even take the trouble to adopt a platform of principles and policies. Rather, the platform was Trump's cult of personality. Old-school conservative Republican philosophies of limited government and the promotion of unfettered free enterprise were rarely spoken of in the Trump era. Voter registration drives were largely tabled as a waste of time or even a threat, since it was now widely understood that the only way for the Party of Trump to retain power was to intensify its voter suppression efforts and double down on the gerrymandering of safe Republican districts. In the end, McConnell and his party followed only one political philosophy: the ends justify the means. Period. Full stop.

The atrophied Republican Party also had to open its gates to every racist, crackpot, and conspiracy theorist, including the new QAnon Caucus members of Congress, such as Marjorie Taylor Greene of Georgia and Lauren Boebart of Colorado, who believe that 9/11 was a hoax, and that the mass murders of students and teachers at Sandy Hook Elementary School in Newtown, Connecticut and Marjory Stoneman Douglas High School in Parkland, Florida were staged "false flag" non-events concocted by gun control advocates.[12]

The Republican Party also ended up with blood on its hands as of January 6, 2021, when its moral bankruptcy and cynical opportunism in promoting Trump's nonsensical election fraud theories became the Frankenstein monster that almost destroyed the U.S. Capitol. The efforts by Trump's band of alternative reality and morally bankrupt lawyers—including Rudy Giuliani, Sidney Powell, and L. Lin Woods—were abysmally unsuccessful in persuading courts, election officials, and state legislators that the election results should be reversed, and the incumbent should be given another four-year term even though he lost. The insurrection and the assault on the country's seat of democracy were the natural, and perhaps inevitable, result of the insistence by some Republican senators and representatives to play along with this charade.

On January 6, McConnell finally realized that the cynical political game played by Trump and the Republicans since election day on November 3, 2020, was getting out of hand and had fueled a full-fledged treasonous insurrection. He sanctimoniously intoned on the Senate floor as he prepared to support the certification of Biden's victory, "I've served 36 years in the Senate. This will be the most important vote I've ever cast."[13] But it was too late. The genie was out of the bottle and the gates of Congress were moments away from being breached by a blood-thirsty mob looking to hang, shoot, and otherwise kill the country's elected representatives gathered to perform their constitutional duty.

After having remained silent for weeks following the November election, McConnell finally said what he should have been saying long before about Congress's limited role in the election process: "We cannot simply declare ourselves a national board of elections on steroids. The voters, the courts and the states have all spoken. If we overrule them, it will damage our Republic forever."[14] On February 13, 2021, in a speech on the Senate floor after he and most of his Republican colleagues had voted in favor of Trump's acquittal in the second impeachment trial, McConnell shed crocodile tears over the four-year Trump debacle, as if he had nothing to do with enabling the now departed president from inflicting maximum damage on the country's body politic. His speech was nothing more than sanctimonious political theater, a simulation of moral righteousness to appease some moderates after having cynically facilitated the Trump program throughout his administration.

Typically, McConnell was too clever by half. After repeatedly leaking to the press that he was considering voting for Trump's conviction at his second impeachment trial, McConnell spinelessly voted not guilty along with all but seven of his Republican Senate colleagues. After the vote, in his totally disingenuous speech, he castigated Trump's conduct, railing against the "outgoing president who seemed determined to either overturn the voters' decision or else torch our institutions on the way out."[15] It was a surreal experience for his fellow citizens watching Dr. Jekyll speak on the Senate floor only a few minutes after Mr. Hyde had voted to acquit the former president, whom he was now denouncing.

Notwithstanding McConnell's two-faced reaction to the capitol insurrection, his indelible legacy as Republican Senate majority leader during the Trump era will be that he did more to damage American democracy than any other person, with the possible exception of Trump himself. He displayed a savvy but toxic mix of craven obsequiousness, political opportunism, and absence of moral character that was truly shocking, even in an era where expectations of our elected leaders are pathetically low.

Before the ascendency of Trump, McConnell had been the chief architect of the Republican scorched earth obstructionist policy from day one of the Obama presidency. In October 2010, McConnell said that "the single most important thing we want to achieve is for President Obama to be a one-term president."[16] *The New York Times* noted early in the Obama years that "on the major issues—not just health care, but financial regulation and the economic stimulus package, among others—Mr. McConnell has held Republican defections to somewhere between minimal and nonexistent, allowing him to slow the Democratic agenda if not defeat aspects of it."[17] Under McConnell, the Republican caucus repeatedly threatened to force the United States to default on its debt, with McConnell saying that the debt ceiling was "a hostage that's worth ransoming."[18] McConnell worked particularly hard to delay and obstruct health care and banking reforms, two of the most notable pieces of legislation that Democrats were seeking to push through Congress early in the Obama years.[19]

In February 2016, when Supreme Court justice Antonin Scalia died, McConnell issued a statement indicating that the U.S. Senate would not consider any Supreme Court nominee put forth by Obama, saying that "this vacancy should not be filled until we have a new president."[20] On March 16, 2016, President Obama nominated Merrick Garland, a highly respected judge of the D.C. Circuit Court of Appeals, to the Supreme Court.[21] Under McConnell's direction, Senate Republicans took the unprecedented step of refusing to consider any nominees or to take any action on the Garland nomination, successfully killing it and turning Supreme Court nominations into a zero-sum battleground.[22]

In January 2017, after the newly sworn-in President Trump nominated Neil Gorsuch to fill the Supreme Court vacancy still open since Scalia's death, McConnell eliminated the filibuster on Supreme Court nominees in order to ram the nomination through the Senate.[23] In July 2018, President Trump nominated Brett Kavanaugh to replace the retiring Anthony Kennedy as an associate justice of the Supreme Court. Kavanaugh was confirmed on October 6, 2018.[24]

In October 2018, McConnell said that if a Supreme Court vacancy were to occur during Trump's 2020 re-election year, he would follow his 2016 decision to let the winner of the upcoming presidential election nominate a justice. He was lying. In September 2020, following the death of Ruth Bader Ginsburg, he announced the Senate would vote on Trump's nominated replacement.[25] This was only two months before the November 3 presidential election. McConnell then set in motion the Senate debate for the confirmation of Amy Coney Barrett to fill Ginsburg's seat, leading to her confirmation on October 26.[26]

During Trump's first impeachment proceedings, McConnell disregarded his oath to act as an impartial juror in the Senate impeachment trial by publicly announcing that he would be working closely with the Trump team to acquit the president. For example, on November 5, 2019, as the House of Representatives began public hearings on the impeachment of President Trump, McConnell stated "I will say I'm pretty sure how [an impeachment trial is] likely to end. . . . If it were today, I don't think there's any question it would not lead to" the removal of President Trump from office.[27] On December 14, 2019, after meeting with White House counsel Pat Cipollone and White House legislative affairs director Eric Ueland, McConnell declared that, for Trump's impeachment trial, he would be in "total coordination with the White House counsel's office" and Trump's representatives.[28] He also declared that there was "no chance" that the Senate would convict Trump and remove him from office, effectively turning the impeachment trial into a kangaroo court.[29]

Three days later, on December 17, McConnell rejected a request to call four witnesses for Trump's impeachment trial, saying that the Senate's role was to "act as judge and jury," not to investigate.[30] Later that day, McConnell told the media: "I'm not an impartial juror [in this impeachment trial]. This is a political process. There's not anything judicial about it."[31]

In response to the COVID-19 pandemic, McConnell initially opposed the Families First Coronavirus Response Act, calling it a Democratic "ideological wish list."[32] He subsequently reversed his position, but only after Trump endorsed the proposed package.[33] The bill passed in the Senate by a vote of 90–8.

After the CARES Act—the largest economic stimulus package in U.S. history—passed both houses of Congress with bipartisan support, McConnell inexplicably waited several months before advancing any additional coronavirus relief measures in the Senate. He failed to do so even after the House had passed another substantial relief package months earlier.[34] In negotiations between congressional Democrats and White House officials for an additional coronavirus relief, McConnell was absent from the talks.[35]

Following Joe Biden's win in the 2020 presidential election, McConnell refused to recognize Biden as the winner of the election.[36] He also publicly defended Trump's failure to concede the results of the election.[37] In his public statements, McConnell did not repeat any of Trump's false claims of voter fraud, but he abnegated his responsibility as the leading Republican in Congress to contradict Trump and to make it clear that the election had been decided and the country had to move forward. Instead, he argued that Trump had the right to challenge the results.[38] At the same time McConnell refused to recognize Biden, he did celebrate Republicans who won their races in the Senate and the House in the same elections.[39]

Finally, on December 15, 2020, one day after the electoral college vote, McConnell belatedly acknowledged Biden's win, stating, "Today, I want to congratulate President-elect Joe Biden."[40] However, McConnell did nothing to stop or speak out against the Trump team's continuing efforts to set aside the 2020 election results. Nor did he do anything to stop the efforts of Republican Senators Josh Hawley and Ted Cruz to derail the counting of the electoral votes in Congress on January 6, 2021 through spurious claims that massive election fraud needed to be investigated by an Electoral Commission.

In short, McConnell shamefully abdicated any real leadership or statesmanship throughout his tenure as Senate majority leader and thus facilitated the rapid erosion of democracy during the Trump era.

## Josh Hawley – Missouri

One photo that will haunt Republican Senator Josh Hawley for the rest of his political career depicts him giving a clenched-fist salute of solidarity as he walked past the mob that was about to attack the U.S. Capitol on January 6, 2021. With the pro-Trump barbarians poised to storm the gates of Congress, Hawley then cynically asked his Senate colleagues "to address the concerns of so many millions of Americans" by investigating the 2020 vote.[41] What he and his Congressional co-conspirators knew, however, was that the public concerns about the legitimacy of the election results had been wholly manufactured by Trump and his loyal band of anti-democratic manipulators, including Hawley himself.

When Hawley persisted in pushing this charade even after the pro-Trump mob had overrun the Capitol, a fellow Republican colleague, Mitt Romney, rebuked him on the Senate floor. "Those who choose to continue to support [Trump's] dangerous gambit by objecting to the results of a legitimate democratic election will forever be seen as being complicit in an unprecedented attack against our democracy," Romney warned. "That will be their legacy," he added, looking in Hawley's direction.[42]

Meanwhile, back home in Missouri, the *Kansas City Star* editorial board declared that Hawley had "blood on his hands," for having masterminded the Electoral College challenge in the Senate that set the stage for the violent siege of the Capitol.[43] Their verdict: only Trump bore more responsibility than Hawley for this "Capitol coup" and "Assault on democracy."[44]

The *St. Louis Post-Dispatch*'s comments were equally harsh, calling for his resignation. "Senator Josh Hawley had the gall to stand before the Senate Wednesday night and feign shock, shock at what happened—hours after he had fist-pumped and cheered the rioters as they arrived on Capitol Hill," the editorial board wrote. "Hawley's tardy, cover-his-ass condemnation of the violence ranks at the top of his substantial list of phony, smarmy and politically expedient declarations." The *Star* further noted Hawley issued a political fundraising solicitation as the siege was underway.[45] As the mob was massing outside the Capitol building, he sent out an email blast to his past contributors, urging them to send him more money so that he could continue to "to relay [your] concerns to Washington."[46]

In widely circulated remarks, former Missouri Senator John Danforth, a Republican and Hawley's political mentor, told the *Associated Press*: "Supporting Josh Hawley . . . was the worst decision I've ever made in my life," adding, "He has consciously appealed to the worst. He has attempted to drive us apart and he has undermined public belief in our democracy. And that's great damage."[47]

Republican Senator Ben Sasse of Nebraska was less articulate in his response, but no less directly on point: "Senator Hawley was doing something that was really dumb-ass," Sasse told National Public Radio. "This was a stunt. It was a terrible, terrible idea. And you don't lie to the American people, and that's what's been going on."[48]

As it took a few days for the January 6 attack on the Capitol to sink into the American subconscious to almost the same level of horror as the September 11, 2001 terrorist attack, Hawley and his Republican Senate colleague Ted Cruz continued to be on the receiving end of much of the blame for this unprecedented assault on the citadel of American democracy. They calculated that it was in their best political interests to continue the charade of challenging Joe Biden's election even after the pro-Trump insurrectionists had succeeded in overrunning much of the Capitol building, leaving death and destruction in their wake.

Hawley, who defeated Democrat Senator Claire McCaskill in 2018, was already being touted by the Republican establishment as a rising star. The ambitious and photogenic Stanford and Yale-educated lawyer was being compared to John F. Kennedy, another Ivy League-educated senator who rose to the presidency at a young age. But this was before Hawley made the calculated gamble to sign onto Trump's campaign to reverse the results of the election with false claims of fraud. Hawley was instrumental in forcing the House and the Senate to take votes on electoral slate challenges that were doomed to failure from the start. His cynical goal, however, was not to ultimately thwart President-elect Joe Biden's certification, but to delay and undermine its legitimacy, thereby winning him the undying gratitude of Trump and his supporters. It was apparently of no concern to Hawley that dozens of courts, state election officials, and even Trump's former attorney general Bill Barr had said there was no evidence of widespread election fraud.

Simon & Schuster reacted to Hawley's January 6 performance on the Senate floor by cancelling the publication of his upcoming book, *The Tyranny of Big Tech*. It said in a statement, "[W]e take seriously our larger public responsibility as citizens and cannot support Senator Hawley after his role in what became a dangerous threat to our democracy and freedom."[49]

## Ted Cruz – Texas

Republican Senator Ted Cruz of Texas, the runner-up behind Trump in the 2016 Republican presidential primaries, worked hard during the entire four years of the Trump presidency to establish himself in the minds of core Trump voters as his logical successor. Nothing was too demeaning for him in his quest to inherit the Trump mantle. He knew he had to work harder than most to achieve his inflated ambitions since he had a well-deserved reputation as a heartless, soulless, and morally bankrupt opportunist. He was probably the least-liked person in the Senate, with rumors circulating that that he was more heartless than most vampires. His smarmy style was as irritating to many as the screeching sound of fingernails being run across a blackboard.

In February 2021, as his home state of Texas was going into a deep freeze with widespread power outages and water treatment plants offline, Cruz and his family were photographed at the airport heading for a resort in Cancun, Mexico. The political optics were unfavorable, to say the least. A storm of outrage erupted, as reporters found his name on flight manifests. Twitter exploded with mocking hashtags including #FlyinTed, a take-off on Trump's famous twitter reference to Cruz as "Lyin' Ted." A photo went viral of the Cruz family poodle Snowflake staring forlornly out the front door of their empty home.

Cruz initially said that he left the state as a chaperone for his daughters, who wanted to go on a trip with friends, in order to be a good dad.[50] But within hours, that story was undercut by leaked text messages from the day before that showed Cruz's wife Heidi complaining about the "FREEZING" temperatures in her home and inviting friends and Houston neighbors to join her family at the Ritz-Carlton in Cancun, where, she said, rooms were only $309 a night.[51] Cruz quickly returned to sub-zero Texas so he could be photographed passing out water and food at an emergency relief center. Not that anyone was fooled by his staged charitable display. It just made him look more hypocritical.

So Cruz was the kind of person that people love to hate, but Cruz knew he had a natural credibility problem. There was little he could do to disguise the faintly sulfurous scent that followed him everywhere. But this only meant that he had to work harder than anyone to hold political power and advance his political career, openly scheming to eventually gain the Republican presidential nomination and grab the ultimate brass ring. Cruz had to out-dissemble Trump himself and other leading Trump supporters by shamelessly promoting the Big Lie, which was that Trump really won the 2020 election in a landslide and that it was stolen from him. While, of course, privately knowing that Biden had decisively won the 2020 election, Cruz cynically became one of the leading advocates of the "Stop the Steal" campaign to reverse the results of the election and deliver a second term to Trump.

Cruz was neither naïve nor stupid enough to actually believe the wild conspiracy theories being tossed around by the White House, Fox News, and other right-wing media talk shows. After all, he was a Harvard Law School graduate and former Texas solicitor general who had previously argued nine cases before the Supreme Court. Even though he well knew that there was no real legal or factual basis for the challenges to the Biden election victory, Cruz—like Hawley—saw it as an opportunity to further ingratiate himself with Trump and his diehard supporters, thus establishing himself as a leading defender of Trump's bogus election challenges. He even went so far as to publicly announce that he would plead the president's case before the U.S. Supreme Court if the opportunity arose.[52] The opportunity, however, did not arise since the Supreme Court summarily rejected a challenge to the 2020 election results filed by Texas Attorney General Ken Paxton and joined by 17 other Republican state attorneys general. But at least Cruz burnished his credentials as a Trump loyalist by letting it be known that he was willing to take this baseless election challenge campaign to the most dangerous of extremes, no matter what the consequences were in terms of undermining public faith in the integrity of the country's electoral processes.

In addition to his willingness to spout baseless theories of election fraud in the Supreme Court, Cruz also joined fellow power-hungry Republican

Senator Hawley in leading the charge against the otherwise ministerial task of counting Biden's electoral votes in Congress on January 6, 2021. They did so by first calling for a delay in the electoral vote count so that an election commission could be formed to investigate the presidential vote counts in Arizona, Pennsylvania, and perhaps other states. Failing this, Cruz, Hawley, and other Republican senators voted against the counting of the Biden electors in Arizona, Pennsylvania, or both, showing America they had the same subversive goal as the insurrectionist mob that had just stormed the Capitol earlier in the day: to overturn the election results through lies, subterfuge, and, if all else failed, violence.

In order to keep his 2024 presidential aspirations alive and to keep on Trump's good side, Cruz had a lot of making up to do. Their relationship got off to a rocky start in 2016 after Trump entered the Republican National Convention that summer with a decisive lead. Cruz was reluctant to endorse Trump in light of the bad blood and nastiness of the primary campaign. Trump had not only personally insulted Cruz himself, but also his father and wife. Trump shamefully suggested that Cruz's father, a Cuban-American, had conspired with Lee Harvey Oswald to assassinate President John F. Kennedy.[53] Despite such personal attacks, Cruz eventually threw his support behind Trump, even though he did not endorse him right away. Instead, he told his delegates at the 2016 Republican Convention to "vote their conscience."[54]

Cruz, a skilled debater, drew a false parallel between the Trump/Biden 2020 race and the Bush/Gore presidential election results in 2000, which, unlike the results of the 2020 election, were razor-thin in Florida. Cruz often pointed out that in 2000, due to the very small number of votes separating the two candidates in Florida, "nobody was saying in the month of November and early December [2000] 'George W. Bush is the president-elect, and how dare anyone dispute it?' No one was insisting, 'Al Gore has no right to litigate these results and present his legal claim.'"[55]

What Cruz well knew as a secretly rational person but would never acknowledge, was that there was no factual basis for Trump's continuing claims of massive election fraud. As Trump said in one of his fantastical "I won" videos after the 2020 election: "This election was rigged. Everybody knows it."[56] This was long after Biden was acknowledged as the winner by all major networks, as well as by every state election official and legislature of the key battleground states. And yet Ted Cruz, along with Josh Hawley and the other Congressional opportunists who were scheming to take political advantage of Trump's dangerous conspiracy theories, continued to provide a thin veneer of legitimacy and rationality to this toxic and combustible mix that exploded with the invasion of the Capitol building on January 6 and continued to inflame the country long afterwards.

## Lindsey Graham – South Carolina

During the Republican primary campaign of 2016, Senator Lindsey Graham of South Carolina called Donald Trump a "nutjob" and "a loser," as well as a "race-baiting, xenophobic, religious bigot."[57] Then, once Trump became the Republican nominee for president and was even more surprisingly elected as president, Graham became Trump's biggest fan and supporter, lavishing praise on him at every opportunity. The senator, who once prided himself on being known as John McCain's best friend, stood silently by while Trump shamelessly tore into the McCain name and legacy, both before and after his death.

Graham and Trump became virtually inseparable. They played golf. They talked on the phone. Graham had found a new BFF, and the bromance survived some very trying moments. Their relationship was temporarily strained when Trump decided—without consulting Graham—to pull U.S. troops out of Syria, leaving our Kurdish allies exposed to an inevitable Turkish invasion of the Kurdish-controlled areas. Graham was well known as one of the Kurds' most enthusiastic supporters. He felt betrayed that Trump would make such a consequential decision without discussing it with him.[58] But this odd couple worked their way through their rough patches, and Graham continued as Trump's most loyal and vocal supporter. After all, Graham had the president's ear, which gave him both the actual and perceived power he craved.

In order to preserve his position as Trump's point man, Graham had to give up all pretense of bipartisanship, which had previously been his claim to fame in the Senate. Graham had been a member of the cross-party "Gang of Eight" that successfully managed to pass an immigration bill extending a citizenship path to 11 million people. When Graham voted for Obama's

Supreme Court nominees Sonia Sotomayor and Elena Kagan, he was lauded as a great statesman by the media and Democrats but left himself open to a primary challenge from the right in deeply conservative South Carolina. However, in his new-found role as Trump's wingman, he has insulated himself from any primary challenge and virtually assured his reelection.

The price for the political security that Trump provided him was that Graham found himself acting as the chief advocate for Trump's most absurd pet projects, such as the border wall. Graham warned Republicans that abandoning Trump's cherished border wall posed an existential threat to the party. "If we undercut the president, that's the end of his presidency and the end of our party," he said hyperbolically.[59]

The hearings for Supreme Court nominee Brett Kavanaugh were a decisive turning point in Graham's political trajectory. At the hearings, Graham angrily blamed Democrats for overplaying their hand with the sexual assault allegations being raised against Kavanaugh. At one point, Graham ferociously accused Democrats on the Senate Judiciary Committee of perpetrating "the most despicable thing I have seen in my time in politics."[60] Trump was impressed with Graham's performance, but the door to any future bipartisanship involving Graham had been firmly slammed shut.

Graham's shapeshifting from a principled and bipartisan leader of the Senate to a Trump apologist became complete when he refused to criticize Trump's racist attacks on a group of four progressive Democratic congresswomen of color—including Alexandria Ocasio-Cortez of New York, Ilhan Omar of Minnesota, Ayanna Pressley of Massachusetts, and Rashida Tlaib of Michigan—known as "the Squad." Trump accused them of "hating America," suggesting that they should return to their countries of origin—which for most of them was the United States, since they were born here.[61] Graham mildly chided Trump, vaguely saying that he should try to "aim higher" when criticizing these women Democrats in Congress.[62] But he astutely refrained from any harsher critique.

*The View's* Meghan McCain, daughter of John McCain, lamented that Lindsay Graham, the man she once saw as an uncle and close family friend, was no longer the person she knew while growing up.[63] Rumors started circulating in Washington that Graham secretly had an evil twin brother who had taken control of the senator, and that the kind, thoughtful, and bipartisan Graham was being hidden away in a basement somewhere.[64]

Even after the Trump-incited attack on the Capitol on January 6, 2021, Graham continued to stand by his man. Following Trump's second impeachment for inciting insurrection, Graham put together a group of well-respected South Carolina lawyers to represent him in the Senate trial. However, Graham was deeply embarrassed when most of the legal team were forced to quit when Trump insisted that they argue that Trump had really won the election and that it had been stolen from him. The more lawyer-like argument was that the Senate trial was unconstitutional since Trump was by then a private citizen, but Trump would not countenance any defense that did not perpetuate the Big Lie.

In other words, Graham found out the hard way that Faustian bargains rarely end well. The price is high and the rewards often turn out to be illusory. Like most affairs, they end badly.

## Lamar Alexander – Tennesee

With experience, gravitas, and seniority, and as a soon-to-retire senator, Lamar Alexander was well-positioned to stand up to the insanity swirling around the Trump White House. But he did not. America desperately waited for someone of Alexander's stature to finally call Trump out, to finally say "Enough is enough" and that the country was fed up and tired of his lies, prevarications, and grandiosity.

Alexander, who announced his retirement from the Senate shortly after the November 2020 election, was a highly respected two-term governor of Tennessee, from 1979 to 1987; president of the University of Tennessee; and U.S. Secretary of Education from 1991 to 1993. First elected to the Senate in 2003, he was generally considered to be one of the most senior and widely respected members of the Republican caucus in the Senate. He had made a respectable run for the Republican presidential nomination in 1996, running on a platform calling for the creation of a "citizen Congress," filled with citizen-legislators more responsive to the American people and less committed to perpetuating their political careers in Washington, D.C.

Alexander's most shameful moment during the Trump Era came on January 31, 2020, during Trump's first Senate impeachment trial. He acknowledged that Trump had acted "inappropriately."[65] At the same time, he inexplicably voted against the motion to call witnesses, such as John Bolton, who had let it be publicly known that they would have testified at the Senate hearing if they had been subpoenaed to appear. Alexander tried to explain away his decision to join with the Senate Republican majority in not calling any witness by saying, "If you've got eight witnesses saying that you left the scene of an accident, you don't need nine."[66] However, the transparent weakness of this argument was that Bolton and some of the other witnesses were in a position to provide first-hand, eyewitnesses testimony of the critical events in question. Bolton, in his position as Trump's national security adviser, was personally asked by President Trump to help him shake down the Ukrainian government in exchange for dirt on former Vice President Joe Biden. Bolton's book—which had not yet been published—revealed that in May 2018 Trump directly instructed Bolton "to help with his pressure campaign to extract damaging information on Democrats from Ukrainian officials."[67] According to Bolton, the president asked him to call Ukrainian President Volodymyr Zelensky and ask him to work with Trump's personal attorney Rudy Giuliani, who was leading the effort to dig up dirt on Biden.

On February 6, 2020, by not joining with Republican Senator Mitt Romney in voting for the conviction of Trump on the impeachment charges for high crimes and misdemeanors relating to attempts to manipulate the Ukrainian government for his own partisan political purposes, Alexander clearly put his principles and obligations to the American people on hold out of misplaced partisan loyalty to the Republican president and his own party. After a lifetime of notable achievements, this one vote was more than just a missed opportunity. It is his enduring legacy.

## Robert "Rob" Portman – Ohio

Before being elected to the Senate in 2010, Republican Rob Portman was a much-admired House member who had also served as U.S. Trade Ambassador and director of the Office of Management and Budget for President George

W. Bush. During the Trump era, Portman rarely spoke out against Trump and went along with appointments he must have known were unacceptable, like approving the politically partisan John Ratcliffe for the sensitive post of director of National Intelligence.

Portman sought to justify his unwavering support for the Trump White House by saying that he was merely reflecting Ohio's strong support for the president. By that logic, however, Richard Nixon would have never been forced to resign the presidency and to leave Washington as a result of his Watergate crimes after winning his reelection bid on November 7, 1972 by taking 49 states—all but Massachusetts—in a landslide victory. Even after the Watergate scandal broke, Nixon still enjoyed widespread support among the Republican base, but that did not stop a group of senior Republican senators, including Barry Goldwater, from visiting Nixon at the White House and telling him that it was time for him to go, and that the Republican Congressional leadership was no longer willing to back him.

During Trump's second Senate impeachment trial, Portman followed the dodgeball strategy employed by Majority Leader Mitch McConnell and several of his Republican colleagues, which was to publicly decry Trump's incitement of the January 6, 2021 attack on the Capitol, but to vote "not guilty" on the impeachment charges on the ill-founded grounds that a former president cannot be found guilty of impeachment. Portman stated: "The question I must answer is not whether President Trump said and did things that were reckless and encouraged the mob [that invaded the Capitol]. I believe that happened. The threshold question I must answer is whether a former president can be convicted by the Senate in the context of an impeachment..."[68] Portman then answered his own question in the negative, saying, "I believe the Constitution reserves the narrow tool of impeachment and conviction for removal of current officeholders and current presidents, and does not apply to former officeholders or former presidents. Impeachment in the Constitution is fundamentally about removing someone from office."[69]

For a Michigan Law School graduate and highly intelligent person, Portman knew that this was not true, and that there was substantial precedent for the Senate to hold impeachment trials of former officeholders. Ex-Secretary of War William Belknap, who had been in Ulysses S. Grant's Cabinet following the Civil War, was impeached by the House and tried by the Senate. The Senate ended up not convicting Belknap, but the mere fact that he had resigned and left his office made no difference whatsoever at the trial held by the Senate.

And if the Belknap impeachment trial was not enough to convince Portman that Trump could properly be tried on the impeachment charges, the nonpartisan Congressional Research Service noted on January 15, 2021 "that most scholars who have closely examined the question have concluded that Congress has authority to extend the impeachment process to officials who are no longer in office."[70] There was also strong evidence that the Founders of our country knew that the British parliament did in fact impeach former officials, not just current ones. If, therefore, they wanted to bar impeachment trials of former officials, they would have said so. But they didn't.

It was clearly not any constitutional scruples that prevented Portman from voting to convict Trump for inciting the Capitol insurrection. Instead, he was disingenuously voting not to convict Trump so that he could glide effortlessly along the easy dodge pathway in order to avoid responsibility for voting in favor of a conviction that would effectively bar Trump from running for the presidency again in 2024 or thereafter.

Thus, Portman helped Trump get off the hook at the impeachment trial on charges of which he was clearly guilty. If recklessly inciting and encouraging a mob to march on the Capitol and to fight like hell is not enough to impeach a president, then what is? Trump had always bragged that he could shoot a person dead in broad daylight on Fifth Avenue in Manhattan and get away with it.[71] As long as he wasn't a sitting president at the time, Senator Portman and most of the Senate Republicans agreed with him.

## Ron Johnson – Wisconsin

Wisconsin Republican Senator Ron Johnson debased himself even more than most of his Republican colleagues in the Senate by becoming the chief spreader of wild conspiracy theories about what happened before, during, and after the January 6 riot at the U.S. Capitol. Johnson suggested that Speaker Nancy Pelosi insisted that former President Donald Trump be impeached over his role in the riot as a way to cover up her own malfeasance on that day.[72]

Although Johnson never quite explained what he thought Pelosi had been doing wrong that day, it was part of his broader strategy to deflect attention from the heinous actions of the former president and his loyal troops who stormed the Capitol. Indeed, Johnson went so far as to say that he did not believe that the attack on the Capitol was an insurrection,[73] despite the fact that many rioters referred to it as a "1776 moment," and searched for the vice president and Speaker Pelosi for the purpose of killing them.[74]

According to the *Milwaukee Journal Sentinel*, Johnson was one of the primary boosters in the Senate for Trump's bogus election fraud campaign to overturn the 2020 presidential election results, writing that Johnson "helped perpetuate the myth that voter fraud cost the former president the election."[75] To that end, he even held a Senate hearing in his role as chairman of the Senate Homeland Security Committee, openly giving credence to the false myth being circulated by Trump and his minions that a nationwide election-rigging scheme was responsible for Biden's victory. Although no court anywhere in the country ever even partially accepted this idea, Johnson continued to promote this false narrative. As the *Journal Sentinel* put it in an editorial calling for his immediate resignation, "Johnson was willing to throw out the legally cast votes of millions of Americans. He was willing to throw away democracy—government of the people, by the people, for the people—to serve Donald Trump."[76]

After the January 6, 2021 attack on the Capitol, Johnson promoted the false narrative that the sacking of the Capitol building was no big deal and was being blown out of proportion by the Democrats and the media. "This didn't seem like an armed insurrection to me. When you hear the word 'armed,' don't you think of firearms? Here's the questions I would have liked to ask: How many firearms were confiscated? How many shots were fired?"[77] Johnson took his disinformation campaign one step further when, during a February 23, 2021 Senate hearing on the law enforcement preparations and response to the January 6 attack, Johnson suggested that the riot was really precipitated by leftist provocateurs posing as pro-Trump demonstrators.[78]

Nothing that Johnson said or suggested was consistent with the mountain of evidence already in the public domain by the date of the February 23 Senate hearing. Much of the video evidence, arrests, and indictments handed down following the January 6 attack showed that a significant number of the most violent participants in the assault on the Capitol were members of right-wing paramilitary groups such as the Oath Keepers and the Proud Boys. Johnson's narrative was also completely at odds with the FBI's assessment of the January 6 siege, which concluded that there was zero evidence that Antifa or any other group of leftist provocateurs had been part of the January 6 crowd, or that they were the ones who incited the violence.[79] Federal prosecutors also announced that paramilitary Trump supporters had discussed transporting weapons across the Potomac River into Washington, DC. The weapons-by-boat plan was mentioned in a court filing from the U.S. Justice Department, seeking to keep in jail Thomas Caldwell, a Virginia man charged with conspiracy and alleged to have helped to organize Oath Keeper and other extremist group rioters.

In short, Johnson grossly abused his elected public position and his oath in order to undermine public confidence in the integrity of our electoral and democratic institutions, and to try to derail a serious Congressional investigation into the nature and causes of the January 6 assault on the Capitol and the domestic terrorist groups that planned and participated in it.

# TRUMP'S HOUSE OF REPRESENTATIVES ENABLERS

Republican members of the U.S. House of Representatives were, if possible, even more cowardly in their submissiveness to the White House than their Senate colleagues. The false post-election narrative being spread by Trump and his enablers—that he had won the 2020 presidential election and that he was being denied his rightful second term due to a vast voting fraud conspiracy by the Democrats—was joined by virtually all members of the Republican House caucus.[1] All of them face re-election every two years. Even if they represented relatively safe Republican districts, they could almost be assured of a primary challenge from their right if they dared to suggest out loud that Trump had not won the presidential election he had clearly lost.

Tuesday, December 8, 2020, was the date when the states were required under the U.S. Constitution to certify the results of the presidential elections in their respective states. Each state did so. Traditionally, this would have been the day that the final Republican (or Democratic) holdouts would acknowledge the obvious to the American people and cease waging any war of words or legal challenges to the election results. However, the 2020 election broke this democratic norm, perhaps irretrievably. Senate and House Republican lawmakers continued their baseless refusal to acknowledge the plain fact that Joe Biden was now the president-elect and Kamala Harris was now the vice-president elect.

On December 9, the Associated Press reported that most Republicans in Congress would keep the country waiting until January 6, 2020 to acknowledge the winner of the election, which was the date when the electoral slates would be counted in Congress and the winner formally declared.[2] Until then, Republican lawmakers intended to either remain mum on the issue or actively support Trump's continued campaign of frivolous lawsuits and baseless claims of fraud.

Congressional Republicans well knew that their foot dragging in acknowledging the results of the election was severely undermining public confidence in America's electoral process. It also was dramatically changing long-accepted civic norms in ways that were not fully predictable, but would in no way be good for the country. Indeed, Republican lawmakers were putting themselves in a predicament partially of their own making. By not simply acknowledging the obvious, that the 2020 election was over and that they had lost, fair and square, they were continuing to feed the frenzy of calls and complaints by their constituents who voted for Trump and still believed in the false, truth-denying narrative emanating from Trump and his inner circle of sycophants.

Trump led his party down this unprecedented and dangerous path by claiming, without any basis in fact, that the election was rigged. But it was the Republican leadership in Congress that allowed Trump's baseless claims of election fraud to swell through their weeks of silence. Eventually, and perhaps inevitably, their cynical decision to fan the flames of doubt over the integrity of the election helped let it grow into the raging fire that engulfed the Capitol on January 6.[3]

Even for those Republican members of Congress who knew that this was a totally made-up, artificial election crisis, they decided to stay silent since they calculated that it would be political suicide for them to publicly declare, in essence, that the emperor had no clothes. To swim against the political currents would inevitably lead to a backlash from Trump supporters back home. Trump was extremely vigilant in keeping the rank-and-file Republican members of Congress in line. No deviations were permitted, and even the faintest sign of disloyalty would be met with a tweet blast that could burn any offending Republican member of Congress. In fact, when *The Washington Post* reported that there were 25 Republican members of Congress who were at least privately acknowledging Trump's defeat, Trump immediately tweeted to his Congressional lieutenants to "send me a list of the 25 RINOS [Republicans in name only]."[4]

Fearful of the consequences of candidly admitting that the election was over and that it was time to move on, almost every Republican voice of reason and truthfulness was silenced. Most of them just decided to "let the process play itself out"[5] until at least January 6, when the electoral votes from the states would be counted in Congress, no matter what the long-term damage to the American public's confidence in the integrity of our electoral system.[6]

What the Republican members of Congress failed to acknowledge was that, for Americans to have faith in the elections, the losing side has to accept defeat and move on. Without that social compact, it is difficult, if not impossible, to continue the 240 years of American tradition of the peaceful transfer of presidential power from one party to the other. Instead of following this honored tradition, the Republican Party continued to take its cues from President

Trump rather than following the high and honorable road of acknowledging that Biden had won the election and that the process for a peaceful transition to the new administration should begin.

Yet even after the mob riot and resulting death and destruction at the Capitol, 139 House Republicans joined eight Senate Republicans—a majority of all congressional Republicans—in voting *not* to certify the election results in at least one state, thereby signaling their tacit support for mob rule and the end of our cherished tradition of passing power peacefully based upon the results of a free and fair election.[7]

## Kevin McCarthy – California

In the aftermath of the 2020 presidential election, House Republican Minority Leader Kevin McCarthy continued to parrot Trump's false claim that he had "won the election,"[8] even after the ballot counting was completed in the closely contested states and Biden was the president-elect in the minds of everyone except the fevered brains of Trump and his cultish followers. McCarthy went further than most, suggesting that Republicans would never give up and never surrender until Trump was declared the winner, saying, "Everyone who is listening: Do not be quiet. Do not be silent about this. We cannot allow this to happen before our very eyes."[9] You would think that McCarthy was trying to rally his countrymen against some foreign invasion, or maybe even an alien attack from another galaxy, given the hysterical nature of his call to arms.

In December 2020, McCarthy was one of 126 Republican members of the House of Representatives who signed an amicus brief in support of *Texas v. Pennsylvania*, a lawsuit filed at the U.S. Supreme Court contesting the results of the 2020 presidential election.[10] The Supreme Court declined to hear the case on the basis that Texas lacked standing under Article III of the Constitution to challenge the results of the election held by another state.

House Speaker Nancy Pelosi issued a statement accurately calling the signing of the amicus brief an act of "election subversion."[11] Additionally, Pelosi reprimanded McCarthy and the other House members who supported the lawsuit: "The 126 Republican Members that signed onto this lawsuit brought dishonor to the House. Instead of upholding their oath to support and defend the Constitution, they chose to subvert the Constitution and undermine public trust in our sacred democratic institutions."[12] New Jersey Democratic Representative Bill Pascrell, citing section three of the 14th Amendment, urged Pelosi to not seat McCarthy and the other Republicans who signed the brief supporting the suit. Pascrell argued that "the text of the 14th Amendment expressly forbids Members of Congress from engaging in rebellion against the United States. Trying to overturn a democratic election and install a dictator seems like a pretty clear example of that."[13]

McCarthy, like Senate Majority Leader McConnell and the rest of the Republican leadership in Congress, permitted their party to be hijacked by an anti-democratic and autocratic leader who somehow managed to pull off a narrow upset in 2016. They then either vocally supported or stood by in silence as Trump committed one outrage after another, culminating in his cataclysmic mishandling of the worst pandemic in a century, which in less than a year claimed more American lives than were lost in World War II.

In October 2019, McCarthy publicly refused to acknowledge that there was anything wrong with the president extorting a foreign country for personal gain when Trump withheld desperately needed military aid in return for an announcement that the Ukrainian government was investigating the Bidens. McCarthy said "there's nothing that the president did wrong" when he requested the Ukrainian president start an investigation into his personal political rival, Joe Biden.[14] McCarthy added, "the President wasn't investigating a campaign rival, the President was trying to get to the bottom, just as every American would want to know, why did we have this Russia hoax that actually started within Ukraine," referring to the discredited Russian-promoted theory that it was really Ukraine that interfered with the 2016 U.S. elections, not Russia.[15]

Similarly, when Trump said, "China should start an investigation into the Bidens,"[16] McCarthy went on *Fox & Friends* to say, "You watch what the president said—he's not saying China should investigate."[17] In other words, McCarthy completely bought into the Trump parallel *Alice in Wonderland* universe where up means down, down means up, and the actual words you speak don't matter.[18]

At any point, McCarthy and the rest of the Republican Congressional leadership, including Representative Steve Scalise, the Republican Minority

Whip from Louisiana, could have stood up to Trump and said enough is enough and no more. But they didn't, and the newly emboldened Trump planned to pull off the first political coup in the history of the country by scheming to get the courts or Congress to overturn the election results and give him the second term that his ego so desperately needed. Or, failing all of that, he would call on his supporters to come to Washington for a "wild"[19] demonstration on January 6, 2021, following their supreme leader's exhortation to "fight like hell" to keep Trump in power, even if that meant an attack on the U.S. Capitol and insurrection.[20]

Without McCarthy and the rest of the Republican Congressional leadership behind this outlandish conspiracy, Trump's election fraud campaign would have been stripped of even the appearance of legitimacy. Within a few weeks after the November 2020 election, the reputations of Rudy Giuliani, Sidney Powell, L. Lin Wood, and other pro-Trump lawyers had become so tarnished that they were practically being laughed out of court and the state legislatures where they were trying to peddle their wild conspiracy theories. Other Trump supporters had started calling for the execution for treason of Vice President Mike Pence, Chief Justice John G. Roberts Jr., Speaker Nancy Pelosi, and anyone else who stood in the way of Trump's continuing Reign of Terror.[21] Without continuing support from Republican members of Congress, Trump's election fraud campaign would have never gained enough traction to pose a serious threat to our democracy. These are the members of Congress who kept Trump's dream alive until the bitter end, making them complicit in the death and destruction at the U.S. Capitol on January 6.

## The House Sedition Caucus

Mo Brooks – Arkansas
Paul Gosar – Arizona
Andy Biggs – Arizona
Pete Sessions – Texas

Standing before thousands of MAGA-clad Trump supporters on the National Mall on the morning of January 6, 2021, Representative Mo Brooks roared out a message that further inflamed the hyped-up crowd before it marched on the U.S. Capitol. "Today is the day American patriots start taking down names and kicking ass," said Brooks. "Are you willing to do what it takes to fight for America? Louder! Will you fight for America?"[22]

Shortly thereafter, urged on by Trump and others at the same rally, rioters stormed the Capitol, disrupting a joint session of Congress that was meeting to formalize Biden's election. They chanted, "Hang Mike Pence," and threatened to shoot House Speaker Nancy Pelosi.[23] Even after the tear gas cleared and the Capitol was secured, the overwhelming majority of House Republicans, including the party's two top leaders—Kevin McCarthy and Steve Scalise—voted to throw out millions of lawfully cast votes and to give Trump what he was looking for: a second term as president even after losing the election.[24]

Some extremist Republican lawmakers went far beyond merely voting to overturn the lawful results of the election. These members of the Sedition Caucus actively supported and endorsed the attempted insurrection on January 6, 2021. In addition to Mo Brooks, Representative Paul Gosar of Arizona, who for weeks enthusiastically promoted the January 6 protest and other "Stop the Steal" events across the country, repeatedly referred to Biden as an "illegitimate usurper" and suggested that Trump was the victim of an attempted coup.[25] "Be ready to defend the Constitution and the White House," Gosar wrote in an op-ed piece.[26]

Several weeks after the November 2020 presidential election, Gosar and Representative Andy Biggs, also of Arizona, appeared in a video produced by the Arizona Republican Party. They claimed there was widespread voter fraud in the 2020 presidential election.[27] Gosar further falsely claimed Arizona's voting machines were faulty and that Wisconsin intentionally paused counting votes to "dump" 100,000 votes into the count for Joe Biden.[28]

Gosar also participated in "Stop the Steal" protests prior to January 6, comparing their efforts to the Battle of the Alamo—which ended in a massacre.[29]

During the actual siege of the Capitol on January 6, Gosar posted a message on the Parler internet site that was sympathetic to the mob action, using a photo of people scaling the walls of the building with a caption, stating: "Americans are upset."[30] Following the storming of the Capitol on January 6, Gosar was the first member of Congress to advance the false conspiracy theory that people associated with Antifa, a loose association of leftist and anti-fascist groups, were responsible for the attack.[31] Meanwhile, back in Arizona, three of Gosar's siblings called for him to be expelled from Congress. "When you talk about what happened the other day, you're talking about treason. You're talking about overthrowing the government. That's what this is. If that doesn't rise to the level of expulsion, what does?" said Tim Gosar.[32]

On the Saturday prior to the January 6 riot and assault on the Capitol, Representative Pete Sessions of Texas posted a photograph on Twitter (later deleted), saying that he "had a great meeting today with the folks from 'Stop The Steal,'" one of the leading groups that organized the January 6 Washington rally and march on the Capitol.[33] In the tweet, Sessions urged the group to "keep fighting," which, based on their actions a few days later, they took quite literally.

Ali Alexander, a far-right activist and conspiracy theorist who was one of the leaders of "Stop the Steal," claimed that he organized the January 6 event along with Representatives Brooks, Gosar, and Biggs. "We four schemed up of putting maximum pressure on Congress while they were voting," Alexander said in a since-deleted video.[34] He added that their goal was for Congress to be "hearing our loud roar from outside" while they were deliberating on the outcome of the election.[35] Alexander also referred to Gosar as "the spirit animal of this movement."[36] Alexander elaborated on his relationship with Gosar: "He's helped out where he could. He's offered to call donors. We actually had our first D.C. march because he called me and he said, 'You need to go to the Supreme Court.' I said: 'All right, my captain.' And that's what started that."[37]

While several of the Congressional promoters of the Capitol riot quickly deleted their tweets and videos from Facebook or other social media platforms after the riot turned deadly, Brooks proudly stood behind his role in encouraging the rioters. "I make no apology for doing my absolute best to inspire patriotic Americans to not give up on our country and to fight back against anti-Christian socialists in the 2022 and 2024 elections," Brooks told a local newspaper.[38] "I encourage EVERY citizen to watch my entire rally speech and decide for themselves what kind of America they want: One based on freedom and liberty or one based on godless dictatorial power."[39]

Representative Tom Malinowski, Democrat of New Jersey, introduced a resolution to formally censure Brooks, asserting that he was responsible for inciting the crowd and "endangering the lives of his fellow members of Congress."[40] Other House Democrats pushed to invoke Section 3 of the 14th Amendment, which disqualifies people who "have engaged in insurrection or rebellion" against the United States from holding public office.[41] The clause was originally enacted to limit the influence of former Confederates in the Reconstruction era. Representative Cori Bush, Democrat of Missouri, introduced a resolution with 47 co-sponsors that would initiate investigations for "removal of the members who attempted to overturn the results of the election and incited a white supremacist attempted coup."[42]

## The House QAnon Caucus

Marjorie Taylor Greene – Georgia
Lauren Boebert – Colorado

One of the driving forces behind the attack on the Capitol was QAnon, a movement centered on the conspiracy theory that President Trump, secretly aided by the military, was elected to smash a cabal of Satan-worshiping and child abusing Democrats, international financiers, and "Deep State" bureaucrats.[43] It prophesied an apocalyptic showdown, known as "the Storm," between Trump and his enemies. During the Storm, their enemies, including Joe Biden and many Democratic and Republican members of Congress, would be arrested and executed.[44]

The mob that attacked the Capitol on January 6 included many visible QAnon supporters wearing "Q" shirts and waving "Q" banners. Among them was Jake Angeli, a QAnon devotee who styled himself the "Q Shaman." Angeli, whose real name is Jacob Chansley, stormed the Capitol wearing horns and animal furs, leaving a note threatening Vice President Mike Pence.[45] Another QAnon acolyte was Ashli Babbitt, who was shot and killed by a Capitol Police officer as she tried to climb through a window in a barricaded door near the House chamber.[46]

Representatives Marjorie Taylor Greene of Georgia and Lauren Boebert of Colorado, both first-term lawmakers and outspoken QAnon advocates, referred to January 6 as their "1776 moment."[47] Greene, who expressed the belief that 9/11 was staged, called QAnon "a once-in-a-lifetime opportunity to take this global cabal of Satan-worshiping pedophiles out."[48] Many of her Facebook posts in recent years reflected language used by the movement, including talk of hanging prominent Democrats or executing FBI agents.[49]

Before being elected to the House of Representatives in 2020, Greene participated in the spreading of false conspiracy theories that the mass killings in Parkland, Florida and at Sandy Hook Elementary School in Newtown, Connecticut were staged events designed to promote gun control legislation.[50] She also promoted a theory that former secretary of state Hillary Clinton murdered a child during a satanic ritual and drank her blood.[51] One of the posts she "liked" suggested getting rid of House Speaker Nancy Pelosi with "a bullet to the head."[52] CNN also found a 2019 video in which Greene harassed David Hogg, a survivor of the Parkland shooting who was making the rounds on Capitol Hill to advocate for gun control. Greene shouted lies at him, calling him "a coward" for not responding to her.[53] She also has said that it is "worth listening to" the QAnon conspiracy theory holding that Donald Trump was secretly fighting a worldwide child-sex-slavery ring that would culminate in the mass arrest of his political opposition.[54] Other theories she has ascribed to include the theory that 9/11 was an inside job,[55] and that Muslims should not be hired by the U.S. government and should be barred from holding public office. Also, according to a Greene Facebook post, the wildfires in California were not natural. "Forests don't just catch fire, you know. Rather, the blazes had been started by PG&E [the public utility company], in conjunction with the Rothschilds, using a space laser, in order to clear room for a high-speed rail project."[56]

And now she is a member of Congress. America is truly the land of opportunity. An argument could possibly be made that there are enough irrational people in America that they too deserve representation in Congress. But a line has to be drawn somewhere, and threatening to kill fellow members of the House is clearly over any such line.

After Congress resumed its certification proceedings following the January 6 attack, Greene was one of the congressional Republicans who still objected to the election results. Video footage also emerged showing her, along with other House Republicans, refusing to wear a mask while sheltering with other lawmakers amid the violence.⁵⁷ At least three House Democrats later tested positive for Covid-19.⁵⁸

Instead of drawing back in horror at what the Georgia voters had sent to Congress, House Minority Leader McCarthy rewarded Greene with a seat on the House Education and Labor Committee, which would give her a role in shaping federal policy with regard to schools. Speaker Pelosi's response was to say that this appointment was "appalling, really beyond the pale."⁵⁹

The calls for Greene to be censured or removed from Congress became louder and more persistent as more and more offensive internet and Facebook posts were made public. Senator Raphael G. Warnock, the newly elected Democratic Senator from Georgia, called Greene's behavior "dangerous and unacceptable," adding, "This extreme and violent rhetoric only fans the flames of division, and we've just seen how deadly those flames can be."⁶⁰ Even some Republicans called for her ouster. Illinois Representative Adam Kinzinger said Greene's actions disqualified her from their party. "She is not a Republican," Kinzinger said on Twitter. "There are many who claim the title of Republican and have nothing in common with our core values."⁶¹

On Thursday, February 4, 2021, after the House Republican caucus refused to discipline Greene for her past violence-filled conspiracy theories, the House voted 230–199 to remove Greene from her committee assignments, citing her past advocacy of QAnon conspiracy theories and circulating a Facebook post depicting her holding a military-grade AR-15 pointed at the heads of three progressive women members of the House, known as "the Squad."⁶² Another significant factor in the vote to oust her from her committee assignments appeared to be the video in which she is seen aggressively confronting David Hogg.⁶³

McCarthy and others in the Republican House leadership forced the House Democrats to bring the matter to a floor vote after they refused to rescind her assignments to the budget and education committees, notwithstanding a cascade of new information confirming her beliefs that the mass shootings of school children never really happened and were "hoaxes." She also openly continued to promote the false narrative that "Trump Won" by wearing a face mask in Congress bearing those words, even after President Biden's inauguration.⁶⁴ On the day that she was stripped of her committee assignments, however, Greene switched face masks, now sporting one reading "Censored."⁶⁵ There were eleven Republicans who sided with the Democrats in ousting Greene from her committee assignments. These included Kinzinger, who was one of only ten House Republicans to vote to impeach Trump for a second time. Among the representatives who joined in disciplining Greene was Young Kim of California, who said conspiracy theories and threats "should never be part of our political discourse. This should not be tolerated by either party."⁶⁶ Nicole Malliotakis of New York called Greene's past comments "deeply disturbing and extraordinarily offensive" and said she fully condemned such remarks, regardless of which side of the aisle they come from.⁶⁷ Carlos Gimenez of Florida, the former mayor of Miami-Dade County, commented that "too often members of Congress are let off the hook when deeply hurtful comments are swept under the rug for the sake of political expedience."⁶⁸

Completely unrepentant as to her disturbing views that led to her rebuke in the House, Greene responded: "I woke up early this morning literally laughing thinking about what a bunch of morons the Democrats (+11) are for giving someone like me free time," referring to the eleven Republicans who joined Democrats in voting to strip her of the assignments.⁶⁹

## Lauren Boebert – Colorado

Representative Lauren Boebert, the owner of Shooters Grill, a restaurant in Rifle, Colorado, also had close connections to QAnon. She was associated with several militia groups, including the so-called Three Percenters, an extremist offshoot of the gun rights movement which includes members who illegally breached the Capitol on January 6, 2021.⁷⁰ While members of Congress were in lockdown and members of the mob were looking for Leader Pelosi to "put a bullet in her head," Boebert tweeted information as to Pelosi's location that could have been helpful to those searching for her.⁷¹ The insurrectionists eventually left the Capitol, no doubt disappointed that they did not achieve this objective.

After the assault, metal detectors were installed in the U.S. Capitol, which Boebert at first refused to use and then refused to hand over her bag for inspection after one of the machines started beeping. This resulted in a standoff with police.⁷²

In January 2021, Boebert also produced a viral digital ad proclaiming her right to carry a Glock pistol on the grounds of the U.S. Capitol and in the streets of Washington. The ad showed Boebert strapping a Glock to her hip before embarking on a walk around Capitol Hill, near federal buildings. "I refuse to give up my rights, especially my Second Amendment rights," she said to the camera.[73]

# TRUMP'S "HERD IMMUNITY" GANG

*We want them infected!*

– Paul Alexander – July 4, 2020

# Paul Alexander

On July 4, 2020, Paul Alexander, a Trump appointee at the U.S. Department of Health and Human Services, expressed his callous contempt for his fellow Americans by encouraging as many Americans to contract the coronavirus as possible. Alexander wrote an email to his boss Michael Caputo, Health and Human Services assistant secretary for public affairs. In the email he urged the department to adopt a strategy of herd immunity, a theory that says when most of the population has been infected with a deadly communicable virus such as COVID-19, it will stop spreading further since there are not enough uninfected people left to infect.[1]

"There is no other way," Alexander's email said, "we need to establish herd [immunity], and it only comes about allowing the non-high-risk groups expose themselves to the virus. PERIOD."[2] In the same message, the previously obscure Canadian health researcher added, "Infants, kids, teens, young people, young adults, middle aged with no conditions etc. have zero to little risk . . . so we use them to develop herd . . . we want them infected."[3]

Alexander and his cohorts in the Trump administration did not invent the concept of herd immunity; it has been around for a long time. However, the danger of a herd immunity strategy was that without a widespread vaccination program in place, it would put millions of healthy Americans at risk of developing long-term health problems while, at the same time, substantially increasing the country's COVID-19 death toll.

According to Johns Hopkins University, depending on how contagious a disease is, herd immunity can be achieved when roughly 50 to 90% of the population is immune, either by contracting the disease and developing natural immunity or through a program of vaccination.[4] "In the worst case (for example, if we do not perform physical distancing or enact other measures to slow the spread of [COVID-19]), the virus can infect this many people in a matter of a few months," according to the John Hopkins University website. "This would overwhelm our hospitals and lead to high death rates."[5]

Despite the likelihood that implementation of a herd immunity strategy would lead to *millions* of more dead Americans rather than hundreds of thousands, Alexander continued to send out a series of messages during the summer of 2020 making the case to other officials to open up college campuses and businesses to increase the spread among the young and relatively healthy while maintaining distancing measures for the elderly.[6]

The shamefulness of Alexander's approach was astonishing, even to the most cynical among us. In a July 3 message, Alexander wrote: "The issue is who cares? If it is causing more cases in young, my word is who cares." He added, "As long as we make sensible decisions, and protect the elderly and nursing homes, we must go on with life . . . who cares if we test more and get more positive tests."[7] Alexander's plan was further flawed by the fact that there was mounting scientific and medical evidence that COVID-19 did not leave all children and young people unscathed, as he was implying, and that there were numerous cases where infection of otherwise healthy Americans—even young ones—caused serious illness, long-term effects, and even death. Even worse, new variants of COVID-19 have appeared around the globe, often proving to be both more virulent and more deadly than the original virus.

In August 2020, President Trump expressed support for the approach, saying the virus would "go away" once herd immunity was reached.[8] Nevertheless, Trump administration officials, including Secretary of Health and Human Services Alex Azar, continued to deny that the administration was pursuing herd immunity as a way to handle the virus, despite the administration's inaction clearly pointed in that direction.

Sweden, the one country that consciously tried this approach (without calling it that), had to acknowledge that it was a failure. The top epidemiologist in Sweden admitted in late November 2020 that, eight months into the pandemic, there were "no signs of immunity in the population that are slowing down the infection right now."[9]

In addition to being herd immunity advocates, Alexander and Caputo gained notoriety in 2020 for their vigorous efforts on behalf of the Trump White House to control COVID-19 messaging from federal scientists and public health agencies.[10] Alexander sought to muzzle federal scientists and public health agencies to prevent them from contradicting the rhetoric coming from the Trump administration.[11]

Alexander's efforts to suppress accurate but politically sensitive statements from the CDC were focused on the CDC's widely read *Morbidity and Mortality Weekly Report* (*MMWR*), which Alexander and Caputo regarded as containing "political content."[12] Alexander tried to get all issues of *MMWR* held up until personally approved by him.[13] Emails written by Alexander and Caputo detailed their attempts to silence career CDC scientists and question their findings as part of what current and former CDC officials called a "campaign of bullying and intimidation" that stretched for five months.[14] For example, after Dr. Anne Schuchat, the principal deputy director of the CDC, had given an interview to the *Journal of the American Medical Association* urging the use of face masks, Alexander emailed Caputo, calling Schuchat "duplicitous," claiming: "Her aim is to embarrass the president."[15] On June 20, 2020, Alexander also sent a message to CDC Director Robert R. Redfield, criticizing a CDC report about risks to pregnant women from COVID-19. Alexander said that the report would "frighten women" and give the impression that "the President and his administration can't fix this and it is getting worse." He said that in his "opinion and sense" the CDC was "undermining the president by what they put out."[16] Shortly thereafter, on August 8, Alexander wrote to Redfield that the "CDC to me appears to be writing hit pieces on the administration," asking Redfield to change reports that had already been published and demanding that he be allowed to review and edit *MMWR* before publication.[17]

In August and early September 2020, Alexander sent several messages to press officers at the National Institutes of Health, attempting to control Dr. Anthony Fauci's media comments.[18] Among his demands were that Fauci should refrain from promoting the wearing of masks by children in school and COVID-19 testing of children.[19] Fauci later said that he had not received the messages and would not have been influenced by them if he had.[20]

In an interview with the *Toronto Globe and Mail* after his departure from HHS, Alexander defended his actions, stating that he had wanted the CDC to make their reports "more upbeat so that people would feel more confident going out and spending money."[21]

## Michael Caputo

Alexander's close connection to the president through his HHS manager, Michael Caputo, made his advocacy of herd immunity all the more dangerous. "It was understood that he spoke for Michael Caputo, who spoke for the White

House," Kyle McGowan, a Trump appointee and former CDC chief of staff, told *Politico*. "That's how they wanted it to be perceived."[22] Ultimately, both Caputo and Alexander left the department after they were caught pressuring CDC officials to amend their weekly COVID reports to be more politically friendly to President Trump.[23]

With no scientific or medical background, Caputo was as close as the Trump administration could come to installing a Soviet-style political commissar in HHS. Caputo had worked for the Reagan Administration with Oliver North, a National Security Council staff member who was one of the chief architects of the Iran–Contra affair, a political scandal of the late 1980s involving the illegal sale of weapons to the Khomeini government of the Islamic Republic of Iran with the goal of illegally diverting the proceeds from the arms sales to support the Contra rebel groups in Nicaragua.

Caputo came under scrutiny during Special Counsel Mueller's Russia investigation. He was also investigated by the U.S. House Permanent Select Committee on Intelligence. Caputo was perhaps the Trump campaign official most familiar with Russia, having moved there in 1994, where he worked as an advisor to President Boris Yeltsin. He was also employed by Gazprom Media in 2000, where his job was to improve the image of Vladimir Putin in the United States.

In a Facebook live video posted on his personal website on September 14, 2020, Caputo literally ranted about a variety of what *The New York Times* charitably described as "false accusations" and "bizarre conspirac[y]" theories.[24] The *Times* reported that Caputo accused the CDC of harboring a "resistance unit" determined to undermine Trump; accused the CDC scientists of "sedition" and "rotten science"; and called upon Trump supporters to prepare for an insurrection.[25] Caputo specifically claimed that "there are hit squads being trained all over this country" to mount armed opposition to a second term for President Trump.[26] He also stated: "You understand that they're going to have to kill me, and unfortunately, I think that's where this is going."[27]

Caputo's now infamous video further claimed that the shooting of a right wing protester in Portland had been "a drill."[28] He said his physical and mental health were deteriorating and he feared being alone, describing "shadows on the ceiling" in his apartment.[29] On September 14, Caputo's hometown newspaper, *The Buffalo News*, released an editorial calling for his removal:

"What's lunacy is for paranoia and political calculations to be coloring the dissemination of scientific knowledge during a pandemic. Caputo's ideas about managing a health crisis need to be put out to pasture."[30]

Two days later, on September 16, HHS announced that Caputo—who was obviously unhinged and in urgent need of psychiatric help—would take a 60-day medical leave of absence from HHS and that Alexander would permanently leave the department.[31] At a Senate hearing the same day, Redfield said he was "deeply saddened" by Caputo's claims, said they were "not true," and that "The scientific integrity of the *MMWR* has not been compromised, and will not be compromised on my watch."[32]

Two days after Alexander was ousted and Caputo went on leave, the CDC reversed its much-criticized statement saying that asymptomatic people who have been in close contact with a person infected with the coronavirus did not need to receive COVID-19 testing.[33] The statement had been placed on the CDC website by HHS leadership and the White House, over the objections of scientists and without going through the usual CDC scientific review process.[34]

When asked about the herd immunity theory at a House coronavirus subcommittee hearing in October 2020, HHS Secretary Azar told the subcommittee that "herd immunity is not the strategy of the U.S. government with regard to coronavirus."[35] However, what Azar failed to tell the Congress members was this strategy was being seriously discussed among Trump administration officials and considered by Trump himself, although Trump had mistakenly referred to it as "herd mentality."[36] What was clear, however, was that the Trump administration was, through its inaction in the face of the COVID onslaught, backing into a herd immunity strategy without actually calling it by that name. Trump's encouragement of resistance to state-ordered COVID lockdowns and the administration's hostility to mass testing was inexorably pushing the nation toward an unofficial and disastrous herd immunity approach.

## Scott Atlas

Scott Atlas, a senior fellow at Stanford University's Hoover Institution, a conservative think tank, was named as an advisor on the White House Coronavirus Task Force in August 2020.[37] In that role, Atlas spread misinformation about COVID-19,[38] including fringe theories that face masks and social distancing were not effective in slowing the spread of the coronavirus.[39] His statements and influence on policies caused such controversy on the task force that the group's leading medical experts—Dr. Deborah Birx and Dr. Anthony Fauci—indicated that they did not "appreciate" Atlas' controversial input or contributions in the Situation Room gatherings.[40] Atlas pushed for establishing herd immunity and a faster reopening of schools and businesses during the COVID-19 pandemic.[41] He advocated that states should not engage in universal testing,[42] and encouraged residents to resist or "rise up" against state restrictions adopted to prevent the spread of the coronavirus.[43]

Despite scientific evidence that children can carry, transmit, develop long-term complications from, and even die by COVID-19,[44] Atlas claimed that children "have virtually zero risk of dying, and a very, very low risk of any serious illness from this disease" and "children almost never transmit the disease."[45] He argued that only symptomatic individuals should be tested for the coronavirus, and pushed for the CDC's August 2020 recommendation that non-symptomatic people should not be tested,[46] even though this position was contradicted by evidence that approximately 40% of people infected with the virus are asymptomatic and can transmit the virus.[47] Contradicting every other recognized public health expert in the country—including Fauci and Birx and Trump's own Surgeon General Dr. Jerome Adams—Atlas repeatedly expressed skepticism that face masks were effective "scientifically" to halt the spread of the virus.[48] In October 2020, Twitter removed a tweet by Atlas for falsely claiming that masks do not prevent the spread of coronavirus.[49]

Finally, unable to take it anymore, Fauci and Birx let it be known that they could not work with Atlas. Nevertheless, Atlas stayed on, since President Trump expressed his delight that Atlas's public statements were aligned with the White House's "do nothing" view on how best to respond to the crisis.[50]

In an interview with Fox News's Brian Kilmeade in July, Atlas confirmed that he was a full card-carrying member of the herd immunity club: "These people getting the infection is not really a problem, and in fact, as we said months ago, when you isolate everyone, including all the healthy people, you're prolonging the problem because you're preventing population immunity. Low-risk groups getting the infection is not a problem. In fact, it's a positive."[51] Facing a storm of public criticism, Atlas denied later that he advocated for herd immunity,[52] saying "there's never been a desire to have cases spread through the community," and that herd immunity "has never been the president's policy."[53]

On November 19, 2020, Stanford University's Faculty Senate passed a resolution condemning Atlas's "view of COVID-19 that contradicts medical science," stating that Atlas's statements discouraging the use of masks and "other scientifically accepted" health measures showed "disdain for established medical knowledge."[54]

Atlas finally resigned from his position in the White House on November 30, but like the other members of Trump's herd immunity gang, he will never be able to wash his hands of the blood of those who became ill and died as a result of his shameful and unscientific views. [55]

## Dr. Deborah Birx

Dr. Deborah Birx finally spoke out publicly on Sunday, January 24, 2021, disclosing on *Face the Nation* the details regarding the mishandling of the coronavirus response by the Trump Administration, of which she was an essential player.[56] By then, the pandemic in the United States had left 400,000 Americans dead and was still raging, virtually uncontrolled, throughout the country. After nearly a year of coordinating the Trump White House's coronavirus response, Birx explained how the Trump administration simply passed the buck, ceding all responsibility to the states and offering them only vague support.[57] She also dropped a bombshell by disclosing that the White House had used "parallel data" that was markedly different than the charts and data that she prepared.[58] She suspected the false data came from Scott Atlas, a Trump-appointed radiologist whose primary function on the task force was to spread dangerous misinformation about COVID-19.[59]

So why did such a highly regarded public health professional as Birx wait so long to come out and tell the truth? Why did she not speak out while she was in a position of power and influence as the leading expert within the White House on the coronavirus task force? Maybe she could have shaken things up in the Trump Administration and saved countless lives, even if she risked getting fired or exiled. After all, Dr. Rick Bright had not been afraid to speak out as to the dangers of untested treatments promoted by the White House even though he was sidelined for having the audacity to speak the truth to Trump and the American people.[60]

It was not until after Trump had finally decamped from the White House and President Biden had been sworn in that Birx publicly complained that her carefully thought-out plans for fighting the virus had been disregarded. She also revealed that the Trump team continually muzzled her, refusing to let her speak with the national press and clearly explain the real threat of the disease to the American people. She also disclosed that no one other than herself and her one aide regularly wore masks in the White House.[61] While this after-the-fact information was interesting, it would have been good to know just how incompetent the Trump administration was back in the spring, summer, or even fall of 2020, when the American people were deciding whether or not Trump deserved another term in office. There was nothing stopping her from at least occasionally standing up to the president and refuting his dangerous lies, the way Dr. Anthony Fauci, director of the National Institute of Allergy and Infectious Diseases, did.[62]

Birx no doubt justified her decision not to forcefully speak out by convincing herself that she could at least try to do some good from within the administration rather than from the outside. But it must have been clear to her fairly early in her tenure on Team Trump that her presence in the White House was doing nothing to stop the president from engaging in his daily routine of lies and denials regarding the seriousness of the pandemic. To be sure, she spent much of her time trying to help the various states with their response efforts. But the near-total abdication of responsibility by the federal government became increasingly clear, even though she kept hanging on as a member of the moribund coronavirus task force. She must have seen from the inside even more painfully the total disregard for science and the total politicization of the virus response by the federal government and the futility of her trying to change the disastrous course of White House policy.

Birx was not completely blameless when it came to the disastrous federal response to the coronavirus crisis. For example, she led the creation of a reopening plan presented by Trump on April 16, 2020, with voluntary and premature standards for states to end coronavirus lockdowns.[63] In doing so, she was the White House's chief proponent for the idea that COVID-19 infections had peaked by April and the virus was fading quickly. This proved to be an overly optimistic and irresponsible position, however, since infections and hospitalizations surged when restrictions were loosened. A board member at the American College of Emergency Physicians, Dr. Ryan A. Stanton, said Birx sounded like "the builders of the *Titanic* saying the ship can't sink."[64] Birx was also accused of squandering her credibility and bringing her independence into question with her public praise of Trump and her defense of the administration's preparedness for the crisis. At times, she started sounding as if she was the designated apologist for the Trump administration's bungled coronavirus response. She also left herself open to the charge that she was being semi-hypocritical by warning her fellow Americans against big family gatherings at Thanksgiving and Christmas, 2020, and then having press reports circulate that she got together with three generations of her family for the holidays.[65]

To her credit, Birx did issue warnings during the states' reopenings that individuals should continue social distancing and other precautions. However, in July 2020, a working group headed by Birx ordered hospitals to bypass the CDC and instead send all COVID-19 patient information to a database at the Department of Health and Human Services. There was really no good explanation for this significant change in traditional federal data gathering, and it raised the very real danger that the data might become politicized or withheld from the public.

On balance, Birx was, by all accounts, a dedicated and sensitive professional trying to do her job. But by the end, she was little more than ornamental window dressing in a deeply dysfunctional White House. When the Trump nightmare was finally over (at least for the time being), Birx was honest enough and sufficiently self-aware to acknowledge that silence may not have been the best approach to Trump's house of lies. "I could have done more, been more outspoken, maybe been more outspoken publicly," she said.[66]

We, too, are deeply disappointed that such an outstanding medical professional did not try to do more. When good people like her remain silent when the country is being led down a perilous path by self-interested men of ill-will, America pays a high price.

## Ronny Jackson

Trump's former White House physician Dr. Ronny Jackson first gained public notoriety through bizarre pronouncements about the former president's "excellent health" and "incredible genes," suggesting that Trump could be expected to live to the age of 200 if he had maintained a better diet.[67] Later, after Jackson had won a Texas congressional seat in 2020 with the president's help, a Pentagon inspector general's report was released on March 3, 2021, revealing that Jackson, who was a rear admiral in the Navy, regularly drank alcoholic beverages and took sleeping pills while on the job in the White House.[68] It also concluded that he had cursed and belittled his subordinates, and that he had sexually harassed a female medical colleague. Referring to a medical associate, Jackson was reported as having said that she "had a nice body," that he wanted "to see more of her tattoos," and that, visibly intoxicated, he confronted her in a Manila hotel room at 1 or 2 a.m., telling her that, "I need you."[69]

According to the report, "Jackson's overall course of conduct toward subordinates disparaged, belittled, bullied and humiliated them." Nearly all of the 60 witnesses interviewed by investigators described Jackson's "screaming, cursing" behavior and his "yelling, screeching, rage, tantrums and meltdowns" when dealing with subordinates. The report also documented numerous instances in which Jackson was drunk or under the influence of a powerful sleeping drug while he was responsible for the president's health and safety.[70]

Jackson's effusive praise for Trump later helped win him a nomination to become the secretary of veterans affairs, but the nomination was withdrawn after several media reports appeared describing him as a bully to his staff. In addition, there were reports that he kept sloppy medical records and drank excessively.[71] It was also reported that he was referred to in the White House as "the Candyman," in that he could be counted on to prescribe various strong medications to senior White House staff members upon demand in order to keep himself in their good graces.[72]

Even though negative media reports prevented Trump from appointing him to head up the department of veterans affairs, Jackson was rewarded with the former president's strong endorsement in a Republican congressional primary in Texas. Trump tweeted that "Ronny is strong on Crime and Borders, GREAT for our Military and Vets."[73] Jackson won both the Republican primary and the general election in November 2020.[74]

# TRUMP'S CABINET

## Attorney General William P. Barr

> *"Bill Barr has resigned as attorney general, as opposed to before, when Barr was simply resigned to his fate of defending every stupid thing that Donald Trump has ever said."*

### James Corden – December 14, 2020

No U.S. attorney general in modern history did more to politicize and debase the Department of Justice than William P. Barr. This will be his shameful legacy for time immemorial. If ever there is a Wall of Shame erected in Washington, D.C., Barr's name will be indelibly written on it, along with several of the other major subverters of our great democracy during the Trump era. Under his name should be engraved this short description of his perfidy:

> As the 85th Attorney General of the United States, William P. Barr indelibly tarnished the reputation of the country's once great Justice Department by protecting President Trump's criminal associates, targeting his political enemies, intervening in cases for partisan purposes, firing honest prosecutors, and effectively creating two standards for justice in the United States: one for Trump and his team and one for everyone else. His treachery will never be forgiven nor forgotten.

This country has both a written constitution and an unwritten one. Everyone knows of the written one, a stroke of genius bequeathed to us by our Founders at the 1787 Constitutional Convention in Philadelphia. It has served us well for over 240 years and hopefully will endure in perpetuity. However, one of the strengths of our democracy is that we have an unwritten set of democratic norms that evolved over time. These have been carefully handed down from one generation of Americans to another as part of our democratic system of government.

One of the primary pillars of these unwritten rules of normative behavior in our democracy is that the U.S. Department of Justice acts independently regarding criminal investigations and prosecutions, without interference from or consultation with the White House. This independence of the investigative and prosecutorial arms of the federal government is one of the major marks of a true and resilient democracy, which—along with an independent judiciary—distinguishes the United States from the DINOs (Democracies In Name Only) that give lip service to democracy, but really are autocracies, plutocracies, or dictatorships, since the rule of law has been fatally compromised.

Then along came William P. Barr. Previously a fairly well-respected member of the political establishment, Barr was named acting attorney general in August 1991 by President George H. W. Bush upon the resignation of Attorney General Richard Thornburgh to run for the Pennsylvania Senate. In 1992, after being overwhelmingly confirmed by the U.S. Senate as Attorney General, Barr published a Justice Department position paper entitled "The Case for More Incarceration," in which he described prison as the best antidote to crime. "The choice," he wrote, "is simple: more prisons or more crime."[1] Barr was not alone in this blood-thirsty campaign to lock more and more Americans—primarily poor people of color—behind bars, which soon left the United States in the unenviable position of having a greater percentage of its population in prison than any other nation.[2] Notably, President Joe Biden, who was then a Senator from Delaware, was also a big fan of increased incarceration as part of the War on Crime and the War on Drugs, which were little more than thinly veiled campaigns to terrorize communities comprised primarily of poor, disadvantaged, and vulnerable people of color.[3] It was a sign of the times, for which at least Biden and a few other of our leaders have since apologized. But Barr, who comes from the same school as Donald Trump when it comes to accepting responsibility (which is to never admit fault), has never apologized.

When President Trump selected Barr to be his attorney general, the general consensus was that he was about as good an appointment as one could expect from Trump, under the circumstances. Viewed as a Washington insider, the expectation was that Barr would act honorably and provide a much-needed buffer between Trump's worst anti-democratic and autocratic impulses and the democratic norms that pre-dated the Trump Administration, and hopefully would survive it.

These expectations were dashed shortly after Barr assumed office as he repeatedly lied to the American public, twisted the law beyond reason, and ran roughshod over longstanding Justice Department norms and principles. Barr aggressively used the Justice Department to carry out Trump's political agenda and, in only two short years, degraded and corrupted the Justice Department like no other attorney general in modern history.

In retrospect, we should have known that the Barr we hoped for would not be the Barr we got. Even before he was ever appointed, he actively campaigned for the office so unceremoniously vacated by Jeff Sessions. During the first two years of the Trump presidency, Barr frequently criticized legal challenges against Trump and investigations into Trump's 2016 campaign and presidency.[4] In 2017, he publicly stated that there was "nothing inherently wrong" with Donald Trump's calls for investigating Hillary Clinton while the two were both running for president, adding that an investigation into the "Uranium One conspiracy" allegedly involving the Clintons was more appropriate than the one looking into whether Trump conspired with Russia to influence the 2016 elections.[5] Barr's criticism of the "lock her up" movement directed at Hillary Clinton was so tepid that it bordered on an endorsement. For example, in 2017, Barr said that "there are [still] things that should be investigated that haven't been investigated," even though the FBI and various Republican-led Congressional committees had already exhaustively investigated allegations relating to the Clinton Foundation and the related Uranium One matter since 2015.[6]

In February 2017, Barr also argued Trump was justified in firing Acting Attorney General Sally Yates over her refusal to defend Executive Order 13769 and her directive to Justice Department lawyers to stop defending Trump's ban on new arrivals to the United States from seven Muslim-majority countries.[7]

In his public campaign to be named attorney general, Barr even went so far as to send an unsolicited 20-page memo in June 2018 to the Justice Department criticizing Robert Mueller's obstruction of justice investigation, calling it "fatally misconceived."[8] Barr also provided copies of the memo to members of Trump's legal team and discussed it with some of them.[9] In his memo, Barr argued that the special counsel should not be investigating Trump for obstruction of justice because Trump's actions, such as firing FBI Director James Comey, were within his powers as head of the executive branch.[10] He characterized the obstruction investigation as "fatally misconceived," "grossly irresponsible," and "potentially disastrous" to the executive branch.[11] Democrats correctly characterized the memo as Barr's job application for the attorney general position.[12]

## Barr's Distortion of the Mueller Report

Later, as attorney general, Barr held up the public release of the Mueller Report long enough to issue a distorted and misleading summary of the report, whitewashing its contents and suggesting that it exonerated Trump. Barr released his four-page summary to Congress on March 24, 2019, misrepresenting the principal conclusion of the report. Among other things, the memo misleadingly stated that the special counsel did not establish conspiracy or coordination between the Trump campaign and Russia's efforts to interfere with the 2016 election.[13] Secondly, Barr's summary stated that the special counsel made no decision as to whether to prosecute Trump for obstruction of justice. Barr misleadingly quoted a small portion of Mueller's conclusions, which actually stated that "while this report does not conclude that the President committed a crime, it also does not exonerate him."[14] Barr and Deputy Attorney General Rod Rosenstein themselves concluded that the evidence did not establish obstruction of justice beyond reasonable doubt and made the decision not to press the charge, stating, "Deputy Attorney General Rod Rosenstein and I have concluded that the evidence developed during the Special Counsel's investigation is not sufficient to establish that the President committed an obstruction-of-justice offense."[15]

Barr also misrepresented the Mueller Report by saying that it gave no indication that Congress could make a determination on obstruction of justice, although the report specifically stated "that Congress may apply obstruction laws."[16] Barr also said the report was not supposed to be made public, which was untrue since Department of Justice regulations give the attorney general wide discretion to release such a report.[17] His summary of the report further stated that "the White House fully cooperated with the Special Counsel's investigation," which was completely false; Trump refused requests by the special counsel's office for an in-person interview.[18] In fact, Trump only agreed to give written responses to interview questions, which the Mueller Report described as "inadequate."[19] The report also documented numerous instances where Trump tried to either impede or end the special counsel's investigation.[20]

Even normally reserved Special Counsel Robert Mueller was so distressed by Barr's distorted summary of the report that he wrote a letter of objection to

Barr, saying in dry and understated language that Barr "did not fully capture the context, nature, and substance of this Office's work and conclusions."[21]

Later, in March 2020, Reggie Walton, a federal district judge originally appointed by President George W. Bush, considered the dispute about the Justice Department's redactions to the Mueller Report. After studying the matter, Walton implicitly agreed with the special counsel's critique of Barr's distorted summary, finding that Barr's public "inconsistencies" with the Mueller report "cause the Court to seriously question whether Attorney General Barr made a calculated attempt to influence public discourse about the Mueller Report in favor of President Trump..."[22] Walton pointedly noted Barr's "lack of candor," which "call[s] into question Attorney General Barr's credibility." He further expressed his concerns that Barr may have made a "calculated attempt to influence public discourse" in favor of President Trump by establishing "a one-sided narrative" about the report contrary to its complete findings. Walton questioned if the report's redactions were actually "self-serving" to avoid conflict with Barr's statements, and if the Justice Department used "post-hoc rationalizations" to defend Barr. Thus, Walton decided to personally review the redacted material to check if the redactions were justified.[23]

While ruling that the redaction of FBI reports of witness interviews was proper,[24] Judge Walton ruled on September 30, 2020 that the DOJ had violated federal law by redacting some portions of the Mueller Report and ordered them to be released before the November election.[25]

## Barr Effectively Becomes Trump's PR Director

Instead of being chastened by such criticism from a federal judge and making a course correction back to the established sea lanes the Justice Department traditionally navigated, Barr apparently decided to double down on his overt political support for Trump and his corresponding sharp break with long-standing Justice Department traditions. It became commonplace during Barr's tenure as attorney general to virtually repeat Trump's latest talking points verbatim. For example, when Barr testified before Congress, he "confirmed" that the FBI's counterintelligence investigation of Trump amounted to "spying."[26] He also suggested that it was lawful for the White House to direct administration officials to defy congressional subpoenas, since Barr viewed the imperial presidency as incapable of doing any wrong.[27]

## Barr Interjects Politics into DOJ Criminal Prosecutions

Perhaps most egregious was Barr's decision to intervene in politically charged cases, undermining his own Justice Department prosecutors by selectively seeking unwarranted leniency for Trump cronies. In the spring of 2019, Barr reportedly attempted to undermine the conviction of Trump fixer Michael Cohen for campaign finance violations. Barr reportedly raised doubts multiple times about the validity of the charges against Cohen, including requesting the Office of Legal Counsel to draft a legal memorandum which could have helped Cohen's case.[28] Ultimately, Cohen's conviction was not changed, which both Trump and Barr must have found extremely frustrating.[29]

Barr was more successful in his attempts to politically interfere on Trump's behalf with the federal prosecutions of Roger Stone and Michael Flynn. Barr went so far as to direct Justice Department prosecutors to seek dismissal of the charges filed against Flynn, an order that some of the career prosecutors refused to carry out and which the U.S. District Court Judge handling Flynn's case refused to do, until Trump issued a pardon for Flynn. When Barr was asked in a media interview if it now meant nothing that Flynn "admitted lying to the FBI," Barr gave a response that was so full of transparent rationalizations and sophistry that only a direct quote can do it justice: "People sometimes plead to things that turn out not to be crimes ... The Department of Justice is not persuaded that this was material to any legitimate counterintelligence investigation. So it was not a crime."[30] Since every rookie federal prosecutor or FBI agent knows that lying to an FBI agent, even when not under oath, is a federal crime under Title 18, United States Code, Section 1001, Barr's nonsensical comments did much to undermine public confidence in federal law enforcement officers, and, inevitably, may have led many Americans to question whether they really should respond truthfully to questions by federal law enforcement officers.

In February 2020, President Trump gave Barr an enthusiastic shout out for interceding in the Justice Department's prosecution of Trump's old friend and associate Roger Stone by recommending a light sentence for Stone.

Trump's tweeted, "Congratulations to Attorney General Bill Barr for taking charge of a case that was totally out of control and perhaps should not have even been brought."[31] Initially, four career prosecutors had recommended that Stone serve a jail term of between seven and nine years. A Trump tweet followed: "Cannot allow this miscarriage of justice!"—after which the Justice Department recommended an unspecified jail term.[32] The DOJ lamely claimed that this decision was made without consulting the White House, but the immediate resignation of the DOJ prosecutors assigned to the case belied the Department's official position.[33]

Barr also kowtowed to White House directives by refusing to respond to virtually every Congressional subpoena or request for information that the White House considered "sensitive." Most notably, he refused to provide Congress with an unredacted version of the Mueller report.[34] On May 8, 2019, the House Judiciary Committee voted along party lines to hold Barr in contempt of Congress for failing to comply with a subpoena for the full Report.[35]

Shortly thereafter, in early June, the House Oversight Committee again moved to hold Barr in contempt of Congress for defying a subpoena regarding the efforts to add a citizenship question to the census.[36] The following month, the House of Representatives voted to hold Barr in criminal contempt of Congress for failing to produce documents required by other congressional subpoenas.[37] Only once before had a sitting Cabinet member been held in criminal contempt of Congress. The House instructed the Justice Department to prosecute Barr, but, unsurprisingly, the Department refused to prosecute the man who ran it.[38]

## Barr Refuses to Investigate the Ukraine Scandal

Barr also violated his oath of office, in which he swore to defend the U.S. Constitution, by demonstrating that his first allegiance was to Trump, not to the country, when he refused to investigate potential wrongdoing relating to the Ukraine scandal that resulted in Trump's first impeachment.[39] Barr then oversaw the Justice Department's issuance of a preposterous memo aimed at preventing Congress and the public from ever learning about the whistleblower's complaint regarding Trump's improper extortion of the Ukrainian government.[40]

In September 2019, the same month that the whistleblower complaint relating to the Trump-Zelensky phone call was released and the impeachment inquiry began, Barr was reported to have been contacting foreign governments on Trump's behalf to ask for help in the Justice Department's baseless "investigation" of the origins of the Trump-Russia investigation.[41] Barr was so committed to doing Trump's political bidding that he personally traveled to the United Kingdom and Italy to seek information. At Barr's request, Trump phoned the prime minister of Australia to request his cooperation, seeking information related to a conspiracy theory that circulated among Trump allies in conservative media.[42] The theory asserted that Joseph Mifsud, the mysterious professor who introduced George Papadopoulos to Russian operatives, was a Western intelligence operative. According to the theory, Mifsud had been directed to ensnare Papadopoulos in order to establish a false predicate for the FBI to open an investigation into Russian interference in the 2016 presidential election.[43]

Barr also refused to refute the debunked conspiracy theory of Ukrainian interference in the 2016 election.[44] In February 2020, Barr confirmed that he had "established an intake process" within the Justice Department for information on Ukraine, including information coming from Rudy Giuliani. Barr explained that the DOJ had an "obligation to have an open door" policy on receiving information from all sources.[45] Barr's comments came a day after Lindsay Graham stated that the Justice Department "is receiving information coming out of the Ukraine" from Giuliani in his capacity as the personal lawyer to President Trump.[46] Neither Barr nor Graham, however, mentioned that Giuliani himself was reportedly being investigated by the Justice Department or that two of his associates with ties to Russian and Ukrainian organized crime—Lev Parnas and Igor Fruman—had been indicted and arrested.[47]

Barr's personal handling of this far-flung and largely fanciful international investigation was so bizarre that one British official observed, "It is like nothing we have come across before, they are basically asking, in quite robust terms, for help in doing a hatchet job on their own intelligence services."[48]

## Barr Attacks His Own DOJ Prosecutors

Barr brought the DOJ to a nadir on September 17, 2020, when he publicly blasted his own Justice Department prosecutors as a "permanent bureaucracy" that all too often "abused" their power by going after high-profile targets in a process he likened to "headhunting."[49]

Barr did not mention any particular prosecutions, but it did not take much imagination to deduce that he was responding to recent strong criticism over his decisions to intervene in cases to help people close to President Trump, including longtime political adviser Roger Stone and former national security adviser Michael Flynn. Some DOJ prosecutors quit in response to Barr's interventions, and two current Justice Department employees had the temerity to testify before Congressional whistleblower hearings about political interference with the DOJ's duties. Barr was so unhinged by the storm of criticism at his politicization of the Justice Department that he likened DOJ junior prosecutors to preschool children: "Letting the most junior members set the agenda might be a good philosophy for a Montessori preschool, but it's no way to run a federal agency."[50]

## General Barr Orders An Attack on Peaceful BLM Protesters

Further cementing his reputation as the worst and most dangerous attorney general in modern history, Barr helped orchestrate the June 1, 2020 unprovoked attack on peaceful protesters in Lafayette Square, directly across from the White House. This became one of the ugliest defining moments of the Trump presidency, and Barr was its chief orchestrator. After all, it was Barr who gave the order that the park be cleared so that Trump, Barr, and other administration officials could stage a photo in front of St. John's Church, which is on the other side of the park.[51] Trump apparently felt he needed to do something dramatic that made him appear decisive in order to compensate for the breaking news that he recently sought refuge from the ongoing Black Lives Matter protests by hiding in the White House basement bunker. This bunker was last occupied by Vice President Dick Cheney in the wake of the September 11th terrorist attacks.

By the afternoon of June 1, the streets near the White House were occupied by only peaceful protesters participating in the George Floyd protests in Washington, D.C. Barr ordered unidentified federal officers in unmarked uniforms to forcibly remove the demonstrators. They rushed the peaceful protesters without notice and employed smoke canisters, pepper balls, riot shields, and batons against them so that the president could score some publicity.[52]

Once Lafayette Park had been cleared of protesters and tear gas, Donald Trump sallied forth as if he had just won a great military victory, like General Douglas McArthur being photographed upon his triumphant return to the Philippines after the defeat of Japanese forces there. Trump then posed for a photo op in front of historic St. John's Church, accompanied by Barr (who by this time preferred being called General Barr), as well as Joint Chief of Staff General Mark Milley (who was dressed in combat fatigues), and other assorted "dignitaries." Ivanka Trump was there too, having dutifully brought in her $1,500 handbag the Bible that Trump then used as a prop.[53]

When the press reports of the incident did not go as the White House expected, Barr reacted to the incident by falsely claiming that pepper balls used by law enforcement on protesters were not chemical irritants, despite the fact that such a description is used by the product's manufacturer.[54]

Barr also went out of his way, amid the George Floyd protests against racism and police brutality, to publicly reject the view "that the law enforcement system is systemically racist."[55] In a CNN news interview in September 2020, Barr denied that systemic racism plays a role in police shootings of unarmed African American men, calling such shootings by white police officers "very rare."[56]

Barr also tried his best to exacerbate the deep divisions that were already tending to tear the country apart, creating two separate Americas, with each one doing little to communicate with the other one. In an August 2020 appearance on Fox News, for example, Barr asserted that the Black Lives Matter movement was "a revolutionary group that is interested in some form of socialism, communism. They're essentially Bolsheviks. Their tactics are fascistic."[57] Barr equated the movement with Antifa, characterizing a loose collective of anti-fascist leftists as "highly organized," claiming "the media doesn't take footage of what's happening" at George Floyd protests.[58] He also asserted that liberals are intent on "tearing down the system" and that the

Democratic party was only "interested in total victory. It's a secular religion. It's a substitute for a religion."[59]

Barr's overheated imagination went into overdrive as the summer of protests in 2020 stretched out for several weeks, and he even started "verifying" some of Trump's own baseless claims about how the largely spontaneous protests around the country came about. In an August 2020 interview, for example, Trump claimed that a plane full of "thugs in dark uniforms," implying Antifa, had recently flown from one unidentified city to another with the intention of fomenting riots.[60] Two days later, Barr falsely confirmed that he had evidence that Antifa activists "are flying around the country" and "we are following them."[61] Despite Barr's vigorous attempts to blame Antifa for orchestrating the George Floyd protests, a review of records of those arrested for serious federal crimes at the protests showed that none of the arrests had been linked to Antifa.[62]

Barr also gave serious consideration to arresting leaders of Antifa and the Black Lives Matter movement.[63] The Wall Street Journal reported in September 2020 that Barr told federal prosecutors to consider charging violent protestors with plotting to overthrow the U.S. government.[64] This legal tool—charges for sedition—has rarely been used by the Justice Department.[65] The charges are reserved for those who "conspire to overthrow, put down, or to destroy by force the Government of the United States."[66] Prosecution of peaceful protesters on sedition charges would mean that the Justice Department's prosecution manual had to be tossed aside, permitting prosecution of individuals based on their political speech.[67]

## Barr Promotes Trump's Election Fraud Fantasy

Finally, in the months leading up to the 2020 election, Barr mindlessly parroted Trump's most baseless and nonsensical claims about the potential for massive voter fraud. The attorney general made wildly exaggerated claims to the media and to Congress about the potential for voter fraud, conspicuously failing to offer up any compelling or reliable evidence.[68] He blamed purported left-wing, so-called Antifa-related extremist groups for widespread violence, but—like Trump—remained conspicuously reluctant to acknowledge the threat of right-wing extremism.

In a September 2020 interview, Barr falsely asserted the Justice Department had indicted a Texas man for fraudulently completing 1,700 mail-in ballots.[69] There was no such indictment, and the matter actually involved a series of errors by election officials during a county election.[70]

Barr also repeated a claim that foreign adversaries could flood the country with counterfeit ballots to disrupt the election, a threat experts characterized as nearly impossible to execute.[71] Senior American intelligence officials flatly contradicted Barr, saying there was no evidence any foreign powers intended to manipulate mail-in voting.[72] On the day after Barr's interview, the Department of Homeland Security issued an intelligence bulletin. It warned that Russia was using social media and other venues to promote false claims that mail-in voting would lead to widespread fraud in order "to undermine public trust in the electoral process."[73] The DHS bulletin, while not naming anyone specifically, made it clear to observers that Trump, Barr, and the Russian disinformation industry certainly appeared to be aligned in their efforts to undermine public confidence in the integrity of the electoral process.

Despite knowing the damage to our democratic system being caused by the false narrative of massive voter fraud he was spreading, Barr irresponsibly continued to use the vast powers of his position as United States attorney general to set the stage for a Trump post-election claim that the election had been stolen. In a September 2020 interview, Barr stated that mail-in voting meant "we're back in the business of selling and buying votes" including "outright coercion, paying off a postman, here's a few hundred dollars, give me some of your ballots."[74] Barr's shameless campaign to undermine the 2020 elections led the 2,000 former DOJ attorneys who had called for Barr's resignation earlier in the year to sign a second open letter on October 1, 2020, accusing him of trying to rig the upcoming election for Trump. They stated, "we fear that Attorney General Barr intends to use the DOJ's vast law enforcement powers to undermine our most fundamental democratic value: free and fair elections."[75]

As the Trump team's baseless claims of voting fraud continued to circulate in the aftermath of his decisive loss in the November 3, 2020 election,[76] Barr sent a memo to DOJ prosecutors authorizing them to investigate "vote tabulation irregularities" before voting results had been certified, a reversal of long-standing department policy.[77] Richard Pilger, director of the Election

Crimes Branch at the DOJ Criminal Division, stepped down from that position in protest hours later.[78] Four days later, sixteen assistant U.S. attorneys of the Election Crimes Branch wrote Barr a letter urging him to rescind the memo because it "thrusts career prosecutors into partisan politics."[79]

Only when it became apparent to all but the most rabid of the Trump faithful that Trump's days in office were nearing an end did Barr make some half-hearted efforts to try to rehabilitate his tattered reputation. He finally and publicly contradicted Trump's continued insistence that he was the victim of widespread voter fraud. On December 1, 2020 Barr announced that the Justice Department "has not uncovered evidence of widespread voter fraud that would change the outcome of the 2020 presidential election."[80] Trump was reportedly livid over Barr's announcement. He was even further angered when it was disclosed that Barr had actually followed Justice Department policy by not disclosing during the campaign that Joe Biden's son Hunter had been under criminal investigation since 2018.[81]

## Barr's Epitaph

Barr's attempt to rehabilitate what was left of his reputation when he realized that he was on his way out the door along with Trump came too late to trigger any rewrite of his shameful legacy, which brought disrepute to both him and the once-great DOJ he tarnished.

Barr's professional epitaph was most eloquently written by 65 law professors and faculty from George Washington University Law School, Barr's alma mater. In a June 2020 letter, they wrote that he had "failed to fulfill his oath of office to 'support and defend the Constitution of the United States.'"[82] They wrote that Barr's actions as attorney general "have undermined the rule of law, breached constitutional norms, and damaged the integrity and traditional independence of his office and of the Department of Justice."[83] Donald Ayer, a former deputy attorney general for whom Barr worked during the George H. W. Bush presidency, added to this damning critique during a House Judiciary Committee hearing, declaring that Barr "poses the greatest threat, in my lifetime, to our rule of law and to public trust in it."[84]

# Michael R. Pompeo

Secretary of State Mike Pompeo, arguably the "Trumpiest" of all Trump's Cabinet members, presided over the substantial dismantling of the State Department and the rapid collapse of America's standing, reputation, and influence in the world. He aggressively pursued Trump's "America First" agenda that alienated the country from its allies and the international community while mimicking the president's inane bombast and flouting of political and democratic norms.

In sharp contrast to both Democratic and Republican predecessors in his post, Pompeo turned traditional diplomacy on its head by praising dictators and criticizing democratic allies. He did little to strengthen our international standing and stood idly by as Trump sought to undermine NATO and our other alliances that had kept us safe since the end of World War II. America is weaker for it, and the damage he has caused will take years to repair.

## Pompeo's Disregard for Both Law and Accepted Norms

In May 2020, Pompeo fired the inspector general who was investigating his attempts to sell arms to Saudi Arabia in violation of a congressional ban on such sales. Pompeo was also under investigation for his alleged personal use of federal resources. Each of the two succeeding acting inspectors general quit after a few months under pressure from Pompeo, who continually attacked their work.

In August 2020, Pompeo spoke by video at the Republican National Convention from Jerusalem, where he was on an official trip. This was a blatant violation of the Hatch Act, which bars government officials from engaging in such overt political activity. In his speech, he praised Trump's "bold initiatives in nearly every corner of the world."[85]

## Pompeo Stands By as Trump and Giuliani Run Amok in Ukraine

One of Pompeo's greatest failures and most shameful moments occurred when he stood silently by as he watched Trump and his personal lawyer, Rudy Giuliani, set up a parallel State Department for Ukraine, with Giuliani and his sketchy Russian-mob affiliates digging around in Ukraine looking for dirt on Joe Biden. Trump's impeachment investigation was then triggered when Trump himself tried to extort the Ukrainian president into launching an investigation of Biden's son Hunter in exchange for the release of desperately needed military aid.

When asked about his knowledge of the controversial call made by President Trump on July 25, 2019, to Ukraine's President Volodymyr Zelensky, Pompeo initially lied, saying he had little knowledge of the call since he had not yet read the transcript.[86] It was later confirmed by officials that he himself had been on the call.[87]

Pompeo also shamefully permitted Giuliani and his cohorts to mount a smear campaign against U.S. Ambassador to Ukraine Marie Yovanovich, resulting in the ambassador's removal. Indeed, as it turned out, Pompeo was an active participant in the scheme to remove the ambassador. She was seen as an obstacle to the campaign to falsely paint Ukraine as the foreign culprit in the 2016 election interference. Pompeo and Giuliani exchanged emails and phone calls in late March 2019 before Yovanovitch was recalled from Ukraine.[88] The documents also showed that the State Department had deliberately deceived Congress about the rationale for Yovanovitch's removal as ambassador to Ukraine.[89] Giuliani later admitted he spoke to Pompeo on the phone in late March 2019 "to relay information he had gathered during his Ukrainian research."[90] Pompeo also gave credence to the bogus investigation into Ukraine's supposed meddling in the 2016 campaign by telling a reporter that the United States had a duty to investigate such claims.[91] By not standing up for the professional diplomats in the State Department, Pompeo permitted some of the best talent in the department to be fired or driven out in a McCarthy-like purge.

## Pompeo Remains Silent As the Saudi Crown Prince Kills a U.S. Journalist

Pompeo hit another low point in his mishandling of the State Department when he refused to hold Mohammed bin Salman, Saudi Arabia's crown prince and heir apparent, accountable for the gruesome killing of Saudi journalist and U.S. resident Jamal Khashoggi. The journalist was slain in October 2018 in the Saudi Consulate in Istanbul, Turkey. Pompeo's acceptance of the obviously fabricated Saudi position—that a "rogue operation" was responsible—was completely inconsistent with the facts, including contemporaneous videos and analysis by independent investigators.[92]

## Pompeo Promotes Trump's Fantasyland Until the End

Following the 2020 election, Pompeo smugly perpetuated the absurd pretense that he fully expected that it would be Trump who would be sworn in as the next president, despite overwhelming evidence showing Biden won the election. He disingenuously promised "a smooth transition to a second Trump Administration."[93]

Goodbye, and good riddance to you, Mike Pompeo. Your name, like that of Benedict Arnold, shall be forever etched in infamy.

# EPA Administrator Scott Pruitt

Scott Pruitt, the former Oklahoma attorney general, was chosen by President Trump to lead the Environmental Protection Agency (EPA). As administrator of the EPA, Pruitt relentlessly presided over the dismantling of many, if not most, of the agency's regulations designed to protect the environment and the U.S. people from the harmful consequences of contamination. During his roughly 16 months in office, Pruitt reversed more than a dozen major Obama-era regulations and dismantled key elements of the agency's approach to scientific research, making it much more corporate friendly. Pruitt unraveled most federal restrictions on greenhouse-gas emissions and toxic-waste discharge from coal-fired power plants. He also successfully pushed Trump to announce the withdrawal of the United States from the Paris Climate Accord, questioning the science of climate change and also the overwhelming scientific consensus that human activity was the primary contributor to global warming. Pruitt even refused to ban the use of a pesticide that was known to cause potential neurological damage in human fetuses.

Pruitt gained national prominence—and Trump's attention—when he sued the EPA 14 times in his capacity as Oklahoma's attorney general. After taking over the EPA, he spent most of his time meeting privately with industry leaders regulated by his agency, including top executives from the fossil fuel, agriculture, and chemical sectors.[94] He then obediently followed their directions on how best to dismantle the agency and its "anti-business" regulations.[95]

In addition to being the Trump administration official most responsible for the degradation of environment, Pruitt was also one of the most corrupt officials in an administration in which there was a crowd of serious contenders for that position. His lavish overspending at public expense—including his insistence on travelling first-class at taxpayer expense[96] and the $43,000 expense for a soundproof phone booth in his office—was unusual even by Trump administration standards.[97] His numerous ethical lapses during his tenure as EPA administrator were also notable, such as the revelation that he had a discounted condominium rental from the wife of a D.C. lobbyist.[98] The *Washington Post* reported that another lobbyist who helped arrange Pruitt's $100,000 trip to Morocco in December 2017 was later rewarded with a $40,000 per month contract to promote Morocco's interests.[99]

Pruitt was also the subject of a series of news reports that he repeatedly enlisted subordinates to help him search for housing, book personal travel, and help search for a six-figure job for his wife.[100] He even went so far as to make a phone call with Chick-fil-A executives in which he discussed his wife's purchase of a franchise with that company. Pruitt tried to explain away this ethical lapse, saying, "I love, she loves, we love Chick-Fil-A as a, as a franchise of faith, and it's one of the best in the country, and so, that's something we were very excited about."[101] Evidence emerged that Pruitt had also intervened on his wife's behalf with a conservative judicial group that eventually hired her.[102]

More than a dozen federal inquiries were conducted into Pruitt's spending and management at the EPA. Apparently undeterred, Pruitt spent thousands of dollars at a fine jewelry and watch store in Washington, D.C., including more than $1,500 on a dozen fountain pens, all purchased with public funds.[103] The news of his fountain pen shopping spree broke only one day after Pruitt appeared on a talk show aired by Sinclair Broadcast Group, where he suggested that he was misunderstood and was actually a very frugal person who cared "so much about taxpayer money." Only a few days earlier, it was reported that in December, 2018 Pruitt attended a University of Kentucky basketball game as a guest of coal baron Joseph W. Craft III.[104] An EPA spokesperson insisted that the get-together was purely social and had nothing to do with Pruitt's recent decisions to rescind numerous environmental regulations that benefitted the coal industry.

The beginning of the end for Pruitt came when several of his top aides either resigned or were told to pack up and leave. For example, Millan Hupp, a top Pruitt aide, resigned after testifying before the House Oversight Committee that part of her daily work routine was to take care of a number of personal tasks for the administrator, including the purchase of a used Trump hotel mattress.[105]

As evidence of Pruitt's overspending and corruption mounted, several congressional Republicans, as well as some governors, conservative groups, and pundits, defended him. These included Senators Rand Paul of Kentucky and Ted Cruz of Texas, Governor Matt Bevin of Kentucky, Governor Phil Bryant of Mississippi, and Governor Pete Ricketts of Nebraska. Bevin tweeted that Pruitt should "ignore the nattering nabobs of negativism," invoking a phrase Vice President Spiro T. Agnew used in 1969 when blasting the media.[106]

At first, Trump continued to back Pruitt, commenting, for example, on June 6, 2018, "People are really impressed with the job that's being done at the EPA."[107] However, Trump's continuing praise of Pruitt started sounding much like President George W. Bush's endorsement of his embattled FEMA chief Michael D. Brown in 2005, just before he was fired in the wake of that agency's disastrous response to Hurricane Katrina: "Brownie, you're doing a heck of a job."

On the night before offering his resignation, Pruitt attended a gathering for military families on the White House lawn. A band played. Families spread blankets on the grass as fireworks exploded over the nation's Capitol. Less than 24 hours after Trump's latest endorsement of him, Pruitt was given the word to submit his resignation.

In a resignation letter, Pruitt wrote that it had been "a blessing" to serve under Trump and to be able to undertake "transformative work" at the EPA.[108] Few doubted that Pruitt—who had made a career representing the interests of coal mining and energy companies—was referring to the near complete dismantling of the agency as a corporate watchdog designed to prevent the trashing of the country's remaining environmental resources and the health of its citizens.

Democrats and environmentalists were unrestrained in their relief at Pruitt's departure. Senator Thomas R. Carper of Delaware, the top Democrat on the Senate Environment and Public Works Committee, commented that Pruitt's "brazen abuse of his position" had surprised even Republican legislators who championed his diligence in dismantling the agency's environmental regulations.[109] "We had a good idea what he was going to be on the policy side. We had no idea how morally bereft he would be," Carper told reporters. "He was all the things this administration said it was opposed to . . . He's done a lot of damage. It can be reversed, but it's going to take some time."

## HUD Secretary Dr. Ben Carson

After an unsuccessful run as a candidate in the 2016 Republican presidential primary, Dr. Ben Carson, a retired neurosurgeon, joined Trump's transition team as vice chairman. Carson was offered a cabinet position in the administration, which he initially declined on the basis that he lacked the experience. An aide stated, "The last thing he would want to do was take a position that could cripple the presidency."[110] He was eventually offered the position of Secretary of Housing and Urban Development (HUD), which he accepted.[111] During the confirmation process, there was a focus on his lack of relevant experience on housing issues, which he readily admitted.[112]

As Secretary of HUD, Carson watched passively as his department's budget was slashed by the Trump administration. Under the federal budget proposed by Trump in 2017, HUD's budget for fiscal year 2018 was reduced by $6.2 billion (13%) and the Community Development Block Grant, a program which Carson praised in a trip to Detroit as HUD secretary, was eliminated.[113] Carson even issued a statement supporting the proposed cuts.[114] He suggested that federal funds for housing in Detroit could be part of an expected infrastructure bill, but such a bill never got off the ground in Congress.[115]

On March 1, 2020, Vice President Mike Pence announced Carson's addition to the White House Coronavirus Task Force.[116] However, on November 9, 2020, Carson tested positive for COVID-19 after attending President Trump's election night party.[117] He initially treated himself with a homeopathic oleander extract on the recommendation of Mike Lindell, the founder of My Pillow, Inc.[118] Oleander was previously rejected by the Food and Drug Administration as a treatment for COVID-19.[119] Carson disclosed on November 20 that he subsequently became "extremely sick" and attributed his recovery to Regeneron's experimental antibody therapy, to which President Trump had given him access.[120]

Carson was criticized justifiably for spending more than $31,000 on a dining set in his office in late 2017.[121] This expenditure was discovered after Helen Foster, a career HUD official, filed a complaint alleging that she had been demoted from her position because she refused to spend more than the legal $5,000 limit for office redecorations.[122] The Government Accountability Office (GAO) found that Carson failed to disclose the purchase.

Carson and his spokesman said that he had little or no involvement in the purchase of the dining set. However, email communications later revealed that Carson and his wife selected the furniture.[123] On March 20, 2018, Carson testified before the United States House Committee on Appropriations that he had "dismissed" himself from the decision to buy the $31,000 dining room set and "left it to my wife, you know, to choose something."[124]

When Trump started issuing a flurry of post-election pardons, one of the felons he favored was Pittsburgh oral surgeon, Alfonso Costa, who committed criminal health care fraud and was a close friend and crony of Carson. It was clear that Carson had used his influence to get the pardon for Costa, who had helped Carson pocket hundreds of thousands—perhaps millions—of dollars.[125] In 2007, Costa and a partner were charged with health care fraud for defrauding insurance companies, including Blue Cross Blue Shield. After Costa pleaded guilty, Carson sent a gushing letter to a federal judge in Pittsburgh asking for leniency for Costa, who he called his "best friend."[126] Costa was eventually sentenced to a mere 100 hours of community service and a fine with no jail time. Costa fulfilled his community service requirement by working for Carson's charity.

What Carson failed to disclose was that Costa was not just a friend; he was also Carson's business partner.[127] Carson had close business links with a real estate firm Costa owned called Costa Land Management. This company helped oversee a lucrative investment for Carson and his wife, which turned into a profitable multi-million dollar commercial real estate investment.¹²⁸ Although pardons are supposed to correct miscarriages of justice, Carson helped Trump turn the process into a corrupt tool for rewarding loyalists and well-connected cronies. Carson thus confirmed his status as just another Trump "swamp creature" in Washington.

## Commerce Secretary Wilber Ross

Even though he had some stiff competition, Commerce Secretary Wilbur Ross was, without doubt, the most corrupt cabinet member in the Trump administration.¹²⁹ At the time he joined the Trump administration, he was involved in numerous shady deals as vice chair of the Bank of Cyprus and faced multiple lawsuits and SEC fines for his practices with his other business holdings.

Like Trump, Ross held onto many of his business interests despite promising to divest. When he was confirmed by the Senate in February 2017, he promised to sell all his stocks before the end of May 2017. He did not do so. Instead, from May to December 2017, when he finally sold his stock in Invesco (originally worth between $10 and 50 million), the value of Ross's holdings in Invesco had actually increased by between approximately $1.2 to 6 million.¹³⁰

In addition to his failure to follow through with his divestiture of his stock holdings, Ross was never completely candid when it came to filling out required financial disclosure statements. In fact, his 2018 financial disclosure statement was outright rejected.¹³¹ He remained on the board of a Chinese joint venture, creating a serious conflict of interest. Ross even failed to divest himself of these interests after he had taken over the primary responsibility of overseeing trade policies relating to China, and the United States and China were in the middle of a trade war.¹³² In June 2018, an investigation by Forbes found that Commerce Secretary Ross owned "stakes in companies co-owned by the Chinese government, a shipping firm tied to Vladimir Putin's inner circle, [and] a Cypriot bank reportedly caught up in Special Counsel Mueller's investigation."¹³³

A *Forbes* magazine investigation also found that his calendar was filled with meetings with corporate executives tied to his own investment portfolio, including meetings with executives of Boeing, Ford, and various other international firms, some with interests in Russia and China.[134]

## Ross Backs Trump On "Sharpiegate"

The *New York Times* disclosed that Ross "threatened to fire top employees" at the National Oceanic and Atmospheric Administration (NOAA) if they did not back up Trump's claim that Hurricane Dorian was headed for Alabama, when in fact it was not.[135] Birmingham's National Weather Service officials were forced to issue a statement reassuring Alabamians that the storm was not coming their way, after fielding calls from people worried whether they should evacuate. That prompted Trump to continue to insist he had been right about his Alabama claim, even using a Sharpie to ridiculously alter a Weather Service map to falsely show the state was within the storm's potential path.

Dubbed by the media as "Sharpiegate," the *Times* reported that Ross phoned Neil Jacobs, the acting administrator of NOAA, and "instructed Dr. Jacobs to 'fix' the agency's perceived contradiction of the president."[136] Under duress, NOAA released an unsigned statement falsely claiming Trump had in fact been given information that Alabama was a possible Hurricane Dorian target, and specifically chiding Birmingham weather officials for correcting the president.

## The Paradise Papers Scandal

In late 2017, Ross became ensnared in the Paradise Papers scandal. A huge trove of up to 13.4 million leaked documents detailed how high-net-worth individuals around the world—including Ross—used complex offshore finance structures for tax evasion purposes, or, at a minimum, to protect their millions from higher taxes. The released documents, which were leaked to the German newspaper *Süddeutsche Zeitung*, came from the computer files of Appleby, a Bermuda-based law firm, that set up the offshore financial structures. The documents consisted of emails, presentations, and other electronic data. These were then shared with the International Consortium of Investigative Journalists, a global network that won the Pulitzer Prize in 2017 for its work on the similarly leaked documents known as the Panama Papers.

Notably, the released documents relating to Ross showed that he failed to properly include all of his financial information in required disclosure filings, including his stake in a shipping company linked to Russian President Vladimir Putin.[137] This shipping company, called Navigator Holdings, had a partnership with Sibur, a Russia-based and Kremlin-connected oil and gas company.[138] Ross's major interest in Navigator (he owned nearly one third of the company) raised national security concerns as well as conflict of interest issues for Ross. Navigator's major partner, Sibur, was closely tied to the Kremlin since Putin's son-in-law, Kirill Shamalov, was a major Sibur shareholder.

Another owner of Sibur was Gennady Timchenko, a Russian billionaire on the Treasury Department's sanctions list. He has been barred from entering the United States since 2014 because authorities consider him a Specially Designated National, or SDN, who was considered by the Treasury to be a member "of the Russian leadership's inner circle."[139] The Treasury Department statement said that Timchenko's activities in the energy sector "have been directly linked to Putin," and that Putin had investments with a company previously owned by Timchenko, as well as access to the company's funds.[140] Another major Sibur shareholder was Leonid Mikhelson, who, like Timchenko, has close ties to the Kremlin. One of his companies, Novatek, Russia's second-largest natural gas producer, was placed on the Treasury's sanctions list in 2014. Ross, as a member of Trump's Cabinet, was thus simultaneously a de facto partner with at least three members of the Kremlin inner circle, including Putin's son-in-law.

## Ross Insists On Including a Citizenship Question in the Census

Even with all of these other financial and conflicts questions swirling around Ross, the most impactful controversy during Ross's tenure was the dispute over whether to include a citizenship question in the 2020 Census. As secretary of commerce, one of Ross's major responsibilities was to oversee the Census Bureau and the 2020 Census. The results of the census, which is conducted every ten years, are critical to the allocation of government funds to the various states, cities, and local governments. However, Ross precipitated a major battle over the content of the census when he approved the addition of the highly controversial question that critics suspected was linked to the Trump administration's war on immigrants and people of color: "Is this person a citizen of the United States?"[141]

Believing that this question was being included in bad faith and would deter many non-citizens and undocumented persons from answering the survey and thereby reduce federal funding for immigrant-heavy communities, New York Attorney General Barbara Underwood led a group of 17 states and the District of Columbia in the filing of a lawsuit to stop the Trump administration from adding the citizenship question on the 2020 Census.[142] Summarizing their position, Underwood issued a statement: "By demanding the citizenship status of each resident, the Trump administration is breaking with decades of policy and potentially causing a major undercount that would threaten billions in federal funds and New York's fair representation in Congress and the Electoral College."[143]

The Department of Justice supported the Commerce Department's position that the question should be included but asked the federal judge to delay any trial of the issue. On July 3, 2018, U.S. federal judge Jesse M. Furman of the U.S. District Court for the Southern District of New York ruled against the Department of Justice and Ross, holding that if the trial was delayed, the appeals process might not be completed by summer 2019, which was the printing deadline for the census.[144]

Furman blocked the proposed census question in a 277-page decision on January 15, 2019, saying that Ross had violated a "veritable smorgasbord" of federal rules and asserting Ross and his aides made false or misleading statements under oath.[145] Democrats in Congress then accused Ross of lying about the citizenship question's origins and of seeking to add the question to the census based on a pretext.[146] They argued that the Trump administration's ulterior reason for including the question was to exclude communities primarily composed of people of color from being counted.[147]

Ross and the Trump administration refused to comply with a congressional subpoena issued by the House Oversight Committee for documents regarding efforts to add a citizenship question to the 2020 Census.[148] After Trump asserted executive privilege over the subpoenaed documents, the House Oversight Committee voted to hold Ross and Attorney General Barr in criminal contempt of Congress, with the committee's chairman saying that Ross and Barr had "blatantly obstructed our ability to do congressional oversight."[149] In July 2019, the House held Barr and Ross in contempt of Congress,[150] which was only the second time in U.S. history that a sitting Cabinet member was held in contempt.[151]

On June 27, 2019, the Supreme Court, in *Department of Commerce v. New York*, left the citizenship question blocked from the 2020 census, in part because of the government's puzzling explanation for why it was added.[152] In its opinion, the Supreme Court found that there was "a significant mismatch" between Ross's decision to add the question and his stated reason that the question would support Department of Justice's Voter Rights Act.[153]

The 2020 Census thus proceeded without the citizenship question, but not before Ross had cemented his reputation as one of the worst members of the rogue's gallery that doubled as Trump's Cabinet.

## Interior Secretary Ryan Zinke

The rise and fall of Ryan Zinke as secretary of the interior is another prime reason why the Trump administration will go down in history as the most corrupt administration since that of Warren G. Harding. Zinke, a former Congressman from Montana, flaunted his penchant for grandiosity from the very start of his tenue. The day after his swearing in by Vice President Mike Pence on March 1, 2017, Zinke rode a United States Park Police horse named Tonto several blocks to the entrance of the Interior Department's main building to his official welcoming ceremony.[154] Thereafter, Zinke ordered Interior Department civil servants to fly his official secretarial flag over the Main Interior Building whenever he was present in the building.[155] According to the Washington Post, "no one can remember [the flag ritual] ever happening in the federal government."[156]

Zinke's flair for the theatrical attracted near-constant attention from the Washington press corps. Even the Interior Department Christmas parties made news, since they were always crowded with energy company lobbyists and right-wing, anti-conservation, "don't-lock-up-the-public-lands" activists. These anti-environmentalists held countless unrecorded private meetings with Zinke and his deputies, which took place in the agency's executive suites throughout the year but especially around holiday time. Zinke rarely tired of posing for photos with the lobbyists he viewed as his primary constituents as interior secretary. These photos often took place in front of a large stuffed polar bear wearing a Santa cap. In addition, mounted animals on the walls also were fitted with ornaments. In fact, Zinke never failed to display a true love of wildlife—as long as they were dead. He worked hard to roll back regulations prohibiting the import of wild game trophies from Africa, which was also a passion of the president's eldest son, Don Jr.

When Zinke commissioned his official portrait to be displayed at the Interior Department's headquarters in Washington, D.C., he chose to base the portrait on a photo of him on horseback before a towering butte that was taken while touring the Bears Ears National Monument in Utah. This was the first national monument ever created at the request of a coalition of indigenous tribes, who considered the site to be sacred.

Zinke's choice of Bears Ears as the backdrop for his official portrait was considered a slap in the face by the Bears Ears Inter-Tribal Coalition and all indigenous and tribal peoples in the United States. Zinke targeted Bears Ears and the Grand Staircase-Escalante National Monument, another national monument park in Utah, for reduction in size by about 50% so that the area could be used for oil, gas, and mining exploitation.[157]

In August 2017, Zinke put these two monument sites on the list of monuments to be shrunk by the Trump administration. In December 2017, Trump signed executive proclamations that reduced Bears Ears National Monument by 85% and Grand Staircase-Escalante National Monument by almost 46%.[158] When Trump followed through on Zinke's recommendation and signed a proclamation to shrink the site, Ethel Branch, the attorney general for the Navajo Nation, slammed the move as "absolutely shocking" and totally "disrespectful" of the decades of work that went into establishing Bears Ears.[159] In addition to the official portrait of Zinke that was displayed with that of other former secretaries at Interior headquarters, a second unofficial portrait of him was also unveiled. Once again atop a horse and wearing a cowboy hat, Zinke was depicted as riding through flames, wielding a battle ax, and fighting a massive serpent.[160] It was cartoonishly reminiscent of Raphael's famous painting of St. George slaying the dragon.

However, Zinke's troubled and scandal-ridden tenure as interior secretary had little to do with dragon-slaying heroics and everything to do with Zinke's own self-aggrandizement, disdain for the natural environment, and overwhelming urge to line his own pockets by leveraging his powerful cabinet position. Zinke misused his power to further ingratiate himself with the oil and gas company executives who coveted the use of pristine public lands that the Interior Department was entrusted to protect and preserve for all the American people as a national treasure.

By the time that Zinke resigned as interior secretary at the end of 2018, he had been the subject of at least 15 ethics and corruption investigations, some of which had been referred by the Interior Department's Inspector General to the Department of Justice's Public Integrity Section.[161] One of these investigations focused on whether Zinke stood to benefit from a Montana development deal linked to Halliburton, the giant energy company. Zinke apparently had several conversations with David J. Lesar, the chairman of Halliburton, about the Montana land deal. This raised serious conflict of interest issues for Zinke, since Halliburton was in a position to benefit from the deregulation decisions being made by the Interior Department. The land deal was in Zinke's hometown of Whitefish, Montana, and involved a development group backed by Lesar and a charitable foundation established by Zinke and headed by his wife, Lolita.[162] It included plans for a hotel, retail shops, and a microbrewery. Among other things, the federal investigation into Zinke established that he used taxpayer resources to advance the land development project and that taxpayer money was improperly spent on Zinke's travel when he met with Halliburton representatives. Zinke's tepid defense to the allegations that he had improperly accepted travel benefits on private jets was to say that he never flew on a private jet, having only flown on private planes that used propellers.[163]

Regarding the microbrewery, Zinke adamantly denied any impropriety: "Neither my wife or I are involved with the building or operation of any planned microbrewery. Any suggestion to the contrary is absurd."[164] In a later text, he said, "At this point in my life, I am more interested in sampling hand crafted beers rather than making them."[165] However, Zinke's denials began to unravel when a Whitefish city planner told *Politico* (and likely federal investigators) that the developers of the Lesar-backed project confirmed that the microbrewery was intended for Zinke.[166] Moreover, a plan for the development was submitted to the city by Zinke's wife, Lolita, who agreed to use land controlled by a Zinke-created foundation to build a parking lot for the development.[167]

Other investigations of Zinke included inquiries into whether he bent or broke government rules to allow his wife to ride in government vehicles and whether he had a security detail travel with him on a vacation to Turkey at considerable taxpayer cost.[168] Perhaps believing the best defense is a strong offense, Zinke lambasted his critics rather than taking a more conciliatory approach to the investigations of him. For example, he accused critic Representative Raúl M. Grijalva, a Democrat from Arizona, of being a drunk. Grijalva, who took over the leadership of the Congressional committee overseeing the Interior Department in January 2018, called for Zinke to step down from his position, based on the multiple investigations swirling around him. "It's hard for him to think straight from the bottom of the bottle," Zinke shot back at him on Twitter.[169]

By October 2018, two months before he resigned, the Department of Justice had opened up another major investigation of Zinke, which included allegations that he lied to the Office of the Inspector General regarding his involvement in reviewing a tribal casino project in Connecticut.[170] The two Connecticut tribes claimed that the Interior Department refused to sign off on the casino project after intense lobbying of Zinke by MGM Resorts International and two Nevada Republican lawmakers.[171]

During his tenure, Zinke tried his best to dismantle the Interior Department. In June 2017, he called for the elimination of 4,000 jobs from the department and supported the White House proposal to cut the department's budget by 13.4%.[172] That same month Zinke ordered 50 Interior members of the Senior Executive Service to be reassigned, forcing many into jobs for which they had little experience and that were in different locations.[173] One reassigned Interior senior executive, scientist Joel Clement, published an op-ed in the *Washington Post* saying that the reassignment was retaliation against him "for speaking out publicly about the dangers that climate change poses to Alaska Native communities."[174] The moves prompted the Interior Department's Office of Inspector General to launch a probe.[175]

Zinke's response to what he considered as a rebellion by some Interior Department employees was to give a speech to the National Petroleum Council alleging that one-third of the department's employees were disloyal to Trump and that "I got 30 percent of the crew that's not loyal to the flag." Democratic Senator Maria Cantwell, the ranking member of the Senate Committee on Energy and Natural Resources, responded that Zinke had a "fundamental misunderstanding of the role" of the federal civil service, which was supposed to be non-partisan.[176]

In August 2018, Zinke said that "environmental terrorist groups" were to blame for the wildfires in California, and that they had "nothing to do with climate change," a position that was considered nonsensical by virtually every climate scientist and forestry expert.[177]

Zinke was eventually given the ultimatum by the White House to resign by the end of the year, which he did in mid-December 2018. In addition to the scandals constantly swirling around him, Zinke left a dubious legacy as the most pro-fossil fuel, anti-conservation Interior secretary in the country's history. Jennifer Rokala, executive director of the Center for Western Priorities, said in a statement. "Surrounding himself with former lobbyists, it quickly became clear that Ryan Zinke was a pawn for the oil and gas industry. We can expect more of the same from Acting Secretary David Bernhardt, but without the laughable Teddy Roosevelt comparisons."[178]

Perhaps Zinke's most accurate political eulogy was that given by Senator Chuck Schumer, who described the Interior secretary's legacy as follows: "Ryan Zinke was one of the most toxic members of the cabinet in the way he treated our environment, our precious public lands, and the way he treated the government like it was his personal honey pot." Schumer continued: "The swamp cabinet will be a little less foul without him."[179]

## Education Secretary Betsy DeVos

Betsy DeVos, Trump's secretary of education, did more to destroy the public education system in this country than any other person in American history. But perhaps that was the plan when Trump nominated her as the education secretary. Although the nation's public school systems have been one of the cornerstones of American greatness for more than a century, DeVos's hostility to public schools was well-known when she was selected by Trump.

DeVos described public schools as "a closed system, a closed industry, a closed market. It's a monopoly, a dead end."[180] In order to break up this "monopoly," DeVos believed the U.S. educational system should encourage the proliferation of charter schools and more private schools via financial assistance programs, often called vouchers. DeVos believed that opening up the education market would offer parents increased choice, when in fact the primary motivation of DeVos and her well-heeled supporters was to privatize American public education, transforming it into a for-profit system.[181]

As part of her campaign to privatize the American education system and to destroy public schools, DeVos was always a "a fierce proponent of school vouchers" that would allow students to attend private schools with public funding.[182] According to *The New York Times*, it "is hard to find anyone more passionate about the idea of steering public dollars away from traditional public schools than Betsy DeVos."[183]

Prior to being chosen as Trump's education secretary, DeVos, who comes from one of the wealthiest families in Michigan and was married to former Amway CEO Dick DeVos,[184] advocated for the Detroit charter school system and was a member of the board of the Alliance for School Choice.[185] Due to her controversial pro-private school bias and open hostility to the public school system that the Department of Education was supposed to be helping, her Senate confirmation hearings were extremely heated and raucous affairs. Her lack of actual experience with public education was one of the points repeatedly raised against her. *Detroit Free Press* editor Stephen Henderson wrote during her confirmation hearings that "DeVos isn't an educator, or an education leader."[186] Similarly, Randi Weingarten, president of the American Federation of Teachers, called DeVos "the most ideological, anti-public education nominee" since the position became a cabinet position.[187]

DeVos did not do much to help her own cause during the confirmation hearings, drawing widespread media attention for suggesting that guns might have a place in some schools due to a threat from grizzly bears.[188] Finally, however, DeVos narrowly squeaked by and was confirmed, with the final confirmation vote in the Senate tied at 50–50, with Vice President Mike Pence breaking the tie in favor of her nomination. This was the first time in

U.S. history that a Cabinet nominee's confirmation was decided by the vice president's tiebreaking vote.[189]

Thereafter, DeVos's tenure as education secretary was even more disastrous than anticipated. In May 2018 *The New York Times* reported that under DeVos, the size of the team investigating abuses and fraud by for-profit colleges was reduced from about 12 members under the Obama administration to three, with their task also being scaled back to "processing student loan forgiveness applications and looking at smaller compliance cases."[190] DeVos also appointed Julian Schmoke as the team's new supervisor. Schmoke was a former dean of DeVry Education Group, which was one of the private institutions the team was supposed to be investigating.[191] It clearly seemed that DeVos was appointing foxes to guard the henhouse, a sure-fire prescription for disaster.

On July 6, 2017, Democratic attorneys general in 18 states and Washington, D.C. filed a federal lawsuit against DeVos for suspending the implementation of rules that were meant to protect students attending for-profit colleges. The rules, developed during the Obama administration, were meant to take effect on July 1, 2017.[192] DeVos lost the lawsuit on September 12, 2018, with the court finding she had improperly delayed implementation of regulations protecting student loan borrowers from predatory practices.[193]

During the coronavirus pandemic, DeVos shamelessly misdirected millions of dollars of coronavirus relief funds intended for public schools and colleges to private and religious schools.[194] She also pushed for schools to re-open while coronavirus cases were still surging in large parts of the country, going so far as to threaten that the Trump administration would pull funding from public schools unless they provided full-time in-person learning during the pandemic.[195] On July 12, 2020 she said, "there's nothing in the data that suggests that kids being in school is in any way dangerous to them," which directly contradicted what most public health experts were saying.[196] She also refused to say whether schools should follow guidelines laid out by the Centers for Disease Control and Prevention on reopening schools.[197]

Like several other members of Trump's cabinet, DeVos also ran afoul of government ethics regulations. According to DeVos's 2018 financial disclosure form certified by the Office of Government Ethics on December 3, 2018,[198] she still had not divested her assets as required under the ethics agreement she signed in February 2017.[199] In addition, in May 2019, the Education Department Inspector General released a report concluding that DeVos used personal email accounts to conduct government business and that she did not properly preserve the emails.[200] It also was reported in September 2020 that the Office of the Special Counsel had investigated DeVos over potential violations of the Hatch Act after she had appeared on Fox News during the 2020 election campaign and attacked Democratic Party presidential nominee Joe Biden. Adding insult to injury, DeVos then had the Department of Education promote her Fox News interview.[201]

It will probably take the U.S. public school system many years to recover from the damage inflicted on it by DeVos in only four short years.

## Transportation Secretary Elaine Chao

According to an inspector general's report released March 3, 2021, Trump's secretary of transportation, Elaine Chao, repeatedly used her office staff to help family members who run a shipping business with extensive ties to China.[202] The inspector general referred the matter for possible criminal investigation to the Justice Department in December 2020, during the transition period prior to President-elect Biden's inauguration on January 20, 2021.

Chao, the wife of then Senate Majority Leader Mitch McConnell of Kentucky, announced her resignation on January 7, 2021, the day after the Capitol riot. However, in retrospect, it appears that Chao's resignation had more to do with the ongoing ethics investigations of her than her purported shock at the attack on the Capitol.

The investigation of Chao came after a 2019 *New York Times* article detailing the ethics issues arising from her interactions with her family while serving as transportation secretary, including a trip to China she had planned to take in 2017 with her father and sister.[203] As transportation secretary, Chao was the top Trump administration official overseeing the American shipping industry, which was in intense competition with Chinese shippers.

In a letter accompanying the 44-page report, Mitch Behm, the Transportation Department's deputy inspector general, stated: "A formal investigation into potential misuses of position was warranted."[204] The inspector general's office also described the investigation as one into "use of public office for private gain."[205] The report disclosed more than a dozen instances where Chao's office took steps to handle matters related to her father James Chao and her sister Angela Chao, who ran the Foremost Group, a New York-based shipping company established after the Chaos' parents immigrated to the United States from Taiwan in the late 1950s.[206]

Chao, who declined to respond to questions from the inspector general, instead provided a memo discussing the importance of promoting her family as part of her official duties.[207] Suggesting that promoting a family shipping business directly impacted by actions and decisions of a transportation secretary who was a member of that family was proper, as long as that family was Asian American, Chao argued in her memo that, "anyone familiar with Asian culture knows it is a core value in Asian communities to express honor and filial respect toward one's parents."[208] While filial respect and honor are important in any culture, conflicts of interest between family interests and public responsibilities are not.

Congressional Democrats responded with a blistering attack at the suggestion that it was acceptable for federal officials to mix public and family business in this manner. Representative Peter DeFazio, Democrat of Oregon and the chairman of the House Committee on Transportation and Infrastructure, said, "Public servants, especially those responsible for leading tens of thousands of other public servants, must know that they serve the public and not their family's private commercial interests."[209]

The investigators also found that Chao repeatedly asked Transportation Department staff members to help do chores for her father, including editing his *Wikipedia* page and promoting his Chinese-language biography.[210] It should be mentioned, however, that according to the report, none of the Department employees interviewed "described feeling ordered or coerced to perform personal or inappropriate tasks for the secretary."[211]

Although the Justice Department declined to pursue the potential criminal case, the report said, the Justice Department notified the inspector general that "there may be ethical and/or administrative issues to address but there is not predication to open a criminal investigation."[212]

Chao also breached various ethics agreements she made in 2016, when she falsely reported that she cashed out the stock options awarded to her during the nearly two years she served on the board at Vulcan Materials, an Alabama-based producer of crushed stone and asphalt used primarily for road construction. Instead, those stock options were converted to shares in Vulcan Materials worth $250,000 to $500,000, which she continued to hold until June 2019. These stocks were held while Chao served as secretary of transportation, a position which had considerable influence over road-building policy in the United States.[213]

★ ★ ★

President Trump had promised to drain the swamp, but his Cabinet was a monument to corruption. The Cabinet was filled with individuals who saw their public service jobs as personal candy stores where they could do and take whatever they wanted. No wonder they never stood up to Trump. They were simply courtiers to an autocrat who was also enriching himself through the U.S. taxpayers.

# TRUMP'S SENIOR ADVISORS

# Kellyanne Conway

By the time she resigned from her position as a senior counselor to the president in August 2020, Kelleyanne Conway had left an indelible mark on American politics and culture. It was not for the better. More than any other creature who inhabited the Trump swamp, she presided over the dismantling of a reality-based worldview during the Trump era. In its place, she ushered in a post-fact world where facts can supposedly be ignored or, better yet, combatted with "alternative facts," and where reason and science take a backseat to passions and prejudice.

Conway epitomized the inner circle of Trump's faithful, who were willing to do anything to defend the most indefensible of Trump's statements and actions at great cost to their own reputations. She either defended or overlooked Trump's constant stream of falsehoods, which mounted on a daily basis. The sheer volume of Trump's lies defied reality to such a degree that they took on a life of their own and formed an alternative reality that Trump believers willingly entered and then found themselves mired, with no way out.

As an establishment Republican when she first signed on as campaign manager of the Trump campaign late in the 2016 election season, Conway served as a bridge between the traditional Republican establishment and the more controversial elements of the Trump coalition that helped him squeak out a victory in the November 2016 election. She also presided over the extinction of the traditional Republican party as it was re-branded in Trump's image with only the name remaining. With Conway's guidance, the GOP became—and remains—the Trump Party.

Conway had a well-deserved reputation as being one of the toughest of Trump's White House advisors. On the evening after Trump's inauguration on January 20, 2017, Conway proved that she was no shrinking violet when she punched a tuxedo-clad man at one of the exclusive inauguration events just hours after Trump was sworn in as president.[1] In an attempt to break up a scuffle, Conway stepped between two men, but when they would not break up the fight, Conway apparently punched one of them in the face at least three times.

Conway's most infamous incident, however, came when she acknowledged that the Trump White House contained a parallel universe of "alternative facts" that allowed Trump and his people to utter false claims as long as they were consistent with Trump's distorted view of reality and inflated ego.

She coined the phrase "alternative facts" while defending White House press secretary Sean Spicer's idiotic claims about the size of Trump's inaugural crowd, which Spicer insisted was the largest ever. When Chuck Todd of NBC News noted that Trump was beginning his presidency with falsehoods, Conway responded: "You're saying it's a falsehood, and . . . our press secretary, Sean Spicer, gave alternative facts to that." Todd, incredulous, responded: "Look, alternative facts are not facts. They're falsehoods."[2]

Conway's "alternative fact" language reminded some commentators of "Newspeak," a garbling language style that is a key element of the society portrayed in George Orwell's dystopian novel *1984*.[3] Soon after Conway's interview, sales of the book increased by 9,500%, which *The New York Times* and others attributed to Conway's use of the phrase, making it the number-one bestseller on Amazon.com.[4]

Shortly before the alternative facts comment, Conway urged the media to be less concerned about the truth or falsity of Trump's words and to focus more on "what was in his heart." While defending Trump for cruelly mocking a reporter's congenital disability, Conway chided the media: "Why is everything taken at face value?" She added, "You can't give him the benefit of the doubt on this, and he's telling you what was in his heart? You always want to go by what's come out of his mouth rather than look at what's in his heart."[5]

When Trump made the false claim and illogical statement that he won the 2016 popular vote and that fraudulent votes deprived him of it, Conway insisted that such a comment was consistent with appropriate presidential behavior. "Well, he's the presidential-elect, so that's presidential behavior, yes," she said.[6] Conway also defended Trump's racist tweet urging minority congresswomen who were born in the United States to "go back" to their countries.[7] She said Trump merely meant the congresswomen should go back to where their families were "originally" from, as if that was better.[8] In the course of another heated debate with the press, she even asked a reporter, "What's your ethnicity?"[9] Conway said later that she simply meant the vast majority of Americans were descended from immigrants, but failed to explain the relevance of that point. Conway also had a bad habit of changing the subject when some critic asked either Trump or her a hard question, regularly stooping to *ad hominem* insults and referring to critics of Trump as "unpatriotic" or "sore losers."

Conway's first major crisis at the White House occurred when she started making comments about the status of national security advisor Michael Flynn. On February 13, 2017, Conway claimed that Flynn had the president's "full confidence." Hours later, however, Flynn resigned.[10] The following day, Conway claimed Flynn had offered to resign, but White House Press Secretary Sean Spicer said Trump asked Flynn for his resignation.[11] It was then reported that Conway had allegedly leaked negative stories about Spicer to the press.[12]

On February 2, 2017, Conway appeared on MSNBC's *Hardball with Chris Matthews*. In order to justify President Trump's immigration ban, she referenced an event allegedly perpetrated by Iraqi terrorists she termed the "Bowling Green massacre." Such an event never took place.[13] While there were two Iraqi refugees arrested in 2011 in Bowling Green, Kentucky for supporting attacks on American troops in Iraq, there was never any evidence or even suggestion that they were planning to carry out any terrorist attacks on the United States.[14]

On February 5, 2017, New York University journalism professor Jay Rosen argued that, given repeated misstatements of fact, Conway should cease being booked as a guest on television news shows. CNN responded positively to this suggestion, opting to stop booking Conway as a guest because of what the network said were "serious questions about her credibility."[15]

On February 15, 2017, *Washington Post* columnist Jennifer Rubin said Conway should be banned from future television appearances. "In recent days, George Stephanopoulos and Matt Lauer blasted her directly, essentially calling her a fabulist. Given all that, it would be irresponsible for any news show to put her out there, suggesting she really does not know what is going on at any given moment," Rubin wrote.[16] Also on February 15, the MSNBC news show *Morning Joe* officially banned her from future appearances. The show's primary host Joe Scarborough said the decision to ban Conway from the show was based on her being "out of the loop" and "in none of the key meetings." He added, "She's not briefed. She's just saying things just to get in front of the TV to prove her relevance."[17] The show's co-host Mika Brzezinski said, "I don't believe in fake news, or information that is not true . . . every time I've ever seen her on television, something's askew, off or incorrect."[18]

For the week following her Flynn comments she did not appear on any television shows. Her week-long banishment finally ended when she appeared on the Fox News program *Hannity* during the Conservative Political Action Conference (CPAC).[19]

In addition to suggesting that Trump should be held to a different standard than every other president, Conway also apparently thought that she did not have to follow political norms and statutory requirements. On multiple occasions she violated the Hatch Act, which prohibits government officials from political activity while serving in their official roles. A government watchdog said her conduct was so blatant and repeated that she should be fired.[20] Ignoring the obvious fact that government officials are not free to say whatever is on their minds if it constitutes political advocacy, Conway responded by suggesting that it was an attempt to stifle her free speech.[21]

Conway also breached a statute prohibiting federal employees from promoting commercial products.[22] On February 9, 2017, during an appearance on *Fox & Friends*, Conway discussed department store Nordstrom's decision to drop products supplied by Ivanka Trump's business. "Go buy Ivanka's stuff is what I would tell you," said Conway, elaborating, "It's a wonderful line. I own some of it. I'm going to give a free commercial here: Go buy it today, everybody. You can find it online."[23]

Within hours, two organizations filed formal ethics complaints against Conway for use of a federal position "for the endorsement of any product, service or enterprise."[24] Public Citizen, one of the organizations, asked the U.S. Office of Governmental Ethics (OGE) to investigate, saying that Conway's remarks reflected "an on-going careless disregard of the conflicts of interest laws and regulations of some members of the Trump family and Trump Administration."[25] The group's president, Robert Weissman, declared: "Since she said it was an advertisement, that both eliminates any question about whether outsiders are unfairly reading into what's being said, and two, it makes clear that wasn't an inadvertent remark."[26] A similar complaint was filed by Citizens for Responsibility and Ethics in Washington with the OGE and with the White House Counsel's Office.[27] Harvard constitutional law professor Laurence Tribe told *The New York Times* that Conway was "attempting quite crudely to enrich Ivanka and therefore the president's family."[28] Richard Painter, chief ethics attorney for George W. Bush, commented, "The events of the past week demonstrate that there is no intent on the part of the president, his family or the White House staff to make meaningful distinctions between his official capacity as president and the Trump family business."[29]

Conway's comments also drew bipartisan Congressional condemnation, with various House members describing her conduct as "clearly over the line," "unacceptable," and "jaw-dropping."[30] Two congressmen wrote to the OGE on February 9, requesting that Conway's behavior be investigated and that the office recommend "suggested disciplinary action, if warranted."[31]

It took close to two years, but on June 13, 2019, the U.S. Office of Special Counsel (OSC) formally recommended that Conway be removed from federal service, citing multiple Hatch Act violations by Conway since the preparation of its 2018 report, including "disparaging Democratic presidential candidates while speaking in her official capacity during television interviews and on social media." The OSC was referring to Conway's criticism from February to May 2019 of candidates such as Amy Klobuchar, Bernie Sanders, Beto O'Rourke, Cory Booker, Elizabeth Warren, Joe Biden, and Kirsten Gillibrand. The report also called Conway's violations "egregious, notorious, and ongoing." The OSC noted that this was the first time they "had to issue multiple reports to the President concerning Hatch Act violations by the same individual."[32] In an interview, Henry Kerner characterized his agency's recommendation as unprecedented, adding, "You know what else is unprecedented? Kellyanne Conway's behavior."[33]

Conway, however, remained unrepentant, continuing to make frequent television appearances and comments on political topics. Conway declared: "If you're trying to silence me through the Hatch Act, it's not going to work… Let me know when the jail sentence starts."[34]

Due to Conway's status as a presidential appointee, the OSC was unable to take any steps to implement its recommendation, other than to recommend to President Trump that she be fired. The White House, however, immediately rejected the OSC findings, with Trump saying he thought the recommendation was "very unfair, it's called freedom of speech."[35]

On June 26, 2019, Conway failed to appear at a hearing by the House Committee on Oversight and Reform, leading that committee to issue a subpoena for her. At that hearing, Special Counsel Henry Kerner testified that

Conway had been found guilty of two Hatch Act violations in 2018 and eleven violations in 2019, more than any other federal employee in the past 30 years.[36]

Conway announced in August 2020 that she would be leaving the White House at the end of the month. This came after months of a public feud between herself and her 15-year old teenage daughter, Claudia, who lambasted her in the media, politically and personally, and threatened to seek legal emancipation.[37] Claudia first made a name for herself as a TikTok influencer famous for her anti-Trump and pro-Black Lives Matter messages, with the intent of "informing people and spreading love."[38] Claudia followed in her mother's footsteps as a person known to speak her mind plainly, no matter what the consequences. She described Trump as "a horrible person" for mocking a young environmental activist working to prevent climate change.[39] She referred to Ted Cruz as "disgusting," Mike Pence as a "closeted" homosexual,[40] and her mother's behavior as "internalized misogyny."[41] In July 2020 she said that her parents' marriage had "failed."[42]

Conway announced on Sunday, August 23, 2020 that she was leaving the White House. Her husband, George Conway, said he was withdrawing from the Lincoln Project, an anti-Trump Republican group. Both cited a need to focus on their family.

However, Kellyanne Conway's legacy will live on in infamy, as one of Trump's most adroit apologists and prevaricators.

## Stephen K. Bannon

Before being named as President Trump's chief strategist and senior counselor, Steve Bannon was well known in right-wing political circles as the co-founder of *Breitbart News*, a far-right website promoting racist, sexist, xenophobic, and antisemitic material.[43] He was also widely considered to be a far-right fringe "flame thrower," given to promoting wild conspiracy theories and using extreme rhetoric.[44] These were the qualities that no doubt made him so attractive to Trump, since one of the primary goals of the Trump presidency appears to have been to wreak havoc on the country's democratic norms and institutions to the maximum extent possible. In four short years, Trump nearly succeeded in blowing up our democracy, and during the first year of his presidency, Bannon was Trump's principal flame-thrower, scorching everything in his path.

Bannon's connection to Trump arose from his work as vice president of the infamous psychological-warfare-turned-political-consulting-firm Cambridge Analytica. Cambridge Analytica, which stole Facebook user data and fashioned it into micro-targeted political advertising, was owned by the Mercer family, who remain colossally influential donors in conservative circles. Set up in the United States to support the pro-Brexit "Vote Leave" campaign while avoiding UK campaign finance regulations, Cambridge Analytica first waded into U.S. politics by working with Ted Cruz on his failed 2016 bid to become the Republican presidential nominee. After Trump became the GOP candidate, the Mercers leveraged their financial might and past donations to Trump, requesting he take on Steve Bannon as chairman of his campaign.[45]

White nationalism and racist ideology had been a longstanding feature at the fringes of American politics. What Steve Bannon and *Breitbart News* did was to bring it further into the mainstream than it had been since the 1940s, creating an online haven for white nationalist and neo-Nazi groups.[46] Bannon also became a prominent member of a Facebook group called Vigilant Patriots, where white nationalists and other extremists could gather online and freely post racist rants and death threats directed at President Obama and other prominent Democrats.[47] Needless to say, white nationalists, the so-called alt-right, and neo-Nazi groups throughout the country were incredibly energized with the election of Donald J. Trump and the selection of one of their own as a senior White House advisor. They could finally come out of the shadows to join the mainstream of political discourse, at least within Trump's Republican Party. They even held a convention in Washington, D.C. with the declared intention that the white nationalism movement, which was now gaining steam with powerful friends in the White House, was going to "change the world."[48]

During his relatively short but eventful tenure in the Trump White House, Bannon's relationship with the mainstream media was particularly combative, even by Trumpian standards. Several days after Trump's inauguration, Bannon laid out in a *New York Times* interview what would become the Trump administration's approach to the press: "The media should be embarrassed and humiliated and keep its mouth shut and just listen for a while. I want you to quote this: the media here is the opposition party. They don't understand this country. They still do not understand why Donald Trump is the president of the United States."[49]

Bannon, along with Stephen Miller, another one of Trump's right-wing advisors, immediately went to work overhauling immigration policy to reflect their racist and xenophobic views. In their worldview, the influx of immigrants into the United States resulted in a far-too-diverse population that was now threatening the continued political and economic domination of the White America that they were both committed to perpetuating. They authored the infamous Executive Order 13769, which resulted in restricted U.S. travel and immigration by individuals from seven countries, suspension of the United States Refugee Admissions Program (USRAP) for 120 days, and indefinite suspension of the entry of Syrians to the United States.[50]

In order for the Trump administration to accomplish its objectives on the immigration front, Bannon and Miller also agreed that Trump's close affinity for Russia could open the door to a mutually beneficial alliance with America's perennial antagonist, which they suspected shared the same prejudices and concerns about the threat posed by the Muslim minorities within its national borders. According to *The Economist*, Bannon and Miller "see Mr. [Vladimir] Putin as a fellow nationalist and crusader against cosmopolitanism."[51] In February 2017, Bannon appeared on the cover of *Time*, on which he was labeled "the Great Manipulator."[52] The headline used for the associated article was, "Is Steve Bannon the Second Most Powerful Man in the World?", alluding to Bannon's formidable influence in the White House.[53]

Bannon's influence during the first year of the Trump administration was so great that he was granted a retroactive blanket exemption from federal ethics rules that allowed him to communicate with editors at *Breitbart News*.[54] This allowed Bannon to continue as the "de facto editorial director of *Breitbart*" while, at the same time, molding much of the Trump White House's policies, which were lurching to the right.[55]

Bannon's Svengali-like influence in the White House set the wheels in motion behind the scenes to have a citizenship question inserted in the 2020 Census. During a March 14, 2019 hearing of the House Committee on Oversight and Government Reform, Commerce Department Secretary

Wilbur Ross was intensively questioned about his conversations with Bannon and the circumstances surrounding adding the citizenship question to the census. Missouri Democratic Representative Lacy Clay accused Ross of being "complicit" regarding his efforts to weaken minority group voting rights, additionally accusing him of committing perjury with respect to his contacts with Bannon and other immigration hard-liners.[56] Clay angrily called for Ross to tender his resignation, saying, "You lied to Congress. You misled the American people and you are complicit in the Trump administration's intent to suppress the growing political power of the non-white population."[57] Ross denied to the end that Bannon and other White Nationalists in the White House were behind it, saying unconvincingly that the change was in response to a request by the Justice Department for statistics to protect voting rights.[58]

With the Trump administration only a couple of weeks old, Bannon's power in the White House was extended to foreign policy and national security when his official title as counselor to the president was added to the list of members of the Principals Committee of the National Security Council (NSC), a Cabinet-level senior inter-agency forum dealing with national security issues.[59] Trump's addition of Bannon to this sensitive and powerful group precipitated a storm of protest. Susan E. Rice, Barack Obama's last national security adviser, bluntly called it "stone cold crazy."[60] The dangers posed by having someone such as Bannon actually inside the epicenter of the U.S. national security apparatus belatedly dawned on U.S. National Security Advisor H.R. McMaster, who removed Bannon from his NSC role in early April 2017. But Bannon ultimately had the last laugh when he engineered the firing of McMaster, who Bannon had originally help select.[61]

One week before Bannon's departure from the White House on August 18, 2017, a right-wing rally in Charlottesville, Virginia degenerated into violence, leading to the death of one counter-protester. Members of both political parties condemned the white nationalists, neo-Nazis, and alt-right activists for fomenting violence and hatred. However, at the urging of Steve Bannon, Trump took a neutral stance, saying that there were "good people" on both sides and that "many sides" shared the blame for the violence.[62] Right wing nationalists throughout the country correctly took Trump's comments to be a green light from the White House to continue and, indeed, intensify their campaign of hatred, bigotry, and violence.[63] Seeing Bannon's hand in this, there were growing calls for Bannon's ouster.⁶⁴ The NAACP released a statement saying that while they "acknowledge and appreciate President Trump's disavowment of the hatred which has resulted in a loss of life today," they called on Trump "to take the tangible step to remove Steve Bannon—a well-known white supremacist leader—from his team of advisers." The statement further described Bannon as a "symbol of white nationalism" who "energized that sentiment" through his current position within the White House.⁶⁵

Even after Bannon officially left the White House, Trump continued to regularly speak to him, using his personal cell phone to call Bannon when Chief of Staff John Kelly was not around.⁶⁶ *The Washington Post* reported in October 2017 that Trump and Bannon still remained in regular contact.⁶⁷ After leaving the White House, Bannon toured Europe to speak at events held by various far-right populist-nationalist parties in France, Hungary, Italy, Germany, Poland, Sweden, Holland, Austria, Switzerland, the UK, and Belgium. Bannon and a European group with whom he was working announced that they planned to establish a right-wing academy at a medieval monastery in Italy, with the aim of creating a "gladiator school for culture warriors."⁶⁸ However, the group's rights to use the former monastery were later revoked by the Italian government due to failure to pay rent and conduct maintenance work.⁶⁹

Bannon campaigned for Republican Roy Moore in his run for the Senate in Alabama in late 2017, continuing to support him even after nine women alleged sexual misconduct by Moore, including some who were underaged at the time of the incidents.⁷⁰ Trump supported Moore's opponent in the Republican primary, which Moore won before losing in the general election to the Democratic candidate, Doug Jones. Ivanka Trump condemned Moore's campaign in Alabama, saying "there's a special place in hell for people who prey on children."⁷¹ Bannon quickly responded, "What about the allegations about [Ivanka's] dad and that 13-year-old?", referring to a woman who accused Trump and sex offender Jeffrey Epstein of raping her at that age.⁷² In what had been considered a safe Republican seat, Moore lost to a Democrat, which somewhat tarnished Bannon's image as a political genius.⁷³

The final break between Trump and Bannon came in January 2018, when Michael Wolff's book *Fire and Fury: Inside the Trump White House* was published. Trump had recklessly given Wolff virtually free rein at the White House to research a book on the first year of Trump presidency. During the time that Wolff was there, he spent much of his time chatting with Steve Bannon, who gave Wolff a treasure trove of quotes and other material that were extremely unflattering to the president and some of his family members. When Wolff's book was released, Trump is reported to have recoiled in horror when he learned what Bannon said on the record about him, Ivanka, and Don Jr. Wolff quoted Bannon as describing Ivanka Trump as "dumb as a brick;"[74] that the meeting among Donald Trump Jr., Jared Kushner, Paul Manafort, and agents of Russia was "treasonous";[75] and that Special Prosecutor Robert Mueller would cause Donald Trump Jr. to "crack like an egg on live television."[76] Bannon also warned that investigators would likely uncover money laundering involving Jared Kushner and his family business loans from Deutsche Bank.[77]

The media went into a virtual feeding frenzy over each juicy morsel that was revealed in the book, with much of it having originated with Bannon.[78] Given the choice of resigning or being fired, he chose to resign.

Undeterred by the fallout from his first go-round with Michael Wolff as his major source for *Fire and Fury*, Bannon also became a major source of Wolff's 2019 book, *Siege*. Wolff wrote, "Trump was vulnerable because for 40 years he had run what increasingly seemed to resemble a semi-criminal enterprise." Bannon was quoted as saying, "I think we can drop the 'semi' part." Wolff wrote that Bannon predicted investigations into Trump's finances would be Trump's political downfall. Bannon reportedly said, "This is where it isn't a witch hunt—even for the hard core, this is where he turns into just a crooked business guy, and one worth $50 million instead of $10 billion. Not the billionaire he said he was, just another scumbag."[79]

Trump's response to finding out what Bannon apparently really thought of him was to say that Bannon had "lost his mind."[80] He also said that Bannon "cried when he got fired and begged for his job" after being relieved of his White House position.

In November 2019, Bannon was subpoenaed to testify at the federal criminal trial of Roger Stone.[81] He testified that Stone was WikiLeaks' "access point" for the Trump campaign, which helped establish that Stone lied to Congress. Stone was subsequently convicted on charges of lying to Congress and witness tampering,[82] but his federal prison sentence was commuted by

President Trump on July 10, 2020, and he was later pardoned.[83] Asked for a comment after Bannon himself was arrested on August 20, 2020, Stone replied, "Karma is a bitch. But I am praying for him."[84]

On June 3, 2020, Bannon added to the already strained relationship between the United States and China when he and exiled Chinese billionaire businessman Guo Wengui (aka Miles Kwok) participated in declaring a "New Federal State of China" (also called the Federal State of New China). Their declared goal was the overthrow the Chinese government. Near the Statue of Liberty in New York City, planes were seen carrying banners which said, "Congratulations to Federal State of New China!"[85]

Bannon also used his prior relationship with Trump and the MAGA-madness of many of Trump's supporters to cash in through a good old fashioned fraud scheme he cooked up with a few of his friends. On August 20, 2020, a federal grand jury indictment was unsealed against Bannon and three others, charging them with conspiracy to commit wire fraud and money laundering. Each charge has a maximum penalty of 20 years in prison upon conviction.[86]

Federal prosecutors of the U.S. Attorney's Office for the Southern District of New York alleged that Bannon, United States Air Force veteran Brian Kolfage, and the two other defendants used funds received from the We Build the Wall fundraising campaign—ostensibly to be used to support the building of a border wall between the United States and Mexico—in a way which was "inconsistent" with how they were advertised for use to the public.[87] Bannon promoted the project until the day before the indictment, saying in a podcast, "You've been the leader of this, assisting President Trump in building this wall in these tough areas."[88] The indictment alleged that more than $1 million of the money they raised through the nonprofit group Citizens of the American Republic went to Bannon and his co-conspirators, not to build any wall.[89] When arrested by U.S. Postal Service agents, Bannon was on board Guo Wengui's luxury yacht on Long Island Sound. Later that day, Bannon pleaded not guilty to the charges and was released pending trial on a $5 million bond.[90]

Following Bannon's indictment, Donald Trump Jr. distanced himself from Bannon's fundraising efforts for the "Trump Wall," for which Trump and Don Jr. had originally expressed their support.[91]

## Stephen Miller

With the possible exception of Steve Bannon, there was no presidential advisor who deserved more blame for Trump's cruel and disastrous immigration policy than Stephen Miller. As a speechwriter for Trump, Miller helped craft Trump's America First policy restricting immigration. He also helped write Trump's inaugural address—dubbed the "American Carnage" speech—which painted a dark dystopian portrait of an American wasteland waiting for resurrection from the ashes by the new president.[92]

As immigration hardliners, Miller and Bannon were the chief architects of Executive Order 13769 ("the Muslim ban"), which sought to restrict U.S. travel and immigration for citizens of seven Muslim countries, suspend the United States Refugee Admissions Program (USRAP) for 120 days, and indefinitely suspend entry of Syrians to the United States.[93] Miller was also the chief policy advisor behind the Trump administration's decision to reduce the number of refugees accepted into the United States.[94] Not content with limiting immigration from the Muslim world, Miller acted as the champion of the Trump administration's decision to separate migrant children from their parents when they crossed the U.S. border.[95] He argued that such a policy would deter migrants from coming to the United States.[96]

Miller also became a key White House operative on several non-immigration-related issues. As a White House spokesman, he made numerous false and unsubstantiated claims regarding widespread electoral fraud during the 2016 campaign, including allegations that Democratic voters were bussed from other states to New Hampshire during the 2016 presidential election.[97]

Trump's decision to fire FBI Director James Comey in May 2017 was, in part, at Miller's behest.[98] Miller and Trump drafted a letter to Comey that was not sent after an internal review and opposition from White House counsel Don McGahn. However, Deputy Attorney General Rod Rosenstein was given a copy, after which he prepared his own letter to Comey, citing various reasons for firing him.[99] In November 2017, Miller was interviewed by Special Counsel Robert Mueller in relation to his role in Comey's dismissal.[100]

In July 2018, Miller was behind the firing of senior White House official Jennifer Arangio after she reportedly advocated that the United States remain in the Global Compact for Migration, a United Nations plan intended to "cover all dimensions of international migration in a holistic and comprehensive manner."[101] Arangio had incurred Miller's wrath by defending the State Department's refugee bureau when Miller was seeking to defund it.[102] When she was fired and escorted from the White House, Arangio was also in the process of correcting misleading information about refugees that Miller was presenting to Trump.[103]

On August 13, 2018, *Politico* published an essay by Miller's uncle, Dr. David S. Glosser, titled "Stephen Miller Is an Immigration Hypocrite. I Know Because I'm His Uncle."[104] In the essay, Glosser detailed the Jewish family's history of coming to the United States from the village of Antopal in present-day Belarus, commenting, "I have watched with dismay and increasing horror as my nephew, an educated man who is well aware of his heritage, has become the architect of immigration policies that repudiate the very foundation of our family's life in this country."[105]

In the lead-up to the 2018 midterm elections, Miller played an influential role in Trump's messaging, which focused on sowing fears about immigration.[106] Miller helped craft Trump's "closing argument" in those elections, which focused on immigration policy and "white identity politics."[107] However, when Republicans lost forty seats in the House in the midterm elections, it caused some commentators to question whether Trump should be relying so heavily on Miller.[108]

Like other senior White House advisors, such as Kellyanne Conway, Miller's relationship with the press could best be described as contentious. In January 7, 2018, for example, Miller appeared on Jake Tapper's *State of the Union* on CNN, describing Trump as "a political genius . . . who took down the Bush dynasty, who took down the Clinton dynasty, who took down the entire media complex." Miller also accused CNN of "sticking knives" in Trump's allies.[109] Tapper accused Miller of dodging questions, and when both participants started talking over each other, Tapper ended the interview and continued to the next news story.[110] After the interview was over, Miller refused to leave the CNN studio and had to be escorted out by security.[111]

In late 2019, Miller faced growing calls to resign after leaked emails showed he promoted the ideas of white nationalists. In the emails, which were uncovered by the Southern Poverty Law Center, Miller recommended articles on the *American Renaissance* website and on another white nationalist website called *VDARE*.[112]

In 2020, during the coronavirus pandemic, leaked conversations showed that Miller wanted to extend temporary border restrictions imposed because of the pandemic in order to restrict immigration in the long term.[113] Emails showed that Miller had already tried to use public health powers to implement border restrictions in 2019.[114]

When Miller's grandmother passed away from complications due to COVID-19 in early July 2020, his uncle issued another public statement, this one blasting the Trump administration's response to the pandemic.[115]

During the 2020 election, Miller said that if Trump were reelected, the administration would seek to limit asylum, target sanctuary city policies, expand the travel ban, and cut work visas.[116] He voiced support for the administration's Asylum Cooperative agreements with Central American governments, and pledged that it would pursue such policies with African and Asian countries if Trump was elected for a second term.[117]

Following Trump's loss in the 2020 election and his failure to get the results overturned in courts and state legislatures, Miller announced support for a plan to send alternate slates of electors to Congress.[118] On December 14, as the official Electoral College votes were being tallied, groups of self-appointed Republican alternate electors met in several swing states and voted for Trump. Since their alternate slates were not signed by the governors of the states they claimed to represent, the strategy Miller urged was to introduce those bogus slates as challenges to the results when Congress counted the electoral votes on January 6, 2021.[119]

Appearing on Fox News on November 14, 2020 in his capacity as a senior adviser to the Trump campaign, Miller brushed off the idea that the Electoral College vote marked the end of Trump's election challenges.[120] "The only date in the Constitution is January 20 [Inauguration Day]. So we have more than enough time to right the wrong of this fraudulent election result and certify Donald Trump as the winner of the election," Miller said on *Fox & Friends*. He continued: "As we speak, today, an alternate slate of electors in the contested states is going to vote and we're going to send those results up to Congress."[121] Miller thus contributed to the dangerous and false narrative that the 2020 election had been stolen from Trump, which culminated in the deadly mob riot at the U.S. Capitol on January 6, 2021.

## Peter Navarro

Peter Navarro served in the Trump administration as the assistant to the president, director of trade and manufacturing policy, and the National Defense Production Act policy coordinator. During the 2016 presidential campaign, Navarro was an economic policy adviser to the Trump campaign who strongly advocated in favor of Trump's isolationist and protectionist foreign policy.[122]

Navarro and private equity investor Wilbur Ross, who later was named as Trump's Secretary of Commerce, authored an economic plan for the Trump campaign in September 2016.[123] Navarro was invited to be a Trump advisor after Trump's son-in-law Jared Kushner was browsing through Amazon book listings and noticed that he co-wrote *Death by China*, which chronicles the alleged threats to America's economic dominance in the 21st century posed by China's Communist Party.[124]

Although Navarro was a professor emeritus of economics and public policy at the Paul Merage School of Business, University of California, Irvine, his economic theories were "considered fringe" by his fellow economists.[125] A *New Yorker* reporter described Navarro's views on trade and China as so radical "that, even with [Navarro's] assistance, [the reporter] was unable to find another economist who fully agrees with them."[126] *The Economist* described Navarro as having "oddball views."[127] According to MIT economist Simon Johnson, the economic plan authored by Navarro and Ross for Trump during the campaign had projections "based on assumptions so unrealistic that they seem to have come from a different planet. If the United States really did adopt Trump's plan, the result would be an immediate and unmitigated disaster."[128]

In June 2018, Navarro gratuitously damaged the previous cordial relationship the United States had with its northern neighbor by saying that there was "a special place in hell" for Canadian Prime Minister Justin Trudeau, after Trudeau said that Canada would respond to U.S. tariffs against Canada with retaliatory tariffs.[129] In May 2019, Navarro further reinforced Trump's delusional views that tariffs should be used as an instrument of political power rather than just economic power by praising Trump's decision to place tariffs on Mexico for its lack of success in stopping illegal immigration to the United States as "a brilliant move."[130]

Navarro and Ross designed a $1.5 trillion infrastructure development plan calling for $137 billion in tax credits for private business, with the hope of inducing them to finance the bulk of infrastructure spending.[131] Economists across the political spectrum derided the proposal.[132] Trump released a version of this plan in February 2018, but in a rare moment of pushback against Trump's will, the Republican-controlled Congress showed little enthusiasm for it.[133] *The Hill* reported, "President Trump's infrastructure plan appears to have crashed and burned in Congress."[134]

On January 29, 2020, Navarro issued a confidential memo to be circulated among the senior White House staff that was not publicly released for three months. The memo warned that the novel coronavirus could "evolve into a full-blown pandemic, imperiling the lives of millions of Americans" and that the "risk of a worst-case pandemic scenario should not be overlooked." He argued for restrictions on travel from China.[135] Navarro wrote another memo on February 23, arguing that the disease "could infect as many as 100 million Americans, with a loss of life of as many as 1–2 million souls" and calling for an "immediate supplemental appropriation of at least $3 billion."[136] However, at the same time Navarro privately issued these warnings, he was publicly and falsely stating that the American people had "nothing to worry about" regarding the coronavirus.[137]

As the COVID-19 crisis quickly unfolded in the United States during 2020, Navarro became one of the administration's major proponents of the use of hydroxychloroquine to treat the virus, even though the drug's effectiveness was unproven.[138] He clashed with Dr. Anthony Fauci, the director of the National Institute of Allergy and Infectious Diseases, on this issue.[139] In July 2020, Navarro touted a widely criticized study as showing that hydroxychloroquine was an effective coronavirus treatment, which had the damaging effect of diverting the administration's attention away from public health measures that were actually helpful in combatting the spreading pandemic in the country, such as social distancing and the wearing of face masks.[140]

On July 14, 2020, Navarro tore into Fauci in an op-ed piece appearing in *USA Today*, accusing him of being "wrong about everything."[141] Navarro wrote: "Dr. Anthony Fauci has a good bedside manner with the public, but he has been wrong about everything I have interacted with him on." Further, Navarro wrote that in February 2020, "Fauci was telling the public the China virus was low risk," and that Fauci was "flip-flopping on the use of masks."[142]

In fact, it was Navarro himself who had been doing the country a great disservice when in May 2020 he criticized stay-at-home orders, arguing that the COVID-19 pandemic lockdowns will kill "many more" people than the coronavirus.[143]

In August 2020, administration officials terminated a contract for the purchase of 42,900 ventilators for use in the pandemic that Navarro had directly negotiated.[144] An oversight subcommittee of the U.S. House of Representatives concluded that the government had overpaid for the ventilators by $500 million.[145]

Following Democratic candidate Joe Biden's win in the 2020 election, Navarro enthusiastically joined in President Trump's enormously destructive scheme to unlawfully overturn the results of the election. Navarro published a report on December 17, 2020, informally titled "Immaculate Deception," containing widely discredited conspiracy theories regarding Trump's unfounded claims of election fraud.[146] In the report, Navarro wrote that large initial leads by Trump in battleground states, which turned to Biden leads as vote counting progressed, were evidence of some impropriety.[147] Navarro's analysis completely ignored the fact that mail-in votes in several states could not be counted before Election Day, and since these votes overwhelmingly favored Biden, Biden surged in most of the late vote counting.[148]

In the report, Navarro proudly cited biased and unreliable sources of information, such as One America News Network, *Newsmax*, Steve Bannon's *War Room: Pandemic* podcast, *Just the News*, and *The National Pulse*, because they provided "alternative coverage."[149]

Navarro had extensive prior experience with inventing facts and sources to support his baseless arguments. Several of his books liberally quoted a fake expert by the name of "Ron Vara," which was actually just an anagram of his own last name. Similarly, Navarro's election "report" was riddled with manufactured examples of supposed election fraud, including what he described as the most "disturbing" instance, where a contract truck driver for the U.S. Postal Service claimed to have transported thousands of ballots from New York to Pennsylvania in October. Navarro neglected to mention that the source of this discredited evidence was a man who moonlighted as a ghost hunter and who also had a lengthy criminal record.[150]

Navarro also cited security camera footage of election workers moving around boxes of ballots in Atlanta, which pro-Trump theorists claimed was actually a smoking gun of fraud. However, these video clips turned out to show nothing more than the normal processing of votes by election officials.[151] Navarro's report further promoted the discredited theory that the Dominion Voting Systems had ties to the dead Venezuelan president Hugo Chavez, and that "deep State CIA operators had used a supercomputer to rig the election."[152] Navarro even made some of the same glaring errors made by other election fraud hunters. For example, Navarro noted that according to Russ Ramsland, an election consultant, 25 out of the 47 precincts in Wayne County, Michigan displayed greater than 100% voter turnout. He failed to mention, however, that not only were Ramsland's numbers wrong, but that the precincts listed in the affidavit Navarro cited were in Minnesota, not Michigan.[153]

✯ ✯ ✯

As it turned out, Trump's senior advisers were no better than the rest of the members of the Trump gang, who almost uniformly exhibited a startlingly low level of ethics, honesty, judgment and compassion. Good riddance to all!

# ALL THE PRESIDENT'S LIARS

# Sean Spicer

Sean Spicer's tenure as White House press secretary for President Trump was marred from the start by his habitual lies and misrepresentations of fact, as well as by his contentious—even combative—style. He initially promised that he would "never knowingly say something that is not factual" to the media.[1] This promise, however, was broken about five seconds later.

Spicer will be remembered best for his cringeworthy performances during the days following Trump's inauguration on January 20, 2017. On January 21, Spicer claimed that the crowds at Trump's inauguration ceremony were the largest ever at such an event, and accused the press of deliberately under-estimating the number of spectators at the inaugural ceremonies.[2] After this statement was widely criticized as easily proven false by a comparison of the photos of the Trump and Obama inaugurations, Spicer refused to back off of his unmoored claims. At his first formal press conference on January 23, he adamantly insisted that the Trump inauguration "was the most-watched inaugural address" in history, seeking to include the TV and online audiences in his analysis.[3] However, as Philip Bump of *The Washington Post* pointed out, Spicer's claim that Trump had more online viewers than Obama was also false, and that "CNN's live-stream numbers for Obama's inauguration" were significantly higher than Trump's.[4]

During this January 23 press conference, Spicer became increasingly agitated as members of the press corps repeatedly pressed him on this point. Finally, he vehemently declared, almost shouting, "This was the largest audience to ever witness an inauguration—PERIOD—both in person and around the globe."[5]

At the same briefing, Spicer also falsely denied that Trump was at odds with the U.S. intelligence agencies. He also denied that Trump's visit to the CIA two days earlier was meant to "dispel the myth that there was a quote-unquote 'rift' between the president and the intelligence community."[6] However, even Spicer was unable to totally obscure the fact that Trump had been in an escalating war of words with the press over the U.S. intelligence community's views of his administration.

This feud broke out in public when CNN reported on January 10, 2017 that a file, or dossier, was circulated within the intelligence agencies containing material suggesting that the Russians had embarrassing personal and financial information on Trump.[7] CNN further accurately reported that intelligence officials who received the file—which later became known as the Steele Dossier—briefed both Trump and President Barack Obama about its existence.[8] On January 11, Trump tweeted "Intelligence agencies should never have allowed this fake news to 'leak' into the public. One last shot at me. Are we living in Nazi Germany?"[9] Trump then expanded on his critique of the intelligence community, saying in response to reporters' questioning, "I think it was disgraceful—disgraceful that the intelligence agencies allowed any information that turned out to be so false and fake out." He went on: "I think it's a disgrace, and I say that—and I say that, and that's something that Nazi Germany would have done and did do."[10]

The response to Spicer's first White House briefing was extremely negative across the entire political spectrum. Conservative political analyst Bill Kristol wrote, "It is embarrassing, as an American, to watch this briefing by Sean Spicer from the podium at the White House."[11] *Vanity Fair* described Spicer's statement as "peppered with lies,"[12] and *The Atlantic* described Spicer's briefing as "bizarre," referring to the "Trump administration's needless lies" and noting that Spicer's statements appeared to involve a "deliberate attempt to mislead."[13]

Trump's team defended Spicer's statements, with White House Chief of Staff Reince Priebus stating that the purpose of Spicer's strange statements was to call out "dishonesty in the media" and their "obsession with delegitimizing the president."[14] Trump's campaign strategist and counselor, Kellyanne Conway, told NBC's Chuck Todd that Trump's inauguration crowd numbers could not be proved nor quantified and that the press secretary was simply giving "alternative facts."[15]

In a January 24, 2017 press briefing, Spicer continued his misrepresentations by saying, with regard to the Electoral College voting, that Trump had "won overwhelmingly with 306 electoral votes," and that this was the "most votes of any Republican since Reagan."[16] Spicer obviously ignored the fact that President George H.W. Bush received 426 electoral votes in 1988, and that Trump's Electoral College victory ranked him near the bottom of the list historically, placing him at number 46 out of 58 presidential elections.

Spicer also continually hyped Trump's false claim that millions voted illegally in the 2016 election, despite a complete lack of evidence supporting this claim. A *New York Times* report, for example, stated that "the overwhelming consensus" among election officials who "have been adding up how many credible reports of fraud they actually received" is that there were "next to none."[17]

At his January 30 press conference, Spicer defended Stephen Bannon's appointment to the National Security Council Principals Committee by falsely stating that the "makeup of the Principals Committee" from 2001 and 2017, during the Bush, Obama, and Trump administrations, had been "literally 100 percent the same," adding, "So this idea that there's been a change or a downgrade is utter nonsense."[18] However, based on a National Public Radio fact check, this claim that Bannon's role on the NSC Principals Committee was not a departure from any past administration was false.[19] Compared with the George W. Bush administration, Trump had far more people in the Principals Committee, especially since Trump added the chief strategist to the committee roster so Bannon would be included.[20]

During his February 7 press briefing, Spicer falsely represented that CNN had retracted its concerns about Counselor to the President Kellyanne Conway's credibility, which lead them to decline to interview her as they no longer considered her a viable source of information.[21] Spicer claimed that it was his "understanding" that CNN "retracted that, they walked that back, or denied it."[22] However, when CNN was contacted, CNN confirmed via Twitter they never retracted their comments about Conway's credibility.[23]

At his February 9 press briefing, Spicer sidestepped a question regarding Judge Neil Gorsuch's remarks that Trump's attacks on judges were "disheartening and demoralizing"[24] by falsely asserting that the White House press corps never called out President Obama when he criticized the Supreme Court's decision in *Citizens United* in his State of the Union address. Spicer stated, "When President Obama did it, there was no concern from this briefing room," suggesting there is "clearly a double standard" in the media's criticism of Trump's numerous critical comments about judges and judicial decisions.[25]

*The Washington Post*'s Callum Borchers debunked Spicer's claim of a double standard in the media's coverage of Trump's attacks on the judiciary. He noted that not only was Trump's "rebuke" of the judiciary "far more intense than Obama's,"[26] but that Obama's comments about the *Citizens United* ruling in his 2010 State of the Union address were "dissected at length on cable news," "covered on the front page," and were brought up "at the first White House press briefing after the State of the Union."[27] According to Borchers, "Once again, Spicer stood before a roomful of journalists and made an assertion that is totally at odds with the facts."[28]

At his February 21 press briefing, Spicer claimed that there could be more than 15 million people in the country illegally. While explaining the Department of Homeland Security's (DHS) list of priorities for deportation, Spicer's final estimate was "13, 14, 15, potentially more, millions of people" in the country illegally.[29] However, research provided by DHS itself, as well as independent research groups, estimated the unauthorized population in the U.S. to be approximately 11 million.[30]

At his February 22 briefing, when asked why Trump "decided to back down"[31] on his Muslim ban and instead make it a ban on immigration based on specific countries, Spicer falsely replied, "I think he's made it very clear . . . from the beginning that this was a country-focused issue . . . ."[32] Spicer's assertion that Trump never proposed a complete Muslim ban was, of course, false, since Trump's website contained a longstanding statement calling for "a total and complete shutdown of Muslims entering the United States."[33] In fact, as early as December 7, 2015 Trump called for "a total and complete shutdown of Muslims entering the United States until our country's representatives can figure out what is going on."[34] Throughout the course of his campaign Trump repeatedly said he would ban Muslims, publicly discussing the policy proposal at least nine times with media figures.[35]

At his March 8, 2017 press briefing, when asked to confirm that there was an ongoing criminal investigation into the alleged theft of cyber tools from the CIA by WikiLeaks, Spicer quickly changed the subject, claiming that Fox News correspondent James Rosen "had his phones—multiple phones tapped" during the Obama administration.[36] However, CNN reported that Rosen himself had shot down the myth that his phones were wiretapped.[37] While he was appearing on *Fox & Friends,* the show's hosts claimed his phones were tapped. Rosen clarified, "I was not wiretapped, my parents were not wiretapped, which is where you place a listening device on someone's telephone line and you listen to their conversations."[38] In reality, Rosen's emails and phone records were subpoenaed by the Department of Justice after he "received classified information from a former State Department contractor."[39]

During the March 8 White House press briefing, Spicer was also asked to clarify Trump's false claim tweeted one day earlier that Obama released 122 detainees from Guantanamo Bay, referring to it as a "terrible decision."[40] In response, Spicer contrasted the release of detainees under George W. Bush and Obama, saying, "Just to be clear, there is a big difference—under the Bush administration, most of those were court ordered."[41] In reality, however, fewer than a dozen of the 532 detainees released from Guantanamo Bay by the Bush administration were released based on a court order.[42]

During a March 10 briefing, Spicer gave a false reason why Secretary of State Rex Tillerson's plane for his trip to Asia could not accommodate reporters. Spicer said that members of the press corps would be "traveling commercially" and that the reason the plane couldn't accommodate reporters was because of "the size of the plane" and because "there's an element of cost-savings at this point that the secretary is trying to achieve."[43] CNN's Brian Stelter debunked Spicer's claim that Tillerson was trying to save money by taking a smaller plane, explaining that "news outlets normally pay for their reporters' seats, compensating the government for the expenses."[44]

At a March 20 press briefing, Spicer falsely portrayed Paul Manafort as nothing more than a bit player in the Trump campaign, claiming that Manafort had "played a very limited role for a very limited amount of time" in the campaign.[45] However, in point of fact, Manafort had been the chairman of the Trump campaign for several months, which could hardly be construed as being a minor role. *The Washington Post* characterized Spicer's claim about Manafort as "laughable" and "completely nonsensical." Manafort, according to *The Washington Post*, "was Trump's de facto campaign manager" and "was guiding the campaign's strategy while the primaries were happening, and he was in charge of ensuring that Trump's delegate lead resulted in him being awarded the nomination at the Republican National Convention."[46]

At the White House press briefing on March 28, Spicer falsely claimed that intelligence officials had reached the conclusion that there was no collusion between the Trump White House and Russia.[47] However, according to the

Associated Press (AP), as of that date, "no conclusions have been reached at all."[48] The AP explained, "The matter is being investigated by the FBI and two congressional committees, so no conclusions have been reached at all."[49] In particular, Spicer's claim that Democratic leaders who had been briefed agreed that there was no collusion was at odds with statements from leading Democrats, including Rep. Adam Schiff of California, the top Democrat on the House Intelligence Committee and a recipient of classified briefings.[50] Schiff said "there is more than circumstantial evidence now" of a relationship between Russian interests and Trump associates.[51]

Spicer resigned as White House Press Secretary on July 21, 2017, although he remained at the White House in an unspecified capacity until August 31.[52] After leaving the White House, Spicer appeared as a contestant on season 28 of *Dancing With the Stars*, dancing a salsa routine in a lime green shirt.[53] He also gave a surprise cameo appearance at the Emmy Awards on September 18, 2017 by walking on stage with a podium to deliver a one-line joke. "This will be the largest audience to witness an Emmys, period—both in person and around the world," Spicer said. However, if Spicer thought that he could undo the damage to his own reputation and the credibility of the White House press office by making light of his history of lies, he was mistaken. His reputation as the most prolific liar in the history of White House press secretaries will long outlive him, and will be an ignominious record that will be difficult—if not impossible—to beat.

## Sarah Sanders

Sarah Huckabee Sanders, the daughter of former Arkansas Governor Mike Huckabee, was the deputy White House press secretary under habitual liar Sean Spicer in 2017. She learned her lessons well from her immediate boss, following in his footsteps as the president's chief dissembler. On May 5, 2017, she held her first White House press briefing, standing in for Spicer, who was serving on Naval Reserve duty. She continued to cover for Spicer until his return to the podium on May 12. Most notably, she stood in for Spicer during the dismissal of James Comey and the controversy following it, continuing

Spicer's deplorable practice of lying to the press while simultaneously blaming them for the negative reporting swirling around the president.

After Trump's dismissal of Comey in May 2017, Sanders falsely stated that Comey had lost the confidence of the rank and file in the FBI, and that she "heard from countless members of the FBI that are grateful and thankful for the President's decision" to fire the Bureau's director.[54] However, it was later disclosed that when Sanders was questioned about her remarks by Special Counsel Mueller's office, she admitted that she lied.[55] Sanders' remarks also conflicted with numerous emails circulating at the time showing that several FBI heads of regional field offices and high-ranking FBI members reacted with shock and dismay to Comey's firing.[56]

Sanders also irreparably tarnished her reputation by vouching for the president's veracity and credibility, which were already near zero by the time she took over as press secretary. For example, after Comey accused Trump of lying about the circumstances of his dismissal, Sanders defended Trump, saying, "I can definitively say the president is not a liar, and I think it's frankly insulting that question would be asked."[57]

Sanders also enthusiastically joined in one of Trump's favorite pastimes, which was bashing the press at every opportunity while amplifying his "fake news" narrative designed to undercut the credibility of the mainstream media. During a press briefing on June 27, 2017, Sanders accused the media of spreading "fake news" against Trump.[58] Two days later, Sanders also falsely stated during a press briefing that the "president in no way, form or fashion has ever promoted or encouraged violence,"[59] despite video recordings from February 2016 of Trump saying during a presidential campaign speech, "So if you see somebody getting ready to throw a tomato, knock the crap out of them, would you? . . . I promise you, I will pay for the legal fees. I promise." *PolitiFact* also found at least seven other examples in which Trump advocated, or at least tolerated, the use of violence by his supporters.[60]

On July 21, 2017, following Spicer's announcement that he was going to resign, newly appointed White House Communications Director Anthony Scaramucci announced that Sanders would take the role of White House press secretary. Sanders quickly became Trump's denier-in-chief regarding the avalanche of allegations as to his alleged mistreatment of women. In October 2017, for example, Sanders was asked by Jacqueline Alemany of

CBS News whether the official White House position was that all 16 women who accused President Trump of sexual harassment were lying. Sanders responded by saying, "Yeah, we've been clear on that since the beginning, and the President has spoken on it," without elaborating.[61]

In February 2018, when Rob Porter left the White House over domestic abuse allegations, Sanders falsely stated that Porter's background check was "ongoing, and the White House had not received any specific papers regarding the completion of that background check."[62] However, FBI director Christopher Wray directly contradicted her, testifying that the FBI finished and submitted Porter's security clearance investigation to the White House in July 2017.[63] The White House press office changed its story regarding the "Porter affair" three times in one day, with Sanders saying that Porter had made a "personal decision" to leave the White House, while her deputy press secretary Raj Shah was simultaneously saying that Porter was "terminated."[64]

In March 2018, regarding the Stormy Daniels–Donald Trump scandal, Sanders misrepresented the facts by stating that "there was no knowledge of any payments from the president" to Daniels.[65] However, Trump's personal lawyer Rudy Giuliani later disclosed that Trump repaid his previous personal lawyer Michael Cohen $130,000 after Cohen paid Daniels.[66] Sanders said that she had been kept in the dark about these payments.[67]

By June 2018, Sanders's credibility itself had become a newsworthy issue that the press felt necessary to cover, forcing Sanders to publicly declare, "I'm an honest person."[68] To many, however, this reminded them of President Nixon's famous quote during the Watergate scandal. Just before he resigned he declared, "I am not a crook."

In mid-June 2018, when questioned on the Trump administration's immigration policies resulting in the separation of migrant children from their parents at the Mexico–United States border, Sanders blamed "legal loopholes that Democrats refuse to close."[69]

By August 2018, one of Trump's favorite themes at his MAGA rallies was to call the media "the enemy of the people," which Sanders refused to comment on.[70] That same month, *The Washington Post* reported that Sanders and her deputy Bill Shine strategized as to when they should release announcements that the security clearances of various Trump critics and officials involved in the probe into Russian interference in the 2016 election had been revoked.[71]

The announcements were intended to be released to distract from news cycles that were unfavorable to the White House.[72]

In early November 2018, Sanders released a video of CNN's Jim Acosta supposedly showing Acosta rebuffing an attempt by a White House intern to take away a microphone from him during a White House press briefing with President Trump. Acosta was in the middle of a heated verbal exchange with Trump and was in the process of asking the president a question when an intern, at the direction of Trump, tried to take away his microphone. Later in the day, Acosta's White House credentials were suspended in a move which was widely criticized as unprecedented.[73] The following day, in order to justify the White House's actions, Sanders released a video of the moment the intern tried to grab the microphone from Acosta's hand. The video originated from conspiracy theorist Paul Joseph Watson of the far-right website *Infowars*, which had been altered to make Acosta seem aggressive and excluded him saying "Pardon me, ma'am" to the intern.[74] CNN Communications Executive called Sanders' sharing of the video "shameful"[75] and the White House News Photographers Association said they were "appalled" by her actions and called video-manipulation "deceptive, dangerous and unethical."[76]

During the 2018–2019 government shutdown caused by Congress's refusal to fulfill Trump's demand for $5.7 billion in federal funds for a U.S.–Mexico border wall, Sanders argued that a border wall was necessary. She backed her assertion by falsely claiming that U.S. Customs and Border Protection agents stopped nearly 4,000 known or suspected terrorists while crossing the Mexico border in 2018.[77] However, official data showed that from October 1, 2017 to March 31, 2018, only six immigrants on the No Fly List (also known as the terror watch list) were detained at the ports of entry on the Mexican border.[78] In an interview with Chris Wallace on *Fox News Sunday*, Wallace confronted Sanders about her claim of the fictitious "nearly 4,000 terrorists," for which she was unable to provide any source material.[79]

On June 13, 2019, Trump tweeted that Sanders would be leaving her role as press secretary for his administration on June 30.[80]

Sanders' legacy is that she brought the reputation of the White House press office to a new low. By the end of her nearly two-year tenure as press secretary, she sounded the death knell of on-camera briefings, first shortening them and then eliminating them altogether. It became apparent that neither Trump nor Sanders felt that it was in the president's interest to expose themselves to direct questioning by a hostile press, and that there was no advantage to providing any meaningful degree of transparency, at least at the same level as provided by past administrations for several decades. Trump tweeted in January 2019, "The reason Sarah Sanders does not go to the 'podium' much anymore is that the press covers her so rudely & inaccurately, in particular certain members of the press. I told her not to bother, the word gets out anyway!"[81]

Sanders once said that she wanted her legacy as press secretary to be that she was "transparent and honest."[82] Instead, it will forever be one of obfuscation and lies.

# Kayleigh McEnany

*I will never lie to you. You have my word on that.*

### Kayleigh McEnany – May 1, 2020

Kayleigh McEnany was hired as White House press secretary on April 7, 2020 by Mark Meadows, immediately after Meadows replaced Mick Mulvaney as White House chief of staff.[83] Starting off as a critic of the Trump presidency while working as a commentator at CNN, McEnany quickly gained the White House's attention when she became the most ardent MAGA acolyte at that network. For example, in August 2019, McEnany turned a blind eye to the overwhelming evidence that Trump repeatedly lied to the public since day one of his presidency, flatly telling CNN's Chris Cuomo, "I don't believe the president has lied."[84] In the weeks before her appointment as White House press secretary, McEnany also praised Trump's handling of the COVID-19 pandemic, saying, "This president will always put America first, he will always protect American citizens. We will not see diseases like the coronavirus come here, we will not see terrorism, and isn't that refreshing when contrasting it with the awful presidency of Barack Obama?"[85] In a radio interview on *The Pat Miller Program* on March 11, 2020, McEnany said Democrats were trying "to politicize" the coronavirus and that they were almost "rooting for" the uncontrolled spread of the virus.[86] When Trump was criticized for spending an inordinate amount of his presidential time on the golf course, McAnany countered by falsely accusing President Obama of having gone golfing on the day that Daniel Pearl was killed. Pearl, a *Wall Street Journal* reporter who had been taken hostage by a terrorist group in Pakistan, was beheaded in a gruesome video on February 1, 2002, six years before the start of Obama's presidency.[87]

Author Grant Stern best summed up her rapid rise to the inner circle of the Trump universe, tweeting, "Kayleigh McEnany is coming to the White House with new 'alternative facts' about #coronavirus. The rest of the world calls them lies."[88]

When Trump was criticized by experts for suggesting during a coronavirus task force briefing that the coronavirus could be treated with disinfectant injections, McEnany said that his remarks were "taken out of context."[89]

On May 1, 2020, as part of her first public press briefing and the first one by a White House press secretary in 417 days, McEnany was asked by an Associated Press reporter, "Will you pledge to never lie to us from that podium?" McEnany replied, "I will never lie to you. You have my word on that."[90] Without missing a beat, McEnany then unleashed a torrent of falsehoods to the assembled reporters on a wide variety of topics. For example, she misrepresented Trump's repeated contradictions of Dr. Anthony Fauci and the science-based advice that he and other medical professionals were givng the public regarding the coronavirus crisis. McEnany claimed, "This president has always sided on the side of data."[91] She also shamelessly asserted that, despite the president's near-pathological compulsion to lie, that "he has always told the truth."[92]

Not content with only spreading COVID-related disinformation, at her first press conference McEnany also falsely claimed that the Mueller Report on Russian interference in the 2016 presidential election had resulted in a "complete and total exoneration of President Trump,"[93] disregarding the plain language of the report itself, which reads, "Accordingly, while this report does not conclude that the President committed a crime, it also does not exonerate him."[94]

One week later, amid reports on May 8 that the White House was shelving the release of COVID-19 re-opening guidelines, McEnany falsely stated that the guidelines had not been approved by Robert Redfield, the director of the Centers for Disease Control and Prevention (CDC).[95] However, the Associated Press had already accurately reported that Redfield cleared the release of the guidelines and that they had been "buried" by the White House because they were at odds with the president's message that it was time to reopen the country back again.[96] Redfield himself confirmed that the guidelines had been released for "interagency review."[97] Also, in response to criticism of the administration's response to the COVID-19 crisis as "chaotic," McEnany told CNN that, to the contrary, the "response has been unprecedented and saved American lives."[98]

In May 2020, McEnany defended Trump's false accusation that MSNBC's Joe Scarborough had a person murdered, offering no evidence in support of the accusation.[99] That same month—and despite the fact that she herself has voted by mail eleven times in ten years[100]—McEnany defended claims that Trump made about the dangers of voting by mail, repeating his inaccurate claims that the voting method has a "high propensity for voter fraud."[101]

After two months as press secretary, the Associated Press gave an assessment that McEnany "has made clear from her first briefing that she's willing to defend her boss's view of himself as well as his most flagrant misstatements."[102]

In June 2020, McEnany defended the decision by the Trump administration to forcibly remove peaceful protestors by using smoke canisters, pepper balls, riot shields, batons, officers on horseback, and rubber bullets, so that Trump could stage a photo op in front of St. John's Episcopal Church, Lafayette Square in Washington.[103] She likened Trump's action to that of Winston Churchill walking the streets to survey bomb damage during World War II, which overlooked the obvious fact that Churchill did not have to have scores of London residents beaten in order for him to take his walks.[104] When General Jim Mattis, former secretary of defense in the Trump administration, condemned Trump's action, McEnany described Mattis' comments as "little more than a self-promotional stunt to appease the DC elite."[105]

In September 2020, *Washington Post* reporter and author Bob Woodward released February 2020 recordings of Trump privately acknowledging the severity of the COVID-19 virus, which Trump was then downplaying in public.[106] McEnany falsely asserted, "The president never downplayed the virus."[107] In fact, in an interview with Woodward recorded March 19, 2020, Trump flatly admitted that he publicly downplayed the risk of the virus and the severity of the pandemic saying, "I wanted to always play it down. I still like playing it down, because I don't want to create a panic."[108] In response to McEnany's comment, *Washington Post* media critic Erik Wemple wrote that she had sacrificed all of her credibility.[109] Joe Lockhart, who served as White House press secretary during the Clinton administration, wrote her answers confirmed that she had become nothing more than a "state propagandist."[110]

While ballots were still being counted on election day, McEnany made an early false declaration of victory for Trump.[111] Six days later, on November 9, 2020, Fox News signaled that McEnany's credibility had been so severely damaged that not even they—the news network generally considered by most of America as Trump's unofficial mouthpiece—could not endure her lies any longer. Fox News cut away from a White House press conference in which McEnany claimed Democrats were "welcoming" voter fraud, adding that the Trump forces had "only begun the process of obtaining an accurate, honest vote count."[112] She specifically attacked Democrats' opposition to voter ID laws and the verification of signatures, as well as the supposed blocking of Republican observers from watching ballots be counted. Fox News cut away from its coverage of the conference when host Neil Cavuto critiqued McEnany's lack of evidence in remarks to viewers: "She is charging that the other side is welcoming fraud and welcoming illegal voting. Unless she has more details to back that up, I can't in good countenance continuing showing you this."[113]

McEnany's relationship with the White House press corps completely unraveled as the post-election days started stretching into weeks, with no end in sight as the White House refused to acknowledge the results. As she left the lectern on December 15, 2020, CNN Chief White House Correspondent Jim Acosta asked, "Kayleigh, isn't it hypocritical for you to accuse others of disinformation when you spread it every day?"[114] Again, on November 20, five days after Republican Senate leader Mitch McConnell had finally acknowledged the obvious about the election results and had congratulated Biden on his victory, McEnany continued to signal to the press corps and the public that she was still a member of the dwindling band of diehard enablers willing to pretend that Trump should be permitted to serve a second term due to the "massive" election fraud. "There are very real claims out there that the campaign is pursuing," she said during a press briefing.[115]

Separately, she lied about Trump's meeting with Michigan legislators in an unsuccessful attempt to persuade them to throw out that state's election results and, instead, send a slate of Trump electors to Congress. McEnany stated that the meeting with the two Michigan legislators was "not an advocacy meeting, there will be no one from the campaign there—he routinely meets with lawmakers from all across the country."[116] McEnany also made the flatly false statement that there was not an orderly transfer of power from Barack Obama's administration to then President-elect Donald Trump's incoming administration, claiming that Trump "was never given an orderly transition of power."[117]

Ironically, McEnany denounced White House reporters on November 20 as "activists," presumably for calling out the president on his scheme to overturn the results of the recent election that he had lost. McEnany apparently lacked sufficient self-awareness to recognize that her conscious choice to support Trump's blatant attempt to dismantle American democracy could more accurately be described as sedition.

# TRUMP'S LAWYERS

*"The first thing we do, let's kill all the lawyers."*

– William Shakespeare's *Henry VI*, Part 2

Lawyers have, for centuries, had difficulty overcoming the popular reputation of the profession as filled with moral relativists who are willing to say or do anything to earn a fee and to get their wealthy and well-paying clients off the hook. While this caricature may accurately apply to only a miniscule percentage of lawyers, the persistent poor repute in which lawyers are held was strongly reinforced during the Trump era. The Liar-in-Chief occupying the White House surrounded himself with members of the bar who were willing to say or do anything, no matter how false and dishonorable it might be, as long as it furthered the perverse goal of keeping the sitting president in power.

As a young New York developer, Donald Trump's first legal mentor was the notorious mob lawyer and fixer Roy Cohn, whose place as consiglieri in the Trump organized crime family was later filled by Michael Cohen. Cohen's role included paying off Stormy Daniels and other embarrassing reminders of Trump's extra-marital dalliances that stood between candidate Trump and the White House.

Finally, after Cohen was indicted, convicted, and imprisoned for lying and cheating on Trump's behalf, Rudy Giuliani, New York City's former mayor, assumed the mantle as Trump's personal lawyer and fixer. Giuliani did everything from attempting to manipulate and extort the Ukraine government into collecting political dirt on Trump's most formidable Democratic adversary, Joe Biden, to leading the despicable campaign to try to find a federal or state judge corrupt enough to accept the lies the Trump team was selling about a "rigged election" and "massive voter fraud" in 2020.

## Rudolph Giuliani

Rudy Giuliani has, at various times in his long public career, reflected both the best and the worst of what it means to be an American. As Mayor of New York City, he became something of an American hero and icon following the terrorist attacks of September 11, 2001, earning the unofficial title of "America's Mayor." He told a shocked America what they needed to hear, balancing a condemnation of the attacks and mourning for the victims with a call for tolerance of New York's Muslim community.

His steady hand and reassuring voice in a time of national crisis transcended partisan politics and primed him for accomplishing great things in either business, law, or government—whichever route he sought to take.

Two decades later, Giuliani's reputation was in tatters, and he had become a national embarrassment. One scandal after another followed him, with perhaps the most prominent being his role in triggering a Ukraine political extortion scandal that resulted in the impeachment of the president to whom he had sworn his undying allegiance. His behavior became increasingly wild and irresponsible, and at times it was virtually incoherent. He bought into and promoted baseless conspiracy theories about Joe Biden and a supposedly massive election fraud that allowed Trump and his millions of true believers to avoid the reality that Trump's tenure in the White House, and the intoxicating power that came with it, was rapidly coming to an end. Rick Wilson, a GOP political consultant, best summed up the situation: "It's a cliché that if you live long enough, you'll see your heroes become villains."[1]

And so it became for Rudy Giuliani. During the Trump era, he descended from the heights of heroism to the ignominy of being Trump's bumbling personal lawyer, henchman, and chief co-conspirator.

From the start of Trump's campaign to win the presidency, Giuliani was willing to do what others could not bring themselves to do. He felt no shame in doing whatever it took to keep close to the intoxicating fount of executive power. On October 9, 2016, he appeared as Trump's only campaign surrogate on the Sunday morning talk shows to defend Mr. Trump's indefensible 2005 *Access Hollywood* interview as "locker room talk."[2] This was the first of many comments by Giuliani that portrayed all men as sexist predators who objectified women with crude and vulgar remarks on a regular basis and further confirmed the public stereotype that members of the legal profession were capable of lying as easily as breathing. For example, Giuliani falsely commented on Fox News that when Michael Cohen used his own funds to pay hush money to Stormy Daniels, this was a common legal practice and nothing unusual.[3]

In Ukraine, Giuliani, acting as a private citizen and Trump's personal lawyer, led the rogue band of Ukrainian Americans to whom he had attached himself in a tireless campaign to dig up (or manufacture) some dirt on Joe Biden and his son Hunter. By acting as a shadow secretary of state for Trump,

Giuliani succeeded in not only eviscerating the legitimate efforts by career U.S. diplomats to assist Ukraine in its struggle to remain a stable and independent country but also set certain wheels in motion that ended in Trump's first impeachment.

In addition to taking the lead on trying to collect dirt from every conceivable and dubious source to use against Biden, Giuliani breathed new life into the debunked conspiracy theory that it was Ukraine, not Russia, that hacked the Democratic National Committee's computer server.[4] Trump loved this false theory since it—with a single stroke—portrayed him as the *victim of Ukraine* rather than Russia's co-conspirator in manipulating the 2016 election. Giuliani even went so far as to buy into the absurd theory that the DNC server had actually been physically stolen and was being hidden away somewhere in Ukraine.[5] The fact that Russian intelligence services originally concocted this theory to throw U.S. investigators off the scent was immaterial to Trump and Giuliani.

Almost all of the "asks" that Trump made of Ukraine President Volodymyr Zelensky in the infamous phone call of July 25, 2019, were based on conspiracy-tinged nonsense that Trump had been fed by Giuliani. "I would like you to do us a favor," Trump said to Zelensky in the phone call. "The [DNC] server, they say Ukraine has it." The president added, "Rudy very much knows what's happening, and he is a very capable guy. If you could speak to him, that would be great."[6] In other words, Trump and Giuliani had fully embraced an alternate reality fueled by conspiracy theories that painted Trump and Russia as blameless for any tampering with the 2016 election.

In his earlier years, either as U.S. Attorney or as Mayor, Giuliani would have never associated himself with the likes of Lev Parnas or Igor Fruman, two Ukrainian Americans with close ties to Russian-Ukrainian organized crime. But during the Trump era, Giuliani formed a close connection with both of them and even went so far as to help Parnas with his oddly named business venture, Fraud Guarantee.[7]

Parnas and Fruman made good on their promise that they could put Giuliani in touch with a former Ukrainian prosecutor who said that he had some damaging material on Hunter Biden.[8] Giuliani also used his connections with Parnas and Fruman to align himself—and President Trump—with Dimitry Firtash, a Ukrainian oligarch with major Russian organized crime links.⁹ At the time, Firtash was under indictment by federal prosecutors in Chicago in connection with an international bribery scheme. Parnas and Fruman actually met with Firtash in Vienna, where he was basically under house arrest. As intermediaries for Giuliani and Trump, they asked Firtash to use his considerable influence in Ukraine to get the government of that country to publicly announce an investigation of the Bidens and to help them dig up some dirt on them.¹⁰

During various interviews, Giuliani could never get it quite straight whether he was acting as a private citizen or whether he was acting on behalf of the Trump administration during his forays to Ukraine. One particularly bizarre interview took place on September 20, 2019, when Giuliani flew off the rails in a wild war of words with Chris Cuomo of CNN. Giuliani at first denied that he had urged the Ukraine government to investigate Joe Biden, then proudly reversed that position. "You want to cover some ridiculous charge that I urged the Ukrainian government to investigate corruption. Well, I did, and I'm proud of it," proclaimed Giuliani.¹¹ Cuomo closed out the interview by offering his condolences to Giuliani. "I'm embarrassed. I'm embarrassed for you," he said.¹²

Giuliani also carried out some of Trump's most shameful dirty work while working on the Ukraine-Biden smear campaign. For example, he schemed to remove the extraordinarily dedicated and skillful U.S. Ambassador to Ukraine Marie Yovanovitch, which was one of the prime objectives of Russian intelligence operatives in Ukraine and their pro-Russian allies there. Trump's national security adviser at the time, John Bolton, foresaw that Trump's reliance on his increasingly reckless and erratic personal attorney would likely be the catalyst that finally brought down Trump's presidency. "Rudy Giuliani is a hand grenade that is going to blow everybody up," Bolton said, according to testimony at the impeachment hearings.¹³ Trump apparently ignored the warnings and even invited Giuliani to attend the 2018 White House Hanukkah Party, with Parnas and Fruman as his guests.

Giuliani himself was under investigation by the U.S. Attorneys' Office for the Southern District of New York, the office he once ran. The possible crimes for which he was under investigation included money laundering, campaign finance violations, making false statements, obstruction of justice, and acting as an unregistered foreign lobbyist. Both Parnas and Fruman already had been indicted by that same federal prosecutor's office in Manhattan on various criminal charges.

By the end of the Trump presidency, Giuliani had been reduced to little more than just another conspiracy theory wingnut peddling coronavirus and election fraud disinformation. "Why did the US (NIH) in 2017 give $3.7m to the Wuhan Lab in China?" Giuliani tweeted.[14] Giuliani could no longer even muster the presence of mind to realize that the National Institute of Health (NIH) was an agency within the U.S. Department of Health and Human Services, which was part of the Trump administration. So if, in fact, the NIH gave money to the same Wuhan Lab in China that conspiracy theorists said was the source of the coronavirus causing COVID-19, then Giuliani should have been asking Trump or one of his Cabinet members for the answer to this burning question.

Shortly before the 2020 election, Giuliani's reputation took another hit when he unwittingly appeared in one of the scenes of the recent hidden-camera comedy film *Borat Subsequent Moviefilm*. In the scene, Giuliani is interviewed in a New York hotel room by an actress (Maria Bakalova) posing as a 15 year-old conservative female reporter, the daughter of fake Kazakh journalist Borat (Sasha Baron Cohen). Giuliani believed she was an up-and-coming conservative journalist, and after an on-camera interview, accepted an invitation—from an ostensible minor—to "have a drink in the bedroom."[15] Giuliani did not know about the hidden cameras. All he knew was that she was an attractive under-aged blond who was heaping large scoops of praise—even adoration—on the aging former mayor. This was enough to lift both Giuliani's ego and libido, and apparently, on the theory that such an opportunity should not go to waste, he asked for her phone number and address before patting Bakalova on the hip, laying back on the bed and shoving his hand down his pants. Giuliani's fantasies were interrupted before they could get any more graphic, as Borat burst into the room shouting something like, "She's only 15!"[16] When later asked about the scene, Giuliani claimed that he was tucking in his shirt.[17] Interestingly, despite QAnon's claims that Trump was working to overthrow an internal cabal of elite pedophiles, there was no outcry from Trump or the conspiracists when Giuliani was caught on camera about to undress with someone he believed to be an underaged girl.

Giuliani was finally able to get people to stop talking about his Chris Hansen-style cameo when, following the November 3 election, he skyrocketed back to prominence in the Trump universe by emerging as the leader of the president's so-called legal team trying to reverse the election results in court by challenging the votes in several key battleground states. Giuliani's cries of fraud in 2020 echoed his statements after the 1989 New York mayoral race and became something of a blueprint for the Trump team's post-election strategy. After narrowly losing to mayoral incumbent David Dinkins, Giuliani claimed "They stole that election from me. They stole votes in the Black parts of Brooklyn, and in Washington Heights."[18]

Giuliani acted as master of ceremonies at the presidential news conference on Saturday, November 7, 2020, which took place at the Four Seasons Total Landscaping parking lot in northeastern Philadelphia. Trump caused some understandable confusion when he tweeted that the press conference would be held at "Four Seasons" in Philadelphia, which members of the press naturally thought would be held at the prestigious hotel bearing that name in downtown Philadelphia.[19] The Trump team had been bragging that it was a near certainty that they were going to snatch victory from the jaws of defeat by overturning the Biden election victory, so both the national and worldwide press gathered there to see if Giuliani and his legal team could pull off a political miracle. However, Trump had to clarify in a follow-up email that the press conference would not be held at the upscale Four Seasons Hotel and Resorts in Philadelphia, but, rather, in the parking lot behind Four Seasons Total Landscaping. For those unfamiliar with this area of the city, the landscaping company can be found next to the Fantasy Island Adult Book Store (offering a wide selection of DVDs, lotions, novelty gifts and viewing booths for those of you who are interested in such amusements). Oh, yes, and the Delaware Valley Cremation Center is immediately across the street, in the event that you may be in the neighborhood and suffer a fatal heart attack after your visit to the Adult Book Store.

This day—November 7—was a significant date in the 2020 election calendar since it was the day the television networks announced that Biden was the projected winner of the presidential race, with a majority projected in the Electoral College as well as the popular vote.

Giuliani, however, was unimpressed with what the networks and cable news outlets were saying about the results of the election. He brought with him to the press conference a key witness he was confident would provide clear evidence of election fraud. As the first witness to speak, this man was described as a Philadelphia resident and GOP poll watcher in Pennsylvania who wasn't allowed to observe ballots being counted. "They did not allow us to see anything," Daryl Brooks told those attending the open-air press conference, adding, "Was it corrupt or not? But give us an opportunity as poll watchers to view all the documents—all of the ballots."[20]

It did not take reporters long to learn that Giuliani's star witness turned out to *not* be a Philadelphia or Pennsylvania resident at all, but rather was a longstanding resident of New Jersey who had frequently and unsuccessfully run for political office there.[21] Brooks was also a convicted sex offender who had been incarcerated on charges of sexual assault, lewdness in connection with his having exposed himself to two girls ages 7 and 11, and endangering the welfare of a minor.[22]

If possible, Giuliani's subsequent press conference on November 19 at the Republican National Committee headquarters in Washington, D.C. was even more bizarre and comical. A heavily sweating Giuliani appeared to have hair dye dripping down his face as he addressed a press conference. Flanked by conspiracy theorist Sidney Powell and other members of Trump's legal "dream team," Giuliani falsely proclaimed that they had "thousands" of affidavits supporting their claims of voter fraud and attacked the voting machine company Dominion, which he said used Venezuelan technology approved by the late Hugo Chavez, president and de-facto dictator of Venezuela. He further claimed that Dominion's vote-rigging scheme was supported by Cuba and China.[23]

Interestingly Russia - the standard boogeyman for conservative American conspiracy theories - was not mentioned by Trump's team as having any hand in the alleged election manipulation. However, just to add a dash of anti-Semitism to the latest conspiracy theories, Giuliani also threw out the name of Democratic billionaire George Soros as one of the members of this far-flung international conspiracy. "This is real. It is not made up. There is no one here who engages in fantasy. I know crimes—I can smell them."[24] There was certainly a strong stench enveloping the entire press conference at the RNC, but it was coming from the profusely sweating Giuliani and his other team members on the podium, who were all beginning to look like they were suffering under the hot lights of the TV cameras assembled around the podium.

Sidney Powell then chimed in, further expanding on Giuliani's conspiracy theories. She said that Dominion workers had gone overnight to closed polling stations to tamper with the ballots, but she could not provide any evidence to support this claim. She added: "We have no idea how many Democratic officials paid to have the election rigged in their favor. This is a massive, well-coordinated effort. It is the 1775 of our generation and beyond."[25]

Giuliani and Powell also implicated another technology company, Smartmatic, with having conspired with Venezuela and other leftist and communist countries to deliver the 2020 election to Biden.[26] But it was soon confirmed that this company only provided technology and software to Los Angeles County during the 2020 election.[27] Since this company's technology was not used in any battleground states, including Pennsylvania, Georgia, Arizona, Nevada, Michigan, and North Carolina, Giuliani and Powell had no explanation as to the relevance of their allegations, even in the unlikely event they were proved true. Also, prior to Giuliani's November 19 press conference, an open letter signed by 59 election security experts stated that was "no credible evidence" that the 2020 election outcome was altered by exploiting technical vulnerabilities in voting machines.[28]

Giuliani appeared to be completely unmoored from reality as he elaborated on his baseless allegations of a massive fraud and conspiracy in the 2020 election. The theory, which was first promoted by the Trump White House and Giuliani, quickly won enthusiastic endorsement not only in the right-wing internet crawl spaces inhabited by the most paranoid of diehard Trump supporters, but also on Fox News and the more mainstream right-wing media outlets. Christopher Krebs, Trump's former director of a Department of Homeland Security cybersecurity unit, described Giuliani's Four Seasons press conference as "the most dangerous hour and 45 minutes of television in American history. And possibly the craziest."[29] The *New York Times*' Maggie Haberman reported that even Trump's aides who watched Giuliani's performance were in shock. "Trump advisers—none of whom are speaking publicly—are saying this press conference and what Giuliani is doing is dangerous."[30] GOP pollster Patrick Ruffini tweeted, "The thing about Rudy is that he wasn't a carnival barker or a second-rate figure who needed to flail wildly for attention. He had mainstream respectability and was a national hero for a time. Why he decided to go down this road is a great mystery."[31] CNN analyst Joe Lockhart may have found the solution to this puzzle: "One explanation of why Rudy is doing what Rudy is doing? He needs a pardon and he's trying to earn it," he tweeted.[32]

Indeed, Lockhart's statement offers a plausible explanation for Giuliani's unhinged performance in a Philadelphia parking lot as it is likely that he was feeling the heat from the federal grand jury investigation of him by the U.S. Attorney's Office. This investigation seemed to have picked up renewed steam following the November 3 election. In fact, CNN's post-election reporting disclosed that "in recent weeks, FBI agents in New York contacted witnesses and asked questions about Giuliani's efforts in Ukraine and possible connections to Russian intelligence."[33] The FBI investigators had apparently come back to witnesses they had spoken to several months previously about emails and documents related to Hunter Biden that appeared to be similar to those that the *New York Post* reported Giuliani and others helped provide.[34]

There also were reliable reports—denied by Rudy Giuliani and his lawyer, of course—that Giuliani has discussed the issue of his own pardon with Trump, and that Giuliani was counting on it to save him from a post-election federal indictment by the U.S. Attorney's Office for the Southern District of New York.[35] These reports of a deal brewing between Trump and Giuliani for a free pass and preemptive pardon of Giuliani as Trump was on his way out the White House door were made even more credible by the fact that Giuliani must have been worried that the federal prosecutors had been holding off announcing an indictment of him during the blackout period leading up to the November 3 election, where it would have been inappropriate and politically motivated for the prosecutors to return an indictment against Trump's personal lawyer. Federal prosecutors, as required, had already informed Giuliani's lawyer prior to November 3 that Giuliani was a subject or target of a federal investigation. Nevertheless, federal prosecutors waited until at least after the election, and then after the transition period, to take any action against Giuliani.

So, as long as Giuliani continued to hold press conferences and perpetuate the myth that the election was still not over and that the process was still working itself out with court cases, it would look improper for any federal prosecutor to indict Giuliani. It would have looked like they were trying to shut Giuliani up, which would have played into the deep state narrative deployed by Trump and QAnon, thus giving credibility to his unfounded conspiracy theories.

One school of thought, therefore, was that Giuliani was crazy like a fox, cynically pouring gasoline on Trump's post-election hysteria because he wanted to stay relevant and prove to Trump once again that he was his most loyal and faithful follower. Giuliani felt that he had to stay at the center of every post-election news cycle since he could be reasonably confident that FBI agents would not be jumping on any stage to handcuff him while the national media had their cameras focused on him. Nor would they be following him into any meetings with state legislators in which he discussed with them how they could overturn the results of the election in their state by submitting their own slate of electors to Congress.[36]

Giuliani knew that his alliance with shady Soviet-born operatives Lev Parnas and Igor Fruman made him vulnerable to a wide range of federal crimes, including violations of the federal election and lobbying laws, money laundering, and other financial crimes. Although both Parnas and Fruman pleaded not guilty and were scheduled to go to trial as soon as the COVID-19 crisis permitted, their lawyers were also intensely talking to federal prosecutors about a possible deal. Giuliani surely knew, therefore, that these two could buy themselves a lot of credit with federal prosecutors by delivering credible evidence against him regarding the financial transactions and exchange of monies between and among them.

An important aspect of the federal investigation was whether, and to what extent, Giuliani and his two cohorts were acting in concert with Russian intelligence operatives such as Andrii Derkach, a Ukrainian lawmaker who was sanctioned by the U.S. Treasury Department in September, 2020 as a Russian agent attempting to interfere with the 2020 presidential election.

But the law of unintended consequences may have been at work here, and Giuliani's strenuous efforts on behalf of Trump's campaign to overturn the 2020 election may have boomeranged on him, making him too controversial a figure for Trump to risk giving him a pardon. After all, it was Giuliani who told the MAGA crowd getting ready to march on the U.S. Capitol on January 6, 2021, that it was time to engage in "trial by combat," which was correctly interpreted by the pro-Trump mob as a license to storm the Capitol.[37]

This was not Giuliani's first time inciting a riot. On September 16, 1992, at a protest organized by the Patrolmen's Benevolent Association, Giuliani was filmed leading chants and egging on a crowd of approximately 10,000 people, many of whom were off-duty NYPD officers. They had gathered to protest Mayor Dinkins and the creation of a new civilian oversight board to address claims of improprieties within the NYPD. The protesters were whipped into a frenzy by Giuliani and police union officials, turning the event into a riot as off-duty cops rushed and occupied city hall. Another part of the crowd halted traffic on the Brooklyn Bridge, telling those trapped in their cars to "call the cops." Members of the crowd hurled racist slurs at African American city council member Una Clarke and a television cameraman. Notably, Giuliani never condemned the rioters or the NYPD's inaction that day.[38]

When Trump was impeached for inciting the January 6, 2021 insurrection, it was Giuliani who helped him pour gasoline on the flames, and a pardon would make it look like Trump was protecting one of his co-conspirators. In other words, Giuliani was just too toxic.

Trump must have also been distressed that Giuliani's campaign to overturn the election results imploded spectacularly, like some dwarf star collapsing into itself. Trump's semi-serious discussions of voting irregularities quickly degenerated under Giuliani's leadership into farcical spectacle more worthy of a theater of the absurd play rather than a serious court of law. So, while Giuliani may have proved himself to be a loyal Trump stalwart, the abject failure of his post-election campaign irredeemably doomed his already battered reputation. Both Trump and Giuliani also became inexorably shrouded with the mantle of "Loser," a term that Trump has always considered to be the most terrifying noun in the English language.

During the January 6 storming and occupation of the U.S. Capitol by pro-Trump forces, Giuliani left a long and rambling message for Tommy Tuberville, the newly sworn in senator from Alabama, urging him to delay the vote on the Electoral College count for as long as possible. However, Giuliani left the message on a different lawmaker's voicemail, which was promptly turned over to the FBI and other law enforcement agencies investigating the insurrection and coup attempt.[39] Oops! Giuliani recorded the voicemail message addressed to Tuberville at approximately 7 p.m., saying that he wanted to discuss how congressional leaders were "trying to rush this hearing and how we need you, our Republican friends, to try to just slow it down so we can get these legislatures to get more information to you."[40] "And I know they're reconvening at 8 tonight, but it . . . the only strategy we can follow is to object to numerous states and raise issues so that we get ourselves into tomorrow-ideally until the end of tomorrow," Giuliani added.

This phone call should have been enough to dispel any remaining doubts in the minds of any federal prosecutors as to whether Giuliani was a full-fledged co-conspirator with Trump in the attempt to interfere with the lawful governmental processes of Congress, which qualifies him for indictment on charges of sedition and treason.

## Sidney Powell

Attorney Sidney Powell—another member of Rudy Giuliani's self-described legal "Elite Strike Force"—promoted some outlandish conspiracy theories that even Giuliani hesitated to embrace.[41] She claimed, for example, that the company Dominion Voting Systems had bribed Georgia Gov. Brian Kemp and Secretary of State Brad Raffensperger, both Republicans, as part of the scheme that supposedly enabled Joe Biden to steal the election.[42] However, Giuliani and Powell were completely on the same page as to most of the other conspiracy theories that were being circulated, such as the theory that the deceased Venezuelan strongman Hugo Chavez, billionaire Democrat George Soros, the Clinton Foundation, and China had colluded to interfere with the 2020 election by using election software designed to flip Trump votes to Biden.

At one of their more bizarre press conferences, Powell said that Democrats also resorted to a secondary plan involving "mail-in ballots, many of which they had actually fabricated, some [of which] were on pristine paper with identically matching perfect circle dots for Mr. Biden."[43] As a result, Biden was shown to be the winner even though it would have otherwise been clear that "President Trump won by a landslide."[44]

After the press conference, Trump distanced himself from Powell, but not Giuliani. *The New York Times* reported that Trump "has been agitated about Mr. Giuliani and Ms. Powell for a few days," particularly by "the black rivulets of liquid" that "dripped down Mr. Giuliani's face" (apparently as his sweat mingled with hair dye) and the fact that the press conference dragged on for over an hour.[45] Fox News host Tucker Carlson, who generally was uncritically receptive to Republican claims of election fraud, also complained that Powell had repeatedly declined to supply evidence that would back up her charges.[46] "She was too crazy even for the president," an unnamed campaign official told *The Washington Post*.[47]

Powell ran into her own legal and ethical problems with some of the lawsuits she was filing around the country challenging the election results. In her lawsuits, Powell included plaintiffs who didn't consent to being part of her case, and there were instances where it appeared she had manipulated evidence presented to the courts.[48] Powell also cited a major figure in the QAnon conspiracy theory movement as a cybersecurity expert to bolster her claims, even though he lacked any professional credentials to qualify as an expert.[49]

These lawsuits all rehashed the same discredited arguments: that voting machines switched votes from Trump to Biden, and that the states should declare Trump the true winner of their electoral votes. While long on allegations, these lawsuits were short on evidence, leading to the summary dismissal of all of them. Powell described her litigation as "releasing the Kraken," a reference to a mythical sea monster unleashed by Zeus in the 1981 fantasy film *Clash of the Titans*. Unfortunately, the claims in her lawsuits were even less plausible than the beast she named them after.

In Atlanta, U.S. District Judge Timothy Batten granted a motion to dismiss Powell's suit against Georgia Governor Brian Kemp, essentially finding that Powell's claims were not based in reality.[50] In Michigan, U.S. District Judge Linda V. Parker said the "people have spoken" and characterized Powell's suit against Governor Gretchen Whitmer as an assault on hard-fought voting rights.[51] "Plaintiffs ask this court to ignore the orderly statutory scheme established to challenge elections and to ignore the will of millions of voters," Parker said in a ruling denying Powell's emergency motion to block election certification and force inspections of voting machines, software, and security footage of polling places. "This, the court cannot, and will not, do."[52] Powell's claims that foreign agents from Iran and China conspired with Democratic officials and poll workers to infiltrate voting machines and switch votes from Trump to Biden were "an amalgamation of theories, conjecture, and speculation" that did not merit the drastic relief order being sought.[53]

Just as the novel coronavirus caused a pandemic by, most likely, jumping from some small mammal to humans, Sidney Powell's "Kraken" lawsuits represented the deadly transmission of fake news, baseless conspiracy theories, and misinformation from the internet and right-wing media to the U.S. court system. The courts had previously been protected from such dangerous and frivolous nonsense by a firewall of ethical requirements imposed upon licensed attorneys who were subject to severe sanctions and disbarment in the event of serious breaches of the threshold due diligence legal requirements for the filing of lawsuits.

Rule 11 of the Federal Rules of Civil Procedure requires an attorney to certify that he or she has conducted a due diligence investigation before filing legal papers in federal court, and that there was a reasonable and substantial factual basis for the allegations and claims being made. Since Sidney Powell, Rudy Giuliani, and the rest of "Team Kraken" were able to bring one frivolous lawsuit after another in federal court without being sanctioned or barred from practicing law before those federal courts, there was an obvious breakdown in the firewall that previously protected these courts from becoming hopelessly infected with false and fictitious claims.

It is true, of course, that by promptly rejecting these claims, judges not only pointed out the lack of merits in each case but reaffirmed the value of the votes these lawsuits were seeking to invalidate. For example, in her opinion dismissing Powell's election challenge in Michigan Judge Linda Parker wrote, "The right to vote is among the most sacred rights of our democracy and, in turn, uniquely defines us as Americans."[54] Nevertheless, the fact that such baseless claims were permitted to be considered by the courts without any penalty or severe consequences for the lawyers signing the legal pleadings served to further promote public cynicism about the legal profession. It also further undermined the public's faith and confidence that the legal system and the lawyers licensed to practice in it are held to some minimum standards of ethical conduct. Lawyers who file such outright frivolous and dishonest lawsuits need to be held accountable for doing so, especially when the stakes are so high and our fragile electoral system is under assault.

The judges who dismissed these frivolous lawsuits are to be commended for their adherence to the rule of law and rejection of legal claims that are not grounded in fact. As discussed in the companion volume *Profiles in Courage in the Trump Era*, some of them deserve to be singled out for their courageous adherence to the law even in the face of considerable countervailing public pressure. However, with the 2020 election finally behind us and the rightful victor sworn in and at work at the White House, the legal system must reckon with the lawyers who interjected this made-up crisis into our court system. Our federal courts proved once again to be a foundational part of the U.S. democratic process and a forum for determining the truth. Lawyers and litigants who do not respect this fact-based function of the courts should pay a high price for their attempt to improperly manipulate the legal system and to convert it into a weapon for sedition.

## L. Lin Woods

Another one of Trump's most prominent conspiracy lawyers, L. Lin Woods of Georgia, spent much of the post-2020 election period denying (unconvincingly) the many credible claims that he was certifiably insane.[55] Long after the 2020 election had been resolved against the incumbent president, Woods continued to insist, despite substantial evidence to the contrary, that the battle for Trump to retain the presidency was just beginning. Woods adamantly stood by his position that Vice President Mike Pence should be arrested, tried, and executed by a firing squad for treason for failing to do his part in overturning the results of the 2020 election.[56] Woods and many die-hard Trump supporters were furious at Pence for asking a court to dismiss a lawsuit against him filed by Representative Louie Gohmert of Texas and other Republicans seeking to overturn the results of the 2020 election. The lawsuit claimed that Pence had the authority to choose which states' electoral votes to count (he didn't).

Woods himself had filed several previous failed lawsuits attempting to overturn the election results in Trump's favor. He was growing a bit testy at the failure of the federal judiciary to acknowledge that an evil conspiracy involving the Democrats, the CIA, and globalists were stealing the election for Joe Biden.

In fact Woods, a full-fledged QAnon advocate, added some of the Republican leadership and judiciary to his list for the final "reaping." Woods wrote: "When arrests for treason begin, put Chief Justice John Roberts, VP Mike Pence, and Mitch McConnell at top of the list."[57] Woods had earlier claimed in a tweet that Supreme Court Chief Justice John Roberts was a murderous pedophile, an accusation that he noted must be true, since Justice Roberts failed to issue any public denial of Wood's charges.[58] Woods even began to question the loyalty of the U.S. Secret Service, as rumors began to circulate that they were formulating a plan as to how best to remove Trump if he overstayed his welcome at the White House on Inauguration Day.[59]

Convinced that Pence, McConnell, and other key Republicans had turned on the president and had joined the opposition, Woods placed his faith in Mike Pompeo. He wrote: "If Pence is arrested, Pompeo will save the election. Pence will be in jail awaiting trial for treason. He will face execution by firing squad. He is a coward and will sing like a bird and confess ALL."[60]

Perhaps the most astonishing thing about the L. Lin Woods phenomenon during the post-2020 election campaign to keep the rightful winner of the presidential race from assuming office was that so many attorneys who apparently were operating in another irrational sphere such as Giuliani, Powell, and Woods were permitted to sow discord and confusion in dozens of state and federal courts with their nonsensical lawsuits. If they drove their cars like they practiced law, their drivers' licenses would have been revoked. They would be quickly deemed to be threats to the public welfare and safety. But when they filed reckless legal pleadings in the courts, they were subject to nothing more than some harsh words, leaving them to move on to the next court to try the same stunt before a different judge. If a legal license is truly intended to protect the public and the legal system from incompetent, unethical, or mentally unstable lawyers, then it is high time that ethical rules should be enforced in cases of national importance.

# TRUMP'S FELONS

Such an extraordinarily large number of President Trump's closest advisors and associates were criminally investigated, indicted, and convicted that, at times, the Trump administration looked more like an organized crime group fending off law enforcement investigations and prosecutions than the executive branch of the U.S. government. Trump then abused his presidential pardon power in order to help those who remained silent about Trump's complicity in their crimes. He pardoned Roger Stone, Michael Flynn, and Paul Manafort, while denying pardons to those who dutifully cooperated with law enforcement, such as former personal attorney Michael Cohen and Deputy Campaign Manager Rick Gates. These were the depths to which the country had sunk in the Trump era.

## Roger Stone

A longtime friend and confidante of Donald Trump,[1] Roger J. Stone, Jr. has been variously described as a lobbyist, "self-proclaimed dirty trickster," and a political fixer.[2] Over the course of the 2016 presidential campaign, Stone—a foppish, colorful, and controversial figure who sported a large tattoo of his hero Richard Nixon—promoted a number of falsehoods and conspiracy theories, including the baseless conspiracy theory that Hillary Clinton, Trump's Democratic opponent, had been involved in the murder of Seth Rich, a Democratic National Committee staffer.[3] Stone's motto was: "Admit nothing, deny everything, launch counterattack."[4] Stone first suggested Trump run for president in early 1998 while he was Trump's casino-business lobbyist in Washington.[5]

Stone officially left the Trump campaign on August 8, 2015. However, he continued to collaborate and coordinate with WikiLeaks founder Julian Assange to discredit Hillary Clinton during the 2016 presidential campaign. Nearly three dozen search warrants were unsealed in April 2020 which revealed contacts between Stone and Assange. They also revealed that Stone orchestrated hundreds of fake Facebook accounts and bloggers to run a political influence scheme on social media.[6]

On January 25, 2019, Stone was arrested at his Fort Lauderdale, Florida home in connection with Robert Mueller's special counsel investigation and charged in an indictment with witness tampering, obstructing an official proceeding, and five counts of making false statements.[7] Most of these offenses related to Stone's attempts to thwart the work of the House Intelligence Committee by, among other things, trying to persuade a key witness to perjure himself.

Two of the witnesses who testified at trial against Stone were former Trump campaign officials: Rick Gates, the deputy campaign chairman, and Stephen K. Bannon, who led the 2016 campaign through its final three months and served as a White House strategist early in the administration.

The evidence against Stone introduced at trial showed that in the months before the 2016 election, Stone sought to obtain emails that Russia had stolen from Democratic computers and then funneled to WikiLeaks. These emails were then strategically released by WikiLeaks so as to inflict maximum damage to Hillary Clinton's campaign. Stone briefed the Trump campaign about whatever he had picked up about WikiLeaks' plans at "every chance he got," according to prosecutors.[8] During Stone's trial, federal prosecutors also established that Stone falsely told a House committee in September 2017 that he never described his conversations with a WikiLeaks intermediary to anyone involved in the Trump campaign.[9]

One of the major questions that the Stone prosecution did not answer was what Stone discussed with Trump in the 21 conversations the two of them had in the six months leading up to the election. Trump refused to be interviewed on these conversations—or anything else, for that matter—and his written answers to questions from Special Counsel Mueller's office were filled with vague "lack of recollection" responses.[10] However, Rick Gates, Trump's deputy campaign manager, recounted a July 31, 2016 phone call between Stone and Trump, just days after WikiLeaks had released a trove of emails embarrassing the Clinton campaign. Gates testified that as soon as Trump hung up with Stone he declared that "more information" was coming, an apparent reference to future releases from WikiLeaks that would damage Clinton even further.[11]

Stone was convicted in federal court on November 15, 2019 on seven felony counts, including obstruction of an official proceeding, witness tampering, and obstruction of justice. Within minutes of Stone's guilty verdict, Trump posted a message on Twitter complaining that it was unfair. "So they now convict Roger Stone of lying and want to jail him for many years to come," Trump wrote, as if the Justice Department that prosecuted Stone was not part of his own administration.[12]

With this conviction, Stone joined a growing list of former Trump associates who had either pleaded guilty or been convicted on federal crimes stemming from Special Counsel Mueller's investigation, including Rick Gates; Michael Flynn; Michael Cohen, the president's former personal lawyer and political fixer; George Papadopoulos, a former Trump campaign aide; and Paul Manafort, Trump's former campaign chairman and onetime partner of Stone in a political consulting firm.

Stone was banned from using social media by Judge Amy Berman Jackson after a series of publicity infractions, including his posting of a photo of the judge with an image of a gun's crosshairs next to her head on Instagram in February 2019. Stone also apparently passed a message to *Infowars'* Alex Jones, asking Jones to intervene with the president on Stone's behalf for a pardon.

Much of the trial revolved around the relationship between Stone and Randy Credico, a New York radio host and comedian. The charge that Stone tried to block Credico from testifying to the House Committee investigating the roles that Stone and Credico played, if at all, as intermediaries between Julian Assange of WikiLeaks and the Trump campaign was the most serious one he faced, carrying a maximum penalty of 20 years. Credico testified at Stone's trial that Stone had alternately flattered, bullied, and threatened to kill him if he testified before the House Committee. Credico ultimately asserted his Fifth Amendment rights against self-incrimination and refused to testify.

At one point, Stone urged Credico to "Do a Frank Pentangeli," referring to a character in the movie *The Godfather: Part II* who gave false testimony during a Senate hearing on organized crime. Stone also used phrases borrowed from the Nixon era during the Watergate cover-up, such as when Stone texted Credico in late 2017: "Stonewall it. Plead the fifth. Anything to save the plan."[13]

One of Stone's most damaging deceptions, prosecutors argued at Stone's trial, was hiding records of his email communications with Credico, falsely telling congressional investigators that he and Credico only spoke on the phone because Credico "was not an email guy."[14] In fact, the evidence introduced at trial was that Stone and Credico exchanged more than 1,500 emails and text messages during a 1 ½ year period, including 72 texts alone on the day of Stone's congressional testimony.[15] Because Stone misled the committee, prosecutors said, investigators failed to pursue promising leads and arrived at inaccurate conclusions in its final report on Russia's election interference. Credico testified that he tried for months to warn Stone that his lies would catch up to him, but to no avail.[16]

On February 10, 2020, prosecutors from the U.S. Attorney's Office for the District of Columbia requested that Stone be sentenced to seven to nine years in prison for his crimes after securing convictions on all seven charges.[17] Trump reacted to reports of this recommendation almost immediately, characterizing it in a tweet as a "horrible and very unfair situation" and declaring, "Cannot allow this miscarriage of justice!"[18] The next morning a senior Justice Department official said the department would recommend a lighter sentence, adding that the decision had been made before Trump commented.[19] That afternoon the Department of Justice filed a revised sentencing memorandum, saying the initial recommendation could be "considered excessive and unwarranted under the circumstances."[20] All four of the Assistant U.S. Attorneys who were prosecuting the case—Jonathan Kravis, Aaron Zelinsky, Adam Jed, and Michael Marando—responded to news reports that their sentencing recommendations were not being accepted by withdrawing from the case. Kravis also resigned from the U.S. Attorney's Office.[21] Senate Minority Leader Chuck Schumer sent a letter to the Department of Justice Inspector General requesting an investigation into potential political interference in Stone's sentencing process.[22] The next day, Trump praised Attorney General Barr for "taking charge" of the case and thanked Justice Department officials for recommending a lesser sentence than was proposed by the prosecutors who tried the case.[23]

The politicization of Stone's sentencing by Trump and senior Trump administration officials at the Justice Department led to what some commentators described as a crisis in the rule of law in the United States.[24] More than 2,000 former employees of the Department of Justice signed an open letter calling on Barr to resign, and the Federal Judges Association convened an emergency meeting on the matter.[25] In testimony before the House Judiciary Committee, Aaron Zelinsky, one of the prosecutors who withdrew from the case, said that the "highest levels" of Justice Department had been "exerting significant pressure" on prosecutors "to cut Stone a break" and "water down and in some cases outright distort" Stone's conduct.²⁶ Zelinsky testified that "What I heard—repeatedly—was that Roger Stone was being treated differently from any other defendant because of his relationship to the president."²⁷ Zelinsky also testified that acting U.S. Attorney Timothy Shea made the request for a lighter sentence for Stone after coming under "heavy pressure from the highest levels of the Department of Justice" and out of fear of Trump.²⁸ Zelinsky also said that in his career as a prosecutor, the Roger Stone case was the sole occasion in which he witnessed "political influence play any role in prosecutorial decision making,"²⁹ opting to resign from the case "rather than be associated with the Department of Justice's actions at sentencing."³⁰

There was also a chorus of criticism and outrage by former Justice Department officials and experts in legal ethics. Former Attorney General Eric Holder commented, "Do not underestimate the danger of this situation: the political appointees in the DOJ are involving themselves in an inappropriate way in cases involving political allies of the President."³¹ Walter Shaub, former director of the Office of Government Ethics, similarly commented that "a corrupt authoritarian and his henchmen are wielding the Justice Department as a shield for friends and a sword for political rivals. It is impossible to overstate the danger."³² Channing D. Phillips, who previously served as U.S. Attorney for the District of Columbia, said that the events were "deeply troubling" and that the withdrawal of all four line prosecutors suggested "undue meddling by higher ups at DOJ or elsewhere."³³

On February 12, 2020, Judge Amy Berman Jackson denied Stone's motion for a new trial. Stone had asserted that a juror was biased against him.³⁴ Stone again requested a new trial on February 14 after the jury foreperson of his trial publicly voiced support for the four prosecutors who withdrew from the Stone case.³⁵

On February 20, 2020, Jackson sentenced Stone to 40 months in federal prison and a $20,000 fine for his crimes but allowed him to delay the start of his sentence pending resolution of Stone's post-trial motions.³⁶ Jackson stated in the sentencing hearing, "The truth still exists. The truth still matters [in spite of] Roger Stone's insistence that it doesn't [pose] a threat to our most fundamental institutions, to the very foundation of our democracy."³⁷ Jackson also rejected Trump's attacks on the investigators and prosecutors, saying:

"There was nothing unfair, phony, or disgraceful about the investigation or the prosecution."[38] Jackson said, "Roger Stone will not be sentenced for who his friends are, or who his enemies are."[39] Three days after sentencing Stone, on February 23, 2020, Judge Jackson rejected a request by Stone's lawyers that she be removed from the case.[40]

On April 16, Jackson denied Stone's motion for a new trial and ordered Stone to federal prison within two weeks.[41] On April 30, it was reported that the Federal Bureau of Prisons planned to delay Stone's surrender date by at least 30 days due to concerns relating to the COVID-19 pandemic.[42] On May 28, Stone was ordered by Jackson to report to prison by June 30.[43] On June 24, Stone filed a motion to delay his transfer to prison, alleging potential health concerns connected to the COVID-19 pandemic.[44] On June 27, Jackson rescheduled Stone's surrender date as July 14,[45] but also ordered him to immediately begin serving time in home confinement before reporting to prison.[46]

Stone's sentence was commuted by President Trump on July 10, 2020, only days before he was scheduled to report to federal prison.[47] Stone was pardoned on December 23, 2020, on the same day that Trump pardoned his former campaign chairman, Paul Manafort, and Charles Kushner, Jared Kushner's father.[48] Unrepentant and unreformed, Stone promptly started appearing at pro-Trump Stop the Steal rallies, surrounded by armed Oath Keepers, members of a far-right militia group that played a prominent role in the storming of the U.S. Capitol on January 6, 2021.

## Paul Manafort

In March of 2016, Trump selected Paul Manafort to become a senior advisor to his presidential campaign. In June, he was promoted to chairman of the campaign, a move seen by many knowledgeable observers as an odd choice. But to those who fully understood that both Trump and Manafort had close ties with Russian and Ukrainian oligarchs close to Russian President Putin, it seemed almost inevitable that Trump and Manafort would eventually work together.[49] Even a cursory background check by the Trump team would have revealed Manafort's longstanding affiliation with Viktor Yanukovich, the pro-Russian former president of Ukraine.[50] In addition, one of Yanukovich's and Manafort's closest Ukrainian oligarchs, Dimitri Firtash, was closely associated with Russian organized crime leader Semion Mogalevich and, therefore, the Kremlin.[51] Putin's Russia is basically an autocratic kleptocracy, where a small group of Kremlin insiders and well-connected Russian oligarchs control the Russian economy and political apparatus with the cooperation and complicity of Russian organized crime.

The Trump campaign team must also have known that Manafort and Firtash were the masterminds for money laundering services which they provided to Russian and pro-Russian Ukrainian oligarchs, helping them move their ill-gotten gains through U.S. and offshore bank accounts to launder the dirty money and to disguise the questionable origin of the funds.[52] A civil RICO suit brought by McCallion & Associates LLP that was publicly filed in the U.S. District Court for the Southern District of New York detailed a scheme whereby Manafort, Rick Gates, and Firtash formed CMZ Ventures with offices in Manhattan and with Mogalevich as a silent partner.[53] FBI agents and prosecutors from the Southern District of New York—and later the Special Counsel's office—followed up on leads provided by this civil RICO case by issuing subpoenas for the records of CMZ Ventures as part of their investigation of Manafort's Russian and Ukrainian ties and his money laundering efforts involving the United States.

Of particular interest to SDNY federal prosecutors and FBI agents working with them were documents filed in federal court on April 4, 2014 in connection with the civil RICO case. These documents showed the depth of Manafort's relationship with Putin and his entire inner circle, particularly Oleg Deripaska, the Russian oligarch who was perhaps the closest of the Kremlin inner circle to Putin.[54] It was later disclosed that Manafort received millions of dollars each year, and court documents relating to Manafort's indictment revealed that Manafort had received a $10 million loan from Deripaska in 2010.[55]

Manafort's known and suspected money laundering expertise provided yet another reason for Trump to hire him, since the laundering of Russian and eastern European money through U.S. condominium projects owned by the Trump Organization had been keeping several of Trump's projects afloat for the decade preceeding the 2016 election.[56]

In late March 2016, when Manafort surfaced in a leadership role with the Trump campaign, he suspiciously offered to work without pay, despite being badly overextended financially at the time.[57] The relationship worked well for both Trump and Manafort, at least for several months. Manafort provided Trump with what he wanted (access to Putin and the Kremlin), and Trump provided Manafort with both the appearance and reality of close connections to the Republican candidate who, although a longshot at that point, could be the next president of the United States.

Whether Trump himself had been previously compromised by Russian intelligence and was acting at the behest of the Kremlin during the 2016 campaign, or whether he just wanted to further ingratiate himself with Putin and the Kremlin leadership in order to get the green light to build his longstanding dream of a Moscow Trump Tower, made little difference. The bottom line was that Trump saw in Manafort a direct link to Moscow, and this was the overwhelmingly decisive factor in his being hired to run the campaign.

Trump's confidence in Manafort as one of his prime liasons to the Russian leadership was well placed. One of Manafort's first acts on behalf of the Trump campaign was to advise Konstantin Kilimnick, an officer in Russia's foreign military intelligence agency (GRU), that they were now again "open for business" and that "private briefings" could be offered to Deripaska and others close to the Kremlin. Kilimnick had worked closely with Manafort in Kyiv, Ukraine while Manafort was a political consultant for the pro-Russian political party there, and Kilimnick had been assigned by his superiors in Russian intelligence to be Manafort's handler or keeper.[58]

When stories began to surface in 2016 of off-the-books cash payments of millions of dollars to Manafort from Ukraine's pro-Russian political party, Manafort formally withdrew from the Trump campaign. However, Rick Gates, Manafort's trusted deputy, continued to work on the Trump campaign and the transition team. Trump and Manafort also continued their relationship, albeit indirectly, since they shared an obsession with money and with all things Russian, especially since Russian money had provided both of them with the lifestyle to which they had become accustomed and which neither one of them could ever give up.

Manafort and Kilimnik were to pull off the intelligence and political coup of the century for Russia, which was to have Trump, by then a de facto

Russian asset and operative, win the U.S. presidency and occupy the White House.[59] Manafort and Kilimnik were in charge of all liaison and coordination between these two working partners, the Trump campaign and Russia's GRU, who were working toward the same ultimate goal: to gain control of the entire vast executive apparatus of the U.S. government by any means. This was an achievement beyond anything possibly imaginable by Putin, even in his wildest vodka-induced fantasies, and Manafort and Kilimnik were the linchpins to this successful campaign.

The two primary perpetrators of this massive intelligence heist suffered no more than a temporary inconvenience for pulling off the crime of the century. Kilimnik never spent a day in jail and is enjoying a very comfortable lifestyle in Moscow, beyond the reach of U.S. law enforcement.[60] Manafort spent several months in federal prison and under house arrest, but he too was pardoned by Trump in the waning weeks of the Trump administration, along with Roger Stone, Michael Flynn, and several other major members of Trump's criminal organization.[61]

On August 18, 2020, the Senate Intelligence Committee issued a 966-page report on Russia's efforts to interfere with the 2016 presidential election. It confirmed what the American public already knew from the Mueller Report and other sources, which was that the Trump campaign actively sought and welcomed the assistance of the Russians and greatly benefited from that help. It also confirmed that Manafort's and Gates's close association with Russian agent Kilimnik posed, in the words of the report, a "grave counterintelligence threat" to the United States.[62]

In fact, the contacts between Russia and their U.S. assets Manafort and Gates were so close that Manafort actually gave Kilimnik proprietary polling data during the 2016 campaign.[63] The Mueller Report said that they could not determine why Manafort gave this data to Kilimnik and what he then did with it, as if they were incapable of using logic or common sense to conclude that two plus two equals four. The polling data could only have been of interest to Russian intelligence for one reason, and one reason alone, which was to help guide its disinformation and influence campaign through social media. The polling information on how to target this media campaign most effectively in the most competitive precincts in the key battleground states was precisely what the Russians needed in the homestretch of the 2016 campaign season.

The Senate Report went even further than the Mueller Report, correctly identifying Kilimnik as a Russian intelligence officer and not just someone with contacts to Russian intelligence, as the Mueller Report described him. By reading between the lines of the heavily redacted portions of the Senate Report, one can see that the report also suggested that Manafort and Kilimnik participated in the Russian hacking of the DNC, the Clinton campaign, and Democratic Party operatives in 2016.

What the Senate Report apparently did not delve into was the fact that Rudy Giuliani met with Manafort after Manafort had been indicted for federal criminal offenses and received from him invaluable contact information.[64] This allowed Giuliani to pick up where Manafort left off in the Trump team's liaisons with Russian intelligence. Manafort provided Giuliani with introductions and contact information for both Firtash and Kilimnik, and it was also arranged that Giuliani would have two additional contacts with Russian intelligence and organized crime—Lev Parnas and Igor Fruman—who quickly provided Giuliani with additional dirt on Joe Biden.[65] The torch was thus passed from Manafort to Giuliani so that Trump and his operatives would continue to have uninterrupted contact with Russian intelligence and the Kremlin.

Manafort was found guilty of tax fraud and bank fraud in a jury trial in August 2018. A month later, he pleaded guilty to conspiracy charges related to money laundering, lobbying violations, and witness tampering.[66] Among other things, he concealed the millions of dollars he was paid as a political consultant for pro-Russian Ukrainian politicians. He was sentenced to seven-and-a-half years in prison and in May 2020 was released to finish his sentence at home due to the coronavirus pandemic.[67] But Manafort never told the FBI or federal prosecutors the full story of how he and Kilimnik managed candidate Trump on behalf of the Kremlin, and for this Manafort correctly assumed that he would be rewarded with a pardon. Both Trump and Manafort may take this full story to their graves, but, in all likelihood, records relating to the Manafort/Kilimnik handling of Trump as a Russian intelligence asset will surface sometime in the future, as has happened several times before with information on U.S. and UK traitors who sold out their countries.

## Michael J. Flynn

Michael J. Flynn holds the record of having the shortest term of any presidential national security advisor, having been sworn in as Trump's national security advisor on January 22, 2017, and resigning under pressure on February 13, 2017. Flynn, having retired from the military in October 2014, became a senior advisor to the Trump campaign, famously leading the chant of "Lock Her Up!" at the Republican National Convention in 2016, referring to Democratic presidential candidate Hillary Clinton.

In December 2015, while affiliated with Flynn Intel Group, which provided intelligence services for businesses and governments, Flynn was paid $45,000 to deliver a speech in Moscow at the ten-year anniversary celebration of RT (formerly Russia Today), a state controlled Russian international television network. A photograph of the celebration dinner shows Flynn seated next to Russian president Vladimir Putin.

But Russia was not the only foreign power with influence over Flynn. During the 2016 presidential campaign, while serving as national security advisor to Trump, Flynn failed to disclose that he was paid for lobbying work by the Turkish government.[68] Flynn did not register as a foreign agent until March 2017.[69]

During his brief tenure as Trump's National Security Advisor, Flynn lied to Vice President Mike Pence about his conversations with Russian Ambassador to the U.S. Sergey Kislyak during the transition period in late December 2016 and early January 2017.[70] At Trump's direction, Flynn successfully persuaded Kislyak that Russia should not retaliate against sanctions imposed on Russia by the outgoing Obama administration for its interference in the 2016 election.[71] Flynn also lied to two FBI agents about his contacts with Kislyak, a crime under the United States Code for which Flynn was later indicted.[72]

In December 2017, Flynn formalized a deal with Special Counsel Robert Mueller to plead guilty to a felony count of "willfully and knowingly" making false statements to the FBI about the Kislyak communications and agreed to cooperate with the Special Counsel's investigation.[73] However, in June 2019, Flynn fired his attorneys and retained "Kraken lawyer" Sidney Powell, who on the same day wrote to attorney general Bill Barr seeking his assistance in exonerating Flynn.⁷⁴ Powell discussed the case on Fox News and spoke to President Trump about it on several occasions.⁷⁵

Two weeks before his scheduled sentencing in January 2020, Flynn moved to withdraw his guilty plea, claiming government vindictiveness and breach of the plea agreement.⁷⁶ At Barr's direction, the Justice Department filed a court motion to drop all charges against Flynn on May 7, 2020. Federal Judge Emmet Sullivan placed the matter on hold pending receipt of an *amicus curiae* brief from a former federal judge. Powell then asked the D.C. Circuit Court of Appeals to compel Sullivan to drop the case, but her request was denied.⁷⁷ However, on November 25, 2020, Flynn was issued a presidential pardon by Trump, short circuiting the legal process and forcing Judge Sullivan to dismiss the criminal charges against Flynn on December 8, 2020.

Flynn's treasonous words and actions became increasingly inflammatory as 2020 wore on, especially as it became apparent to any rational person that Trump had lost the election and would have to vacate the White House. On July 4, 2020, Flynn actually took an Independence Day oath for pro-Trump QAnon conspiracy theorists.⁷⁸

Moreover, as Trump sought to overturn the results of the 2020 presidential election in which he was defeated, Flynn suggested the president should suspend the Constitution, silence the press, and hold a new election under military authority.⁷⁹ He appeared at a Stop the Steal rally in Washington, D.C. in December 2020 following the decision by the U.S. Supreme Court not to hear *Texas v. Pennsylvania*, the election challenge brought by the Republican attorney general of Texas and joined by 17 other Republican state attorneys general. Flynn dismissed the court's decision, saying, "I will tell you one more time—because I've been asked—on a scale of one to ten, who will be the next president of the United States, and I say Donald Trump. Ten. A ten."⁸⁰ Flynn likened the protesters at Stop the Steal events to the biblical soldiers and priests breaching the city walls in the Battle of Jericho, echoing the rally organizers' call for "Jericho Marches" to overturn the election result.⁸¹

Flynn later met with Trump and their mutual attorney Sidney Powell in the Oval Office to discuss the president's options, including a declaration of martial law and suspension of the various constitutional rights.⁸² Trump denied reports that Flynn's martial law idea had been discussed, which, given Trump's abysmal track record for truthfulness, virtually assured that the martial law option had been discussed. On January 8, 2021, following the failed insurrection at the U.S. Capitol and as Flynn, Powell, and Trump continued to broadcast and promote the false narrative that Trump had actually won the election, all three were permanently banned from Twitter.[83]

## Rick Gates

The former deputy chairman of Trump's campaign pleaded guilty in February 2018 to conspiracy against the United States and lying to investigators.[84] Gates agreed to cooperate with former Special Counsel Robert Mueller and testified as a prosecution witness against his former business partner Paul Manafort and Roger Stone. Gates was sentenced in December 2019 to three years of probation and 45 days in jail. When Trump's term was drawing to an end he started handing out pardons to his convicted former associates who had refused to cooperate with law enforcement, or agreed to cooperate and then lied instead of telling the truth. Trump rewarded Stone, Manafort, and Flynn with pardons. Although Gates publicly begged for a pardon, Trump refused to comply with his request.[85] Like some Mafia boss, Trump reasoned that since Gates had failed to remain silent and had partially cooperated with the Justice Department, he should be punished.

## George Papadopoulos

George Papadopoulos, a former Trump campaign aide, played a role in the Russian meddling in the 2016 presidential election. The former Trump campaign advisor was sentenced in September 2018 to 14 days in prison after pleading guilty to lying to the FBI about his contacts with Russian officials and a Maltese professor who told him the Russians had dirt on Clinton.[86]

## George Nader

George Nader, an informal Trump advisor on foreign policy and a witness in the Mueller investigation, was sentenced in June, 2020 to ten years in prison by a federal judge in Virginia.[87] He pleaded guilty to possessing child pornography and illegally bringing a boy to the United States for sex.[88]

## Alex van der Zwaan

Alex van der Zwaan, the Dutch son-in-law of Russian billionaire German Khan, was sentenced to 30 days in prison and fined $20,000 for lying to U.S. Special Counsel Robert Mueller's investigators about contacts with an official in Trump's 2016 campaign.[89]

## Michael D. Cohen

Michael Cohen, a lawyer and fixer who served as an attorney for Trump from 2006 to 2018, was a vice-president of the Trump Organization. During the course of Special Counsel Robert Mueller's investigation of Russian interference in the 2016 presidential campaign and related matters, Cohen pleaded guilty on August 21, 2018, to eight counts, including campaign finance violations, tax fraud, and bank fraud.[90] Cohen admitted to violating campaign finance laws at the direction of Trump and "for the principal purpose of influencing" the 2016 presidential election.[91] In November 2018, Cohen entered a second guilty plea for lying to a Senate committee about efforts to build a Trump Tower in Moscow.

Cohen's guilty plea to campaign finance law violations at Trump's direction related to his payments to Karen MacDougal and Stormy Daniels, two women with whom Trump had affairs and agreed to pay for their silence regarding the matter. In July 2018, the FBI seized tapes secretly recorded by Cohen of his conversations with Trump about hush payments to Karen McDougal, which contradicted earlier statements by Trump denying knowledge of the payments and raising questions about whether there were violations of campaign finance laws.[92]

Regarding his payments to porn star Stormy Daniels on behalf of Trump, Cohen at first lied about it, telling *The New York Times* in February 2018 that he paid the $130,000 to Daniels from his own pocket. He also said that the payment was not a campaign contribution and he was not reimbursed by either the Trump Organization or the Trump campaign. He later admitted to having been reimbursed by Trump for these hush money payments.[93]

Cohen also admitted to federal prosecutors that then-candidate Trump knew in advance about the June 2016 Trump Tower meeting between his son Donald Jr. and other Trump campaign officials with Russians who claimed to possess information damaging to the Hillary Clinton campaign, contradicting the President's repeated insistence that he was not aware of the meeting until long after it had taken place.[94]

On December 12, 2018, Cohen was sentenced to three years in federal prison and ordered to pay a $50,000 fine. On February 26, 2019, he was officially disbarred by the New York Supreme Court, Appellate Division. He reported to the federal prison near Otisville, New York, on May 6, 2019, but on May 21, 2020, he was released from prison early due to concerns regarding COVID-19. The rest of his sentence would be served under house arrest. He was never given a pardon by Trump since he had committed the unforgiveable sin (in Trump's eyes) of cooperating with federal authorities.

# TRUMP'S CORPORATE BOOSTERS

# Cambridge Analytica

Cambridge Analytica (CA), a British analytics firm that was hired by the Trump campaign in 2016, misappropriated the Facebook data of almost 100 million Americans while working to help Donald Trump get elected.[1] CA and its parent company, SCL Elections, used the data it collected to develop psychological models on each voter's preferences and behavior and predict how they would react to various messaging.[2] Facebook itself admitted that CA had access to personal data on up to 87 million people, mostly in the United States.[3]

Billionaire Robert Mercer, who was CA's main financial backer, developed close ties with the Trump campaign after Ted Cruz withdrew from the 2016 Republican presidential primary. In addition, Steve Bannon, Trump's former campaign manager and chief strategist, held a position on CA's board. Alexander Nix, the CEO of CA, approached Julian Assange of WikiLeaks with a proposal to join forces against the Hillary Clinton campaign.[4] Given the known close association between Assange and WikiLeaks with Russian intelligence operations, it was logical for investigators to conclude that Nix was trying to close the circle with Russian disinformation expertise by having CA join with WikiLeaks as an intermediary between the Russians and the Trump campaign.[5]

CA's relationship with the Trump campaign started in June 2016, when it sent three staffers to the campaign's San Antonio office. The CA team working on the Trump campaign eventually grew to thirteen people working under Trump's Digital Media Director Brad Parscale and alongside his staff and outside consultants.[6] CA bragged that it had a massive data trove with over 5,000 data points on every American.[7] It further claimed to have built extensive personality profiles on every American, which it used for so-called "psychographic targeting," based on people's personality types.[8] In a sense, CA conducted a kind of psychological warfare against the American people, although CA officials later denied that they specifically used psychographic targeting during the 2016 election campaign. Parscale described CA's work for the campaign as "persuasion online media buying," as well as the creation of "a visualization tool that showed in each state which areas were most persuadable and what those voters care about."[9]

CA collapsed in 2018 after undercover reporters from a British TV station caught its executives bragging about electoral "dirty tricks," including the secret use of proxy organizations and super PACs to buy ads targeted at individuals in the United States that could not be traced back to the Trump campaign.

The four-month investigation by *Channel 4 News*, a British public service station, started in November 2017. An undercover reporter posed as a potential customer for CA hoping to help Sri Lankan candidates get elected. Video footage from this operation, published on March 19, 2018, showed Alexander Nix and other CA executives saying they worked on over 200 elections across the world, using "honey traps," bribery stings, and prostitutes to collect opposition research.[10] For example, Nix offered to discredit political opponents in Sri Lanka with suggestive videos using "beautiful Ukrainian girls" and offers of bribes, which could be made to look compromising even if the opponents did not accept the offers.[11] He also said he used "Israeli companies" to entrap political opponents with bribes and sex, which the *Wall Street Journal* confirmed was a reference to Psy-Group, an Israeli private intelligence agency operating from Petah Tikva, Israel, which specialized in "perception management" and clandestine influence and manipulation campaigns.[12] Nix also said that CA "ran all the digital campaigns" for Trump and that any communications used in the operations would self-destruct, leaving no incriminating evidence.[13]

After the news segment was broadcast, the board of CA suspended Nix as chief executive officer, but the entire company collapsed shortly thereafter.[14]

*Channel 4 News* also disclosed that not only did CA have secret files on about 200 million Americans, but that it also labeled 3.5 million Black Americans in their database as "deterrence"—meaning they were specifically targeted with disinformation in an effort to trick them out of voting for Hillary Clinton in the 2016 election.[15]

The seedy relationship between CA and the Trump campaign also raised serious questions regarding possible violations of campaign finance law. During the 2016 election, CA was employed both by Trump's campaign and Robert Mercer's Make America Number 1 super PAC, which supported Trump. While PACs are not limited in the amount of funds they can spend on behalf of a candidate, they are not allowed to coordinate strategy with the campaigns they are supporting. Nix's statements in the video recorded by *Channel 4 News* describe how the Trump campaign itself could "take the high road" and "stay clean," while the negative attacks were handled by CA and the super PAC in ways which made the attacks "unattributable" and "untrackable."[16] These statements strongly suggest unlawful coordination between Trump's campaign and the PAC.

## My Pillow, Inc.
### Michael Lindell, "The My Pillow Guy"

Mike Lindell, the CEO and owner of My Pillow, Inc. emerged as one of Donald Trump's most avid corporate supporters during the 2016 presidential campaign. Before establishing the My Pillow company in 2004, Lindell had experienced a couple of decades of adversity, both through various failed business ventures and in his personal life.

During the 1980s and 1990s, he was addicted to cocaine, crack cocaine, and alcohol, leading to the foreclosure of his house and to his first wife's filing for divorce. Lindell stated that he achieved sobriety in 2009 through prayer, as described in his self-published book, titled *What Are the Odds? From Crack Addict to CEO*.

Following Trump's election to the presidency in November 2016, Lindell described Trump as "the most amazing president this country has ever seen in history."[17] In a speech at Liberty University in August 2019, Lindell said, "When I met with Donald Trump, it felt like a divine appointment, and when I walked out of that office I decided I was going to go all in."[18] Lindell spoke at the 2019 Conservative Political Action Conference (CPAC), in which he again promoted Trump as "the greatest president in history" and "chosen by God."[19]

As the pandemic started hitting the United States in March 2020, Lindell seized on it as a business opportunity. In an appearance on Fox News, Lindell said that his company's bedding factories had been refocused on face mask production.[20] Later that month, he appeared with Trump at a White House coronavirus press conference at which Lindell praised Trump and suggested that the pandemic scourge was ravaging the country because we live in "a nation [that has] turned its back on God." He strongly suggested the best way to combat COVID-19 was to "read our Bible and spend time with our families."[21]

In November 2020, Lindell was identified as among those who paid for the bail of Kyle Rittenhouse, the accused killer of two protesters at a rally in Kenosha, Wisconsin, in August 2020. As a consequence, some major retailers stopped carrying My Pillow products, including outlets like Kohl's and Bed Bath & Beyond.[22]

In various White House meetings with Trump and public appearances, Lindell promoted a plant extract, oleandrin, as a cure for COVID-19, saying: "This thing works—it's the miracle of all time."[23] Lindell has a financial stake in Phoenix Biotechnology, a company that makes oleandrin, and sits on its board.[24] Lindell's unsubstantiated claims set off alarm bells throughout the scientific community since there was no scientific evidence supporting the claim that oleandrin was effective or safe as a coronavirus treatment. The plant is also known to be poisonous, even at low doses. Lindell was joined in his promotion of oleandrin by U.S. Secretary of Housing and Urban Development Ben Carson,[25] leading to President Trump's announcement that his administration would "look at" the substance.[26]

After Trump's defeat in the 2020 presidential election, Lindell played a major role in supporting and financing Trump's attempts to overturn the election result. Lindell helped sponsor a bus tour that sought to challenge the election results. The two-week tour ended in Washington, D.C. on December 14, 2020, and Lindell spoke at five stops along the way.[27]

On January 15, 2021, Lindell was photographed carrying a document into the West Wing of the White House which, when enhanced, referred to martial law and the Insurrection Act.[28] This was about the same time that Mike Flynn and others were encouraging Trump to declare martial law and order a redo of the November 2020 presidential election.

The conspiracy theory that got Lindell into the most trouble was the false claim that voting machine companies Smartmatic and Dominion had conspired with foreign powers to rig voting machines to steal the election from Trump. In January and February 2021, Dominion warned Lindell and others, including Rudy Giuliani, that it planned to file a lawsuit against them. The company stated in its letter, "You have positioned yourself as a prominent leader of the ongoing misinformation campaign."[29]

The defamation complaint was filed on February 22, 2021, with Dominion suing Lindell and MyPillow for $1.3 billion. Dominion claimed that Lindell and MyPillow used "a defamatory marketing campaign—with promo codes like 'FightforTrump,' '45,' 'Proof,' and 'QAnon'—[which have] increased MyPillow sales by 30–40% and [continued] duping people into redirecting their election-lie outrage into pillow purchases."[30] Dominion further stated its intent was to "stop Lindell and MyPillow from further profiting at Dominion's expense." Lawyers for Dominion argued in court filings that none of Lindell's claims about election fraud were based in reality, adding: "Lindell—a talented salesman and former professional card counter—sells the lie to this day because the lie sells pillows."[31]

## Goya Foods, Inc.
### Robert Unanue, CEO

On Sunday, February 28, 2021, Goya Foods CEO Robert Unanue gave a speech at the Conservative Political Action Conference in Orlando, Florida, defying reality and the election results, falsely calling Trump "the real, the legitimate, and still the actual president of the United States."[32] The executive also referenced baseless claims that mail-in ballots were fraudulent. "As a citizen of the United States, I think I'm allowed to vote once, once—not twice, or three times, or ten times," Unanue said.[33] Ignoring the undeniable fact that Trump lost to Biden by more than seven million votes in the 2020 election, Unanue emphasized that his devotion to Trump, like that of most of the pro-Trump believers, was based more on pure faith than facts. "We still have faith that the majority of the people in the United States voted for the president," Unanue said, referencing Trump.

Unanue's comments sparked renewed outrage on social media, with some calling for action against the company with a #BoycottGoya hashtag on Twitter. Citing Trump's anti-immigrant rhetoric and controversial immigration policies, national figures like Democratic Representative Alexandria Ocasio-Cortez of New York, former Democratic presidential candidate Julián Castro, and chef José Andrés condemned the remarks.[34]

The initial backlash against Unanue and Goya unfolded in the summer of 2020 when the CEO compared Trump to his grandfather, the founder of Goya, which is the largest Hispanic-owned food company in the United States. "We're truly blessed at the same time to have a leader like President Trump who is a builder, and that's what my grandfather did," Unanue said during a speech at the Rose Garden in July 2020. "We pray for our leadership, our president, and we pray for our country that we will continue to prosper and grow." Trump reveled in Unanue's effusive support, circulating a photograph of Ivanka holding a can of Goya black beans atop the Resolute Desk in the Oval Office.[35]

In January 2021, Unanue joined the ranks of Trump's election-result deniers by calling the results "unverified" in a Fox News interview.[36] Days later, the *New York Post* reported the majority of Goya's nine-member board voted to censure their CEO. "Bob [Unanue] does not speak for Goya Foods when he speaks on TV," Goya board member and company owner Andy Unanue told the paper. "The family has diverse views on politics, but politics is not part of our business. Our political points of view are irrelevant."[37] After that controversy, the CEO promised that he would refrain from publicly commenting on politics and religion on Goya's behalf.[38] He appeared to have broken that promise by speaking at the CPAC Conference in Orlando. The negative reaction was swift. "No more chickpeas from Goya for me," tweeted *The View's* co-host Joy Behar.[39] Others questioned how Goya could allow Unanue to continue making such claims. "Folks at Goya should be embarrassed by their CEO," tweeted journalist Soledad O'Brien.[40]

★★★

Like all the other categories of Trump enablers, corporate bosses and wealthy business people who helped Trump undermine America's democratic pillars and who supported the Big Lie about the outcome of the 2020 election must be held accountable for their irresponsible actions. This country's free market system gave people like Robert Unanue and Michael Lindell a chance to be wildly rich and successful. But with wealth and power comes the civic responsibility to support the forces of truth, justice, and democracy - not those promoting baseless conspiracy theories that can only lead us inexorably towards authoritarian rule.

# CONCLUSION

Trump's Congressional enablers, Campaign officials, corrupt Cabinet members, White House advisors, press secretaries, and charlatan medical advisors and lawyers all permitted a rogue president to inflict much greater damage on the country and its body politic than otherwise would have occurred. This motley collection of cowards, connivers, and kooks cynically bent the knee and kissed the ring of this insecure tin-horn tyrant for their own personal gain and perverse gratification without regard to what they and the megalomaniac in the White House were doing to shred the Constitution and undermine our democracy. Their names should forever live on in infamy for the betrayal of their basic duties of citizenship and their sworn oaths to God and Country.

# ENDNOTES

## Quote

1. Gerson, Michael. "Opinion | Let the Anti-Constitutional Republicans Reveal Themselves." The Washington Post, WP Company, 5 Jan. 2021, www.washingtonpost.com/opinions/let-the-anti-constitutional-republicans-reveal-themselves/2021/01/04/d3fafee0-4eb6-11eb-83e3-322644d82356_story.html.

## Vice President Mike Pence

1. Pence @Mike_Pence, Mike. "Pence: Election Integrity Should Be a National Imperative." The Daily Signal, 4 Mar. 2021, www.dailysignal.com/2021/03/03/election-integrity-is-a-national-imperative/.
2. Mike Pence's remarkable op-ed highlights the GOP's choice on voting rights - *The Washington Post*, 03 03 21.
3. Palmer, Ewan. "Donald Trump Tweeted Attack on Mike Pence Minutes after Hearing VP Was Fleeing Capitol Rioters." Newsweek, Newsweek, 11 Feb. 2021, www.newsweek.com/donald-trump-tweeted-attack-mike-pence-minutes-capitol-rioters-1568568.
4. Larson, Erik (December 28, 2020). "Pence Sued by GOP Congressman Over Competing Electors". *Bloomberg News*.
5. Cheney, Kyle; Gerstein, Josh (December 31, 2020). "Pence: Gohmert's fight to overturn the 2020 election results is with Congress, not me". *Politico*.
6. Gerstein, Josh; Cheney, Kyle (January 2, 2021). "Judge throws out Gohmert suit aimed at empowering Pence to overturn 2020 election results". *Politico*.
7. Smith, Stewart (January 7, 2021). "SCOTUS rejects Gohmert's last-minute appeal". KLTV.
8. Schmidt, Michael S. (January 5, 2020). "Trump Says Pence Can Overturn His Loss in Congress. That's Not How It Works". *The New York Times*
9. Haberman, Maggie; Karni, Annie (January 5, 2020). "Pence Said to Have Told Trump He Lacks Power to Change Election Result". *The New York Times*.
10. https://www.foxnews.com/politics/trump-says-he-pence-in-total-agreement-vp-has-power-to-block-certification-of-illegal-election 01 05 21
11. Mike Pence rejects Trump's call to overturn Biden election (*CNBC*.com)
12. ibid.
13. Savage, Charlie (January 10, 2021). "Incitement to Riot? What Trump Told Supporters Before Mob Stormed Capitol". *The New York Times*.
14. Haltiwanger, John (January 7, 2021). "Trump attacks Pence for not having the 'courage' to overturn the election as the president's supporters storm the Capitol". *Business Insider Australia*.
15. Parker, Ashley; Leonnig, Carol D.; Kane, Paul; Brown, Emma (January 15, 2021). "How the rioters who stormed the Capitol came dangerously close to Pence". *The Washington Post*.
16. ibid.

17  ibid.
18  Forgey, Quint. "'It Must Stop Now': Pence Tells Rioters to Leave the Capitol." POLITICO, POLITICO, 6 Jan. 2021, www.politico.com/news/2021/01/06/pence-capitol-rioters-455584.
19  Trump attacks Pence as protesters force their way into Capitol | The Hill 01 06 21
20  Brewster, Jack (January 7, 2021). "Lin Wood—Lawyer Closely Tied To Trump—Permanently Banned From Twitter After Claiming Capitol Siege Was 'Staged'". *Forbes*.
21  Welker, Kristin; O'Donnell, Kelly; Alba, Monica (January 9, 2021). "Pence to attend Biden inauguration; Trump never called him in the Capitol bunker, sources say". *NBC News*.
22  Acosta, Jim; Brown, Pamela (January 7, 2021). "Trump pressured Pence to engineer a coup, then put the VP in danger, source says". *CNN*.
23  Colvin, Jill; Miller, Zeke (January 11, 2021). "After frosty few days, Pence, Trump appear to reach détente". WTMJ. *Associated Press*.
24  Cannon, Jay. "Watch VP Pence confirm 2020 election win for Joe Biden hours after mob breaches Capitol". *USA TODAY*.
25  ibid.

# Trump's Senate Enablers

1  Hampton, Rachelle, and Marissa Martinelli. "Here's the Moment Fox News Called the Election for Biden." Slate Magazine, Slate, 7 Nov. 2020, slate.com/news-and-politics/2020/11/fox-news-biden-winner-presidential-election.html.
2  Darcy, Oliver. "Analysis: Fox News, Last to Call Election, Offers Subdued Coverage of Biden's Victory." CNN, Cable News Network, 7 Nov. 2020, www.cnn.com/2020/11/07/media/fox-news-joe-biden-elected/index.html.
3  "'He's a Race-Baiting, Xenophobic, Religious Bigot': Lindsey Graham Speaks out against Trump-in 2015." Daily Kos, www.dailykos.com/stories/2020/1/28/1914694/--He-s-a-race-baiting-xenophobic-religious-bigot-Lindsey-Graham-speaks-out-against-Trump-in-2015.
4  Lange, Jeva. "Lindsey Graham: Donald Trump Is a 'Race-Baiting, Xenophobic Religious Bigot'." The Week - All You Need to Know about Everything That Matters, The Week, 8 Dec. 2015, theweek.com/speedreads/592955/lindsey-graham-donald-trump-race-baiting-xenophobic-religious-bigot.
5  Colarossi, Natalie. "Graham Tweet about Being 'Destroyed' If Trump Nominated Resurfaces as Dems Appear to Win GA." Newsweek, Newsweek, 6 Jan. 2021, www.newsweek.com/graham-tweet-about-being-destroyed-if-trump-nominated-resurfaces-dems-appear-win-ga-1559354.
6  Colarossi, Natalie. "Graham Tweet about Being 'Destroyed' If Trump Nominated Resurfaces as Dems Appear to Win GA." Newsweek, Newsweek, 6 Jan. 2021, www.newsweek.com/graham-tweet-about-being-destroyed-if-trump-nominated-resurfaces-dems-appear-win-ga-1559354.
7  Marcin, Tim. "Donald Trump Insulted Ted Cruz's Wife, Father And Faith, But They're Having Dinner Anyway." International Business Times, 1 Dec. 2020, www.ibtimes.

com/donald-trump-insulted-ted-cruzs-wife-father-faith-theyre-having-dinner-anyway-2504948.

8. "Donald Trump's #LittleMarco Is the Internet's New Favorite Thing." U.S. News & World Report, U.S. News & World Report, www.usnews.com/news/articles/2016-03-04/donald-trump-called-marco-rubio-little-marco-at-the-gop-debate-and-twitter-went-crazy.

9. Tatum, Sophie. "Rubio on Trump: 'He's Not Gonna Make America Great, He's Gonna Make America Orange' - CNN Politics." CNN, Cable News Network, 29 Feb. 2016, www.cnn.com/2016/02/28/politics/marco-rubio-donald-trump-make-america-orange/index.html.

10. Goldberg, Dan. "'It's Going to Disappear': Trump's Changing Tone on Coronavirus." POLITICO, POLITICO, 19 Mar. 2020, www.politico.com/news/2020/03/17/how-trump-shifted-his-tone-on-coronavirus-134246.

11. Cohen, Ben. "Mitch Connell: A Profile In Fear And Cowardice." The Banter - Washington DC, The Banter - Washington DC, 15 Apr. 2019, thebanter.substack.com/p/mitch-connell-a-profile-in-fear-and.

12. Hohman, Jim. "QAnon's Catalogue of Conspiracies; 'Batshit Crazy' Doesn't Even Begin to Describe America's New Favorite Brand of Nuts." Newsmakerblogdotcom, 7 Feb. 2021, newsmakerblog.com/2021/02/06/qanons-catalogue-of-conspiracies-batshit-crazy-doesnt-even-begin-to-describe-americas-new-favorite-brand-of-nuts/.

13. Fink, Jenni. "Full Text of Mitch McConnell's Speech before 'Most Important' Vote of His Career." Newsweek, Newsweek, 6 Jan. 2021, www.newsweek.com/full-text-mitch-mcconnells-speech-before-most-important-vote-his-career-1559426.

14. "McConnell on Impeachment Procedures: The Senate's Duty Is To Conduct a Trial, Not Re-Do House Democrats' Homework For Them: Republican Leader." Remark | Remarks | THE NEWSROOM | Republican Leader, 17 Dec. 2019, www.republicanleader.senate.gov/newsroom/remarks/mcconnell-on-impeachment-procedures-the-senates-duty-is-to-conduct-a-trial-not-re-do-house-democrats-homework-for-them.

15. McConnell, Mitch. McConnell Speech After Trump's Impeachment Trial Acquittal, www.msn.com/en-us/news/politics/read-mcconnell-speech-after-trump-s-impeachment-trial-acquittal/ar-BB1dFZkf.

16. Kessler, Glenn. "When Did Mitch McConnell Say He Wanted to Make Obama a One-Term President?" The Washington Post, WP Company, 15 Aug. 2018, www.washingtonpost.com/news/fact-checker/wp/2017/01/11/when-did-mitch-mcconnell-say-he-wanted-to-make-obama-a-one-term-president/.

17. Nagourney, Carl Hulse and Adam. "McConnell Strategy Shuns Bipartisanship"

18. Kruse, Kevin; Zelizer, Julian (2019). Fault Lines: A History of the United States Since 1974. W.W. Norton

19. Koger, Gregory (2016). Party and Procedure in the United States Congress, Second Edition. Rowman & Littlefield. p. 223.

20. Everett, Burgess; Trush, Glenn (February 13, 2016). "McConnell throws down the gauntlet: No Scalia replacement under Obama". *Politico*.

21. Shear, Michael D.; Harris, Gardiner (March 16, 2016). "Obama Chooses Merrick Garland for Supreme Court". *The New York Times*.

22   Totenberg, Nina (September 6, 2016). "170-Plus Days And Counting: GOP Unlikely To End Supreme Court Blockade Soon". All Things Considered. *NPR*.

23   Adam Liptak; Matt Flegenheimer (April 8, 2017). "Neil Gorsuch Confirmed by Senate as Supreme Court Justice". *The New York Times*. p. A1.

24   Foran, Clare (October 7, 2018). "Brett Kavanaugh confirmed to Supreme Court". *CNN*.

25   Foran, Clare; Raju, Manu; Barrett, Ted (September 19, 2020). "McConnell vows Trump's nominee to replace Ginsburg will get Senate vote, setting up historic fight". *CNN*.

26   Senate takes up Barrett nomination". *CBS News*.

27   Levine, Marianne (November 5, 2019). "McConnell says Senate would acquit Trump if trial held today". *Politico*.

28   Carney, Jordain (December 12, 2019). "McConnell says he'll be in 'total coordination' with White House on impeachment trial strategy". *The Hill*.

29   Egan, Lauren (December 13, 2019). "McConnell: 'There's no chance' Trump is removed from office".

30   "McConnell on Impeachment Procedures: The Senate's Duty Is To Conduct a Trial, Not Re-Do House Democrats' Homework For Them: Republican Leader." Remark | Remarks | THE NEWSROOM | Republican Leader, 17 Dec. 2019, www.republicanleader.senate.gov/newsroom/remarks/mcconnell-on-impeachment-procedures-the-senates-duty-is-to-conduct-a-trial-not-re-do-house-democrats-homework-for-them.

31   Coogan, Steve (December 17, 2019). "Trump impeachment debate". *USA Today*.

32   Carney, Jordain (March 12, 2020). "McConnell: House coronavirus bill an 'ideological wish list'". *The Hill*.

33   Allen, Jonathan (March 12, 2020). "The twisted politics of Washington's coronavirus response". *NBC News*.

34   Hulse, Carl (May 15, 2020). "With Go-Slow Approach, Republicans Risk Political Blowback on Pandemic Aid". *The New York Times*.

35   Hulse, Carl (August 5, 2020). "In Stimulus Talks, McConnell Is Outside the Room and in a Tight Spot". *The New York Times*.

36   Cochrane, Emily; Fandos, Nicholas (November 9, 2020). "President-Elect Joe Biden's Transition: Live Updates as McConnell Backs Trump's Refusal to Concede". *The New York Times*. ISSN 0362-4331.

37   Axios. "McConnell defends Trump's refusal to concede to Biden". *Axios*.

38   ibid.

39   MMcConnell-Led Republicans Hold Steady against Trump ... www.politico.com/news/2020/11/09/mcconnell-backs-trump-election-435506.

40   "McConnell for the first time recognizes Biden as President-elect". *CNN*. December 15, 2020.

41   Dyke, Tyler Van. "Hawley Pivots from Condemning Violence to Concerns of Voting Irregularities." Washington Examiner, 7 Jan. 2021, www.washingtonexaminer.com/news/hawley-pivots-condemning-violence-concerns-voting-irregularities.

42. Cillizza, Chris. "Analysis: How Josh Hawley's Political Ploy Backfired Massively." CNN, Cable News Network, 7 Jan. 2021, www.cnn.com/2021/01/07/politics/josh-hawley-kansas-city-star-electoral-college/index.html.

43. MO Sen. Josh Hawley to Blame for ... - The Kansas City Star. www.kansascity.com/opinion/editorials/article248317375.html.

44. ibid.

45. "Editorial: Hawley Should Resign. Silent Enablers Must Now Publicly Condemn Trumpism." STLtoday.com, 22 Jan. 2021, www.stltoday.com/opinion/editorial/editorial-hawley-should-resign-silent-enablers-must-now-publicly-condemn-trumpism/article_beae190c-9c42-5c18-bb54-e3e3877192d7.html.

46. ibid.

47. Moore, Elena. "GOP Leaders Condemn Sen. Josh Hawley After Pro-Trump Riot At U.S. Capitol." NPR, NPR, 9 Jan. 2021, www.npr.org/2021/01/08/955103447/gop-leaders-condemn-sen-josh-hawley-after-pro-trump-riot-at-u-s-capitol.

48. Beaumont, Thomas, and Jim Salter. "'Really Dumb-a\*\*': Backlash from Many Fellow Republicans Is Swift for Josh Hawley and Ted Cruz." Chicagotribune.com, 9 Jan. 2021, www.chicagotribune.com/election-2020/ct-josh-hawley-capitol-backlash-20210108-775mnvr2mbfmpofydrparxpuii-story.html.

49. Harris, Elizabeth A., and Alexandra Alter. "Simon & Schuster Cancels Plans for Senator Hawley's Book." The New York Times, The New York Times, 7 Jan. 2021, www.nytimes.com/2021/01/07/books/simon-schuster-josh-hawley-book.html.

50. Hutzler, Alexandra. "Ted Cruz Took His Kids to Cancun to Be a 'Good Dad," Confirms Return to Texas This Afternoon." Newsweek, Newsweek, 18 Feb. 2021, www.newsweek.com/ted-cruz-took-his-kids-cancun-good-dad-confirms-return-texas-this-afternoon-1570316.

51. Goldmacher, Shane, and Nicholas Fandos. "Ted Cruz's Cancún Trip: Family Texts Detail His Political Blunder." The New York Times, The New York Times, 18 Feb. 2021, www.nytimes.com/2021/02/18/us/politics/ted-cruz-storm-cancun.html.

52. Bowden, John. "Cruz Offers to Argue Pennsylvania Election Case before Supreme Court." TheHill, The Hill, 8 Dec. 2020, thehill.com/homenews/senate/529146-cruz-offers-to-argue-pennsylvania-election-case-before-supreme-court.

53. Mccaskill, Nolan D. "Trump Accuses Cruz's Father of Helping JFK's Assassin." POLITICO, 3 May 2016, www.politico.com/blogs/2016-gop-primary-live-updates-and-results/2016/05/trump-ted-cruz-father-222730.

54. Weigel, David. "Ted Cruz Booed by Angry Delegates after Failing to Endorse Trump." The Washington Post, WP Company, 28 Apr. 2019, www.washingtonpost.com/news/post-politics/wp/2016/07/20/ted-cruz-rallies-his-troops-before-closely-watched-convention-speech/.

55. "Ted Cruz Tried to Defend Trump's Coup. He Then Praised the White Supremacist Compromise of 1877." Salon, Salon.com, 11 Jan. 2021, www.salon.com/2021/01/07/ted-cruz-tried-to-defend-trumps-coup-he-then-called-for-a-return-to-a-white-supremacist-comprise/.

56. Miller, Hayley. "Trump Claimed Election 'Rigged' Or 'Stolen' Over 100 Times Ahead Of Capitol Riot." HuffPost, HuffPost, 9 Feb. 2021, www.huffpost.com/entry/trump-rigged-stolen-capitol-riot_n_602188e2c5b6173dd2f88c4f.

57   Slade, David. "Sen. Lindsey Graham Doesn't Buy the Idea That Donald Trump Has Divided the Country." Post and Courier, The Post and Courier, 14 Sept. 2020, www.postandcourier.com/news/sen-lindsey-graham-doesnt-buy-the-idea-that-donald-trump-has-divided-the-country/article_30c0a2fc-a8bc-11ea-868f-a72d037d3414.html.

58   Chappell, Bill, and Richard Gonzales. "'Shocking': Trump Is Criticized For Pulling Troops From Syrian Border." NPR, NPR, 7 Oct. 2019, www.npr.org/2019/10/07/767904589/shocking-trump-is-criticized-for-pulling-troops-from-syrian-border.

59   Weber, Peter. "Sen. Lindsey Graham Tells Sean Hannity That Trump's Speech Was 'Presidential,' 'Compelling,' and 'True'." The Week - All You Need to Know about Everything That Matters, The Week, 9 Jan. 2019, theweek.com/speedreads/816604/sen-lindsey-graham-tells-sean-hannity-that-trumps-speech-presidential-compelling-true.

60   "WATCH: Graham Calls Dems' Treatment of Kavanaugh 'Despicable'." PBS, Public Broadcasting Service, 27 Sept. 2018, www.pbs.org/newshour/politics/watch-graham-calls-dems-treatment-of-kavanaugh-despicable.

61   BRESNAHAN, JOHN, and BURGESS EVERETT . "Trump Ambushes Republicans with Attacks on Minority Congresswomen." POLITICO, 15 July 2019, www.politico.com/story/2019/07/15/trump-republicans-racist-tweets-1415952.

62   ibid.

63   Baragona, Justin. "Meghan McCain Goes After 'Uncle' Lindsey Graham: 'Not the Person I Used to Know'." The Daily Beast, The Daily Beast Company, 15 July 2019, www.thedailybeast.com/meghan-mccain-goes-after-uncle-lindsey-graham-not-the-person-i-used-to-know.

64   McLeod, Paul. "Democrats Are Wondering What The Hell Happened To Lindsey Graham." BuzzFeed News, BuzzFeed News, 16 Jan. 2019, www.buzzfeednews.com/article/paulmcleod/lindsey-graham-bipartisan-what-happened.

65   Eidler, Scott. "Republicans Say Conduct 'Inappropriate,' but Not Impeachable." Newsday, Newsday, 3 Feb. 2020, www.newsday.com/news/nation/trump-impeachment-1.41347207.

66   Allyn, Bobby. "GOP Sen. Alexander To Vote Against Witnesses; Trump Impeachment Trial Could End Friday." NPR, NPR, 31 Jan. 2020, www.npr.org/2020/01/30/801437236/mcconnell-now-likely-has-votes-to-block-witnesses-trial-could-end-soon.

67   Haberman, Maggie, and Michael S. Schmidt. "Trump Told Bolton to Help His Ukraine Pressure Campaign, Book Says." The New York Times, The New York Times, 31 Jan. 2020, www.nytimes.com/2020/01/31/us/politics/trump-bolton-ukraine.html.

68   Portman, Rob. Portman Statement on the Constitutionality of the Senate's ... www.portman.senate.gov/newsroom/press-releases/portman-statement-constitutionality-senates-impeachment-trial.

69   ibid.

70   The Impeachment and Trial of a Former President - Congress. crsreports.congress.gov/product/pdf/LSB/LSB10565.

71   Reilly, Katie. "Donald Trump: I 'Could Shoot Somebody' and Not Lose Voters." Time, Time, 23 Jan. 2016, time.com/4191598/donald-trump-says-he-could-shoot-somebody-and-not-lose-voters/.

72. "Editorial: Hawley Should Resign. Silent Enablers Must Now Publicly Condemn Trumpism." STLtoday.com, 22 Jan. 2021, www.stltoday.com/opinion/editorial/editorial-hawley-should-resign-silent-enablers-must-now-publicly-condemn-trumpism/article_beae190c-9c42-5c18-bb54-e3e3877192d7.html.

73. Seipel, Brooke. "Ron Johnson Says Capitol Attack 'Didn't Seem like an Armed Insurrection'." TheHill, The Hill, 16 Feb. 2021, thehill.com/homenews/senate/538919-ron-johnson-says-capitol-attack-didnt-seem-like-an-armed-insurrection.

74. Edmondson, Catie, and Luke Broadwater. "Before Capitol Riot, Republican Lawmakers Fanned the Flames." The New York Times, The New York Times, 12 Jan. 2021, www.nytimes.com/2021/01/11/us/politics/republicans-capitol-riot.html.

75. Editorial: Ron Johnson's Whitewash of the U.S. Capitol Riot Shows Why Wisconsin's Senior Senator Has to Go, www.msn.com/en-us/news/politics/editorial-ron-johnsons-whitewash-of-the-us-capitol-riot-shows-why-wisconsins-senior-senator-has-to-go/ar-BB1dO0CS.

76. Milwaukee Newspaper Takes 'Rare Step' of Fact-Checking Ron Johnson Op-Ed with 19 Detailed Footnotes: 'How About Telling the Truth?', www.msn.com/en-us/news/politics/milwaukee-newspaper-takes-rare-step-of-fact-checking-ron-johnson-op-ed-with-19-detailed-footnotes-how-about-telling-the-truth/ar-BB1cTKuv.

77. Cillizza, Chris. "Analysis: This Republican Senator Just Said That January 6 Wasn't an 'Armed Insurrection'." CNN, Cable News Network, 16 Feb. 2021, www.cnn.com/2021/02/16/politics/ron-johnson-january-armed-insurrection/index.html.

78. ibid.

79. Rodrigo, Chris Mills. "FBI: No Evidence Antifa Involved in Capitol Riot." TheHill, The Hill, 10 Jan. 2021, thehill.com/policy/national-security/533432-fbi-no-evidence-antifa-involved-in-capitol-riot.

## Trump's House of Representatives Enablers

1. Raju, Manu. "Big Lie? Big Whoop: Many Republicans on Capitol Hill See Little Reason to Bat down Trump's Election Lies." CNN, Cable News Network, 26 Feb. 2021, www.cnn.com/2021/02/25/politics/republican-reaction-donald-trump-party-future-big-lie/index.html.

2. Mascaro, Lisa. "President-Elect? GOP May Wait for January to Say Biden Won." AP NEWS, Associated Press, 9 Dec. 2020, apnews.com/article/joe-biden-donald-trump-elections-electoral-college-mitch-mcconnell-1fd5fd27a95e3ab-214c8b3f1a8f32216.

3. Crowley, James. "Rep. Ted Lieu Says Republicans' Spreading of 'Big Lie' Poses Security Threat to Capitol." Newsweek, Newsweek, 6 Mar. 2021, www.newsweek.com/ted-lieu-republicans-big-lie-security-threat-capitol-1574238.

4. Williams, Jordan. "Trump Demands Names of the Congressional Republicans Who Said They Recognize Biden as Winner." TheHill, The Hill, 5 Dec. 2020, thehill.com/homenews/campaign/528899-trump-demands-names-of-the-congressional-republicans-who-said-they.

5   Carrasco, Maria. "Scalise: 'Let the Legal Process Play out'." POLITICO, POLITICO, 13 Dec. 2020, www.politico.com/news/2020/12/13/house-minority-whip-scalise-legal-election-444849.

6   Carrasco, Maria. "Scalise: 'Let the Legal Process Play out'." POLITICO, POLITICO, 13 Dec. 2020, www.politico.com/news/2020/12/13/house-minority-whip-scalise-legal-election-444849.

7   Gross, Jenny, and Luke Broadwater. "Here Are the Republicans Who Objected to Certifying the Election Results." The New York Times, The New York Times, 7 Jan. 2021, www.nytimes.com/2021/01/07/us/politics/republicans-against-certification.html. qwerwertyuiogfjhdZKfhk

8   Vlamis, Kelsey. "Kevin McCarthy Echoed Trump's False Claim That He Won the Election, Saying Republicans 'Will Not Back down'." Business Insider, Business Insider, 6 Nov. 2020, www.businessinsider.com/kevin-mccarthy-trumps-false-claim-that-he-won-the-election-2020-11.

9   Robins-Early, Nick. "Fox News' Biggest Hosts Go Full Election Conspiracy For Trump." HuffPost, HuffPost, 6 Nov. 2020, www.huffpost.com/entry/fox-news-election-trump-hannity_n_5fa5b864c5b64c88d400747f.

10  Diaz, Daniella. "READ: Brief from 126 Republicans Supporting Texas Lawsuit in Supreme Court." CNN, Cable News Network, 11 Dec. 2020, www.cnn.com/2020/12/10/politics/read-house-republicans-texas-supreme-court/index.html.

11  "Nancy Pelosi: 'Republicans Are Engaged in Election Subversion That Imperils Our Democracy'." CNSNews.com, cnsnews.com/index.php/article/washington/cns-newscom-staff/nancy-pelosi-republicans-are-engaged-election-subversion.

12  ibid.

13  Solender, Andrew. "House Democrat Calls To Exclude 126 Republicans From Next Congress For Supporting Texas Lawsuit." Forbes, Forbes Magazine, 11 Dec. 2020, www.forbes.com/sites/andrewsolender/2020/12/11/house-democrat-calls-to-exclude-126-republicans-from-next-congress-for-supporting-texas-lawsuit/.

14  Willis, Oliver. "GOP Leader Says Trump 'Wasn't Investigating' Biden Even after Trump Publicly Said He Was." The American Independent, 16 Oct. 2019, americanindependent.com/kevin-mccarthy-trump-investigating-biden-ukraine-call-rudy-giuliani/.

15  Nelson, Joshua. "Andrew McCarthy: Trump's Ukraine Call Not a 'High Crime,' Doesn't Reach Impeachment Threshold." Fox News, FOX News Network, 25 Sept. 2019, www.foxnews.com/media/trump-ukraine-not-high-crime-andrew-mccarthy.

16  "'China Should Start an Investigation Into the Bidens,' Trump Says in Extraordinary Request." The New York Times, The New York Times, 3 Oct. 2019, www.nytimes.com/video/us/politics/100000006749777/trump-china-biden.html.

17  Benen, Steve. "GOP Leader Struggles with Reality (Again) Trying to Defend Trump." MSNBC, NBCUniversal News Group, 25 Sept. 2020, www.msnbc.com/rachel-maddow-show/gop-leader-struggles-reality-again-trying-defend-trump-msna1287961.

18  Benen, Steve. "GOP Leader Struggles with Reality (Again) Trying to Defend Trump." MSNBC, NBCUniversal News Group, 25 Sept. 2020, www.msnbc.com/rachel-maddow-show/gop-leader-struggles-reality-again-trying-defend-trump-msna1287961.

19. Holland, Steve, et al. "Trump Summoned Supporters to 'Wild' Protest, and Told Them to Fight. They Did." Reuters, Thomson Reuters, 6 Jan. 2021, www.reuters.com/article/us-usa-election-protests-idUSKBN29B24S.

20. Mascaro, Lisa, et al. "Trump Says He'll 'Fight like Hell' to Hold on to Presidency." PBS, Public Broadcasting Service, 5 Jan. 2021, www.pbs.org/newshour/politics/trump-says-hell-fight-like-hell-to-hold-on-to-presidency.

21. Moye, David. "Pro-Trump Lawyer Mocked For Claiming Mike Pence Guilty Of Treason." HuffPost, HuffPost, 1 Jan. 2021, www.huffpost.com/entry/l-lin-wood-pence-execution-treason_n_5fef9625c5b6fd33110de8de.

22. Lemon, Jason. "Mo Brooks Attacks 'Weakling, Cowering, Wimpy' GOP Congressmen during D.C. Protest Speech." Newsweek, Newsweek, 6 Jan. 2021, www.newsweek.com/mo-brooks-attacks-weakling-cowering-wimpy-gop-congressmen-during-dc-protest-speech-1559345.

23. Staff, TMZ. "Rioters Were Looking to Hurt Pelosi, 'Hang Mike Pence' in Capitol Siege." TMZ, TMZ, 9 Jan. 2021, www.tmz.com/2021/01/09/rioters-wanted-hurt-nancy-pelosi-hang-mike-pence-capitol/.

24. Demsas, Jerusalem, and Emily Stewart. "A Majority of House Republicans Voted to Reject Results from Arizona and Pennsylvania." Vox, Vox, 7 Jan. 2021, www.vox.com/2021/1/7/22218225/house-republicans-senate-electoral-college-votes-storm-capitol-election-stop-the-steal-trump-biden.

25. Mathias, Christopher. "Paul Gosar Spoke At A White Nationalist Conference. The GOP Doesn't Care." HuffPost, HuffPost, 5 Mar. 2021, www.huffpost.com/entry/paul-gosar-white-nationalist-republican_n_60415a1ec5b60208555d4f60.

26. ibid.

27. Hansen, Ronald J. "FACT CHECK: Reps. Andy Biggs, Paul Gosar Still Touting Baseless Election-Fraud Claims." The Arizona Republic, Arizona Republic, 18 Nov. 2020, www.azcentral.com/story/news/politics/fact-check/2020/11/17/andy-biggs-paul-gosar-still-touting-baseless-election-fraud-claims/6334872002/.

28. ibid.

29. O'Brien, Luke. "Republican Congressman Helped Organize Far-Right Protest Against Election Result." HuffPost, HuffPost, 13 Nov. 2020, www.huffpost.com/entry/paul-gosar-far-right-protest-arizona_n_5fada218c5b6370e7e311861.

30. Tolan, Casey, et al. "GOP Lawmakers' Fiery Language under More Scrutiny after Deadly Capitol Riot." CNN, Cable News Network, 13 Jan. 2021, www.cnn.com/2021/01/12/politics/gop-lawmakers-fiery-language-under-scrutiny-invs/index.html.

31. "Rep. Paul Gosar: DC Riot Had 'Hallmarks of Antifa Provocation.'" News Break, www.newsbreak.com/arizona/phoenix/news/2139940803598/rep-paul-gosar-dc-riot-had-hallmarks-of-antifa-provocation.

32. Fung, Katherine. "GOP Rep. Paul Gosar's Siblings Call for His Removal, Citing Involvement in Capitol Riot." Newsweek, Newsweek, 13 Jan. 2021, www.newsweek.com/gop-rep-paul-gosars-siblings-call-his-removal-citing-involvement-capitol-riot-1561201.

33. GOP Lawmaker Deletes Tweet Saying He Met With 'Stop The Steal', Urged Them To 'Keep Fighting' (theguardiansofdemocracy.com) 01 11 21.

34  Armus, Teo. "A 'Stop the Steal' Organizer, Now Banned by Twitter, Said Three GOP Lawmakers Helped Plan His D.C. Rally." The Washington Post, WP Company, 14 Jan. 2021, www.washingtonpost.com/nation/2021/01/13/ali-alexander-capitol-biggs-gosar/.

35  ibid.

36  Burkhalter, Eddie. "Brooks Helped Plan Jan. 6 Event, Activist and Organizer of Rally Says." Alabama Political Reporter, 12 Jan. 2021, www.alreporter.com/2021/01/12/brooks-helped-plan-jan-6-event-activist-and-organizer-of-rally-says/.

37  Armus, Teo. "A 'Stop the Steal' Organizer, Now Banned by Twitter, Said Three GOP Lawmakers Helped Plan His D.C. Rally." The Washington Post, WP Company, 14 Jan. 2021, www.washingtonpost.com/nation/2021/01/13/ali-alexander-capitol-biggs-gosar/.

38  Gattis, Paul. "Mo Brooks on 'Kick Ass' Speech: 'I Make No Apology'." Al, 9 Jan. 2021, www.al.com/news/2021/01/mo-brooks-on-kick-ass-speech-i-make-no-apology-for-inspiring-patriotic-americans.html.

39  ibid.

40  "Some House Democrats Move to Censure Trump Ally Rep. Mo Brooks." Yahoo! News, Yahoo!, news.yahoo.com/some-house-democrats-move-to-censure-trump-ally-rep-mo-brooks-173203941.html.

41  Carney, Jordain. "Democrats Float 14th Amendment to Bar Trump from Office." TheHill, The Hill, 22 Jan. 2021, thehill.com/homenews/senate/535467-democrats-float-14th-amendment-to-bar-trump-from-office.

42  Clancy, Sam. "'They Have Broken Their Sacred Oath of Office': Cori Bush Calls for Expulsion of Representatives Who Opposed Electoral College Certification." Ksdk.com, 6 Jan. 2021, www.ksdk.com/article/news/politics/national-politics/missouri-congresswoman-cori-bush-calls-expulsion-representatives-opposed-electoral-college-certification/63-9d5c2b69-7616-40e3-934f-2eec3d34b6f2.

43  Roose, Kevin. "What Is QAnon, the Viral Pro-Trump Conspiracy Theory?" The New York Times, The New York Times, 18 Aug. 2020, www.nytimes.com/article/what-is-qanon.html.

44  ibid.

45  Mangan, Dan. "QAnon 'Shaman' Jacob Chansley Held without Bail after Storming Senate during Capitol Riot by Trump Supporters." CNBC, CNBC, 15 Jan. 2021, www.cnbc.com/2021/01/15/trump-rioters-planned-to-kill-congress-members-fed-probe.html.

46  "Woman Shot and Killed in Storming of US Capitol Named as Ashli Babbitt." The Guardian, Guardian News and Media, 7 Jan. 2021, www.theguardian.com/us-news/2021/jan/07/ashli-babbitt-woman-shot-and-killed-in-storming-of-us-capitol-named.

47  Edmondson, Catie, and Luke Broadwater. "Before Capitol Riot, Republican Lawmakers Fanned the Flames." The New York Times, The New York Times, 12 Jan. 2021, www.nytimes.com/2021/01/11/us/politics/republicans-capitol-riot.html.

48  Rodrigo, Chris Mills. "QAnon-Supporting Congressional Candidate Embraced 9/11 Conspiracy Theory." TheHill, The Hill, 13 Aug. 2020,

thehill.com/policy/technology/511888-qanon-supporting-congressional-candidate-embraced-9-11-conspiracy-theory.

49. "Rep. Marjorie Taylor Greene's Old FB Posts Called for Death of Dems." TMZ, TMZ, 27 Jan. 2021, www.tmz.com/2021/01/27/rep-marjorie-taylor-greene-old-facebook-posts-death-democrats/.

50. Hananoki, Eric. "A Guide to Rep. Marjorie Taylor Greene's Conspiracy Theories and Toxic Rhetoric." Media Matters for America, www.mediamatters.org/congress/guide-rep-marjorie-taylor-greenes-conspiracy-theories-and-toxic-rhetoric.

51. ibid.

52. ibid.

53. LeBlanc, Paul. "Video Surfaces of Marjorie Taylor Greene Confronting Parkland Shooting Survivor with Baseless Claims." CNN, Cable News Network, 28 Jan. 2021, www.cnn.com/2021/01/27/politics/marjorie-taylor-greene-david-hogg-video/index.html.

54. Steadman, Otillia. "Donald Trump Is Gone, But QAnon's Sex Trafficking Conspiracies Are Here To Stay." BuzzFeed News, BuzzFeed News, 24 Apr. 2021, www.buzzfeednews.com/article/otilliasteadman/qanon-sex-trafficking-conspiracy-extremism.

55. Sheth, Sonam. "Marjorie Taylor Greene Says She Endorsed Assassinating Democrats and Questioned Whether 9/11 Happened Because QAnon Made Her 'Believe Things That Weren't True'." Business Insider, Business Insider, 4 Feb. 2021, www.businessinsider.com/marjorie-taylor-greene-qanon-support-house-speech-2021-2.

56. ibid.

57. Enriquez, Keri. "Republican Members of Congress Refuse to Wear Masks during Capitol Insurrection." CNN, Cable News Network, 9 Jan. 2021, www.cnn.com/2021/01/09/politics/republican-congress-members-refuse-masks-trnd/index.html.

58. Freking, Kevin. "3 House Democrats Test Positive for COVID-19; Jayapal Blames GOP Members Who Refused to 'Wear a Damn Mask' during Capitol Lockdown." Chicagotribune.com, Chicago Tribune, 12 Jan. 2021, www.chicagotribune.com/coronavirus/ct-nw-capitol-lockdown-congress-covid19-20210112-jpd2xiawzje6xarz7loixdp67m-story.html.

59. "Pelosi Slams Marjorie Taylor Greene's Appointment to House Education and Labor Committee: 'What Could They Be Thinking?'." Yahoo! News, Yahoo!, news.yahoo.com/pelosi-slams-marjorie-taylor-greenes-170220940.html.

60. Rep. Marjorie Taylor Greene's Endorsement of Conspiracy Theories, Violence Sparks Calls for Her Resignation - Again, www.msn.com/en-us/news/politics/rep-marjorie-taylor-greene-endorsed-the-execution-of-democrats-in-old-facebook-posts-report-says/ar-BB1d7JWN.

61. Summers, Madison, et al. "Rep. Kinzinger Slams GOP Rep. Marjorie Taylor Greene: She Is 'Not a Republican'." IJR, 28 Jan. 2021, ijr.com/kinzinger-gop-greene-not-a-republican/.

62. Segers, Grace. "Marjorie Taylor Greene Removed from House Committee Assignments." CBS News, CBS Interactive, 5 Feb. 2021, www.cbsnews.com/news/house-votes-to-remove-gop-rep-greene-from-committees/.

63   LeBlanc, Paul. "Video Surfaces of Marjorie Taylor Greene Confronting Parkland Shooting Survivor with Baseless Claims." CNN, Cable News Network, 28 Jan. 2021, www.cnn.com/2021/01/27/politics/marjorie-taylor-greene-david-hogg-video/index.html.

64   Mastrangelo, Dominick. "Rep. Marjorie Taylor Greene Wears 'Trump Won' Mask on House Floor." TheHill, The Hill, 4 Jan. 2021, thehill.com/homenews/532534-rep-elect-marjorie-taylor-greene-wears-trump-won-mask-on-house-floor.

65   "QAQ'non Congresswoman Mocked for Wearing Mask Saying 'Censored' While Speaking to the Nation on Live TV." The Independent, Independent Digital News and Media, 13 Jan. 2021, www.independent.co.uk/news/world/americas/us-election-2020/marjorie-taylor-greene-mask-trump-impeachment-b1786952.html.

66   "SoCal Congresswoman Breaks with Republicans in Vote to Remove Greene from Committees." ABC7 Los Angeles, KABC-TV, 5 Feb. 2021, abc7.com/rep-young-kim-congresswoman-orange-county-marjorie-taylor-greene/10315732/.

67   Malliotakis Votes Against GOP Colleague for Incendiary Views, www.ny1.com/nyc/all-boroughs/news/2021/02/05/malliotakis-one-of-11-in-gop-to-vote-against-colleague-for-supporting-conspiracy-theories.

68   "Gimenez Votes to Remove Congresswoman Marjorie Taylor Green from Committee Assignments." Representative Carlos Gimenez, 5 Feb. 2021, gimenez.house.gov/media/press-releases/gimenez-votes-remove-congresswoman-marjorie-taylor-green-committee-assignments.

69   Hudak, Zak. "House Committee Assignments Once Were the Seat of Power. Do They Matter Anymore?" CBS News, CBS Interactive, 15 Apr. 2021, www.cbsnews.com/news/house-committees-impact-matt-gaetz-marjorie-taylor-greene/.

70   Staeger, Steve. "New Colorado Congresswoman Has History of Associating with Militias." KUSA.com, 19 Jan. 2021, www.9news.com/article/news/local/next/boebert-colorado-congresswoman-militias/73-b52b98e0-303d-4921-8ba7-14469403fd1c.

71   Person. "QAnon Congresswoman Who Live-Tweeted Nancy Pelosi's Location to Rioters Now Facing Calls for Arrest." Salon, Salon.com, 11 Jan. 2021, www.salon.com/2021/01/11/qanon-congresswoman-who-live-tweeted-nancy-pelosis-location-to-rioters-now-facing-calls-for-arrest_partner/.

72   Batchelor, Tom. "Lauren Boebert Faces $5,000 Fine after Setting off Capitol Metal Detector." Newsweek, Newsweek, 25 Jan. 2021, www.newsweek.com/lauren-boebert-fine-capitol-metal-detector-1563660.

73   Flynn, Meagan. "In Ad, Lawmaker Vows to Carry Her Glock around D.C. and on Hill." The Washington Post, WP Company, 4 Jan. 2021, www.washingtonpost.com/local/legal-issues/boebert-capitol-guns/2021/01/04/a59f70f8-4e9d-11eb-83e3-322644d82356_story.html.

# Trump's "Herd Immunity" Gang

1   Diaz, Daniella, and Betsy Klein. "Former Trump Appointee Encouraged Herd Immunity Strategy for Covid-19, Internal Emails Reveal." CNN, Cable News Network, 17 Dec. 2020, www.cnn.com/2020/12/16/politics/trump-administration-herd-immunity/index.html.

2   ibid.

3   ibid.

4   Rogers, Lindsay Smith. "What Is Herd Immunity and How Can We Achieve It With COVID-19?" Johns Hopkins Bloomberg School of Public Health, 14 Oct. 2020, www.jhsph.edu/covid-19/articles/achieving-herd-immunity-with-covid19.html.

5   ibid.

6   Rogers, Lindsay Smith. "What Is Herd Immunity and How Can We Achieve It With COVID-19?" Johns Hopkins Bloomberg School of Public Health, 14 Oct. 2020, www.jhsph.edu/covid-19/articles/achieving-herd-immunity-with-covid19.html.

7   Levin, Bess. "'Who Cares': A Trump Administration Official Wanted to Purposely Infect 'Infants, Kids," and the 'Middle Aged' With COVID-19." Vanity Fair, www.vanityfair.com/news/2020/12/trump-administration-herd-immunity-paul-alexander.

8   Lee, Bruce Y. "Trump Says With 'A Herd Mentality' Covid-19 Coronavirus Will Go Away." Forbes, Forbes Magazine, 17 Sept. 2020, www.forbes.com/sites/brucelee/2020/09/16/trump-says-with-a-herd-mentality-covid-19-coronavirus-will-go-away/.

9   Jewers, Chris. "Sweden Admits It Is Seeing No Sign of Herd Immunity Slowing the Spread of Covid-19." Daily Mail Online, Associated Newspapers, 24 Nov. 2020, www.dailymail.co.uk/news/article-8983053/Sweden-admits-seeing-no-sign-herd-immunity-slowing-spread-Covid-19.html.

10  Blackwell, Tom (September 16, 2020). "Canadian professor at heart of controversy over White House push to control COVID-19 messaging". *National Post*.

11  Owermohle, Sarah (September 9, 2020). "Emails show HHS official trying to muzzle Fauci". *Politico*.

12  Sun, Lena H. (September 12, 2020). "Trump officials seek greater control over CDC reports on coronavirus". *The Washington Post*. Retrieved September 14, 2020.

13  ibid.

14  Weiland, Noah (September 18, 2020). "Emails Detail Effort to Silence C.D.C. and Question Its Science". *The New York Times*.

15  ibid.

16  Sun, Lena H.; Dawsey, Josh (July 9, 2020). "CDC feels pressure from Trump as rift grows over coronavirus response". *The Washington Post*.

17  Diamond, Dan (September 11, 2020). "Trump officials interfered with CDC reports on Covid-19". *Politico*.

18  Owermohle, Sarah (September 9, 2020). "Emails show HHS official trying to muzzle Fauci". *Politico*.

19  ibid.

20  ibid.

21  Morrow, Adrian. "McMaster Professor Embroiled in White House Controversy over Reports He Attempted to Muzzle Scientists." The Globe and Mail, 17 Sept. 2020, www.theglobeandmail.com/world/us-politics/article-mcmaster-university-professor-embroiled-in-white-house-controversy-for/.

22  Diamond, Dan. "'We Want Them Infected': Trump Appointee Demanded 'Herd Immunity' Strategy, Emails Reveal." POLITICO, POLITICO, 17 Dec. 2020, www.politico.com/news/2020/12/16/trump-appointee-demanded-herd-immunity-strategy-446408.

23  Trump Appointee Reportedly Pushed for Herd Immunity: 'We Want Them Infected', www.msn.com/en-us/news/politics/trump-appointee-reportedly-pushed-for-herd-immunity-we-want-them-infected/ar-BB1bZmGw.

24  LaFraniere, Sharon (September 14, 2020). "Trump health aide pushes bizarre conspiracies and warns of armed revolt". *The New York Times*.

25  ibid.

26  LaFraniere, Sharon (September 14, 2020). "Trump Health Aide Falsely Alleges Conspiracies and Warns of Armed Revolt" – via NYTimes.com.

27  Jiang, Weijia. "HHS Spokesman Michael Caputo Claims He Received Death Threat during Facebook Live Session." CBS News, CBS Interactive, 15 Sept. 2020, www.cbsnews.com/news/michael-caputo-hhs-facebook-live-video-death-threat-claims/.

28  Yeo, Patricia Kelly (September 14, 2020). "Trump Health Aide Goes on Batshit Attack Against CDC, Warns of Left-Wing Hit Squads". *The Daily Beast*. New York City: IAC. Retrieved September 15, 2020.

29  LaFraniere, Sharon (September 14, 2020). "Trump Health Aide Falsely Alleges Conspiracies and Warns of Armed Revolt" – via NYTimes.com.

30  "The Editorial Board: It's time for Caputo to go". The Buffalo News. September 14, 2020. Archived from the original on September 15, 2020.

31  Feuer, Will (September 16, 2020). "HHS spokesman Caputo to take medical leave after reportedly accusing CDC officials of plotting against Trump". *CNBC*.

32  Abutaleb, Yasmeen; Dawsey, Josh; Sun, Lena H. (September 16, 2020). "Top Trump health appointee taking medical leave after incendiary remarks". *Washington Post*.

33  Weiland, Noah (September 18, 2020). "Emails Detail Effort to Silence C.D.C. and Question Its Science". *The New York Times*.

34  Mandavilli, Apoorva (September 18, 2020). "C.D.C. Testing Guidance Was Published Against Scientists' Objections". *The New York Times*.

35  Higgins-Dunn, Noah. "Top Health Official Says Coronavirus 'Herd Immunity Is Not the Strategy of the U.S. Government'." CNBC, CNBC, 2 Oct. 2020, www.cnbc.com/2020/10/02/top-health-official-says-coronavirus-herd-immunity-not-us-strategy.html.

36  Lee, Bruce Y. "Trump Says With 'A Herd Mentality' Covid-19 Coronavirus Will Go Away." Forbes, Forbes Magazine, 17 Sept. 2020, www.forbes.com/sites/brucelee/2020/09/16/trump-says-with-a-herd-mentality-covid-19-coronavirus-will-go-away/.

37  Varadarajan, Tuunku (September 4, 2020). "Trump's Covid Adviser Gets a Washington Welcome". *The Wall Street Journal*.

38  Monica Alba & Carol E. Lee. "Atlas on the outs with coronavirus task force but still pushing Trump's pandemic claims".

39. Abutaleb, Yasmeen; Rucker, Phillip; Dawsey, Josh; Costa, Robert (October 19, 2020). "Trump's den of dissent: Inside the White House task force as coronavirus surges". *The Washington Post.*

40. Monica Alba & Carol E. Lee. "Atlas on the outs with coronavirus task force but still pushing Trump's pandemic claims". *NBC News.*

41. Bruggeman, Lucien; Cathey, Libby. "Former Stanford colleagues warn Dr. Scott Atlas fosters 'falsehoods and misrepresentations of science'". *ABC News.*

42. *CNN*, John Avlon, Michael Warren and Brandon Miller. "Atlas push to 'slow the testing down' tracks with dramatic decline in one key state". *CNN.*

43. LeBlanc, Paul; Diamond, Jeremy (November 15, 2020). "Trump coronavirus adviser Scott Atlas urges Michigan to 'rise up' against new Covid-19 measures". *CNN.*

44. Weiland, Noah; Stolberg, Sheryl Gay; Shear, Michael D.; Tankersley, Jim (September 2, 2020). "A New Coronavirus Adviser Roils the White House With Unorthodox Ideas". *The New York Times.*.

45. Weiland, Noah; Stolberg, Sheryl Gay; Shear, Michael D.; Tankersley, Jim (September 2, 2020). "A New Coronavirus Adviser Roils the White House With Unorthodox Ideas". *The New York Times.*.

46. Abutaleb, Yasmeen; Dawsey, Josh (August 31, 2020). "New Trump pandemic adviser pushes controversial 'herd immunity' strategy, worrying public health officials". *The Washington Post.*

47. ibid.

48. Smith, Allan (October 18, 2020). "Twitter removes tweet from top Trump Covid adviser saying masks don't work". *NBC News*. Archived from the original on November 30, 2020.

49. ibid.

50. Stolberg, Sheryl Gay; Haberman, Maggie; Weiland, Noah (October 19, 2020). "Trump Calls Fauci 'a Disaster' and Shrugs Off Virus as Infections Soar". *The New York Times.*.

51. Abutaleb, Yasmeen; Dawsey, Josh (August 31, 2020). "New Trump pandemic adviser pushes controversial 'herd immunity' strategy, worrying public health officials". *The Washington Post.*

52. Kashmira Gander (September 1, 2020). "'Overt Lie': White House Adviser Scott Atlas Denies Herd Immunity Strategy Claims". *Newsweek*; Stabile, Angelica (September 1, 2020). "Dr. Atlas blasts reports he backed 'herd immunity': 'I've never said that to the president'". *Fox News.*

53. "President Trump News Conference". *C-SPAN.*

54. University, Stanford. "Faculty Senate Condemns COVID-19 Actions of Hoover's Scott Atlas." Stanford News, 20 Nov. 2020, news.stanford.edu/2020/11/20/faculty-senate-condemns-actions-hoover-fellow-scott-atlas/.

55. Kaitlan Collins, Jim Acosta and Devan Cole, Dr. Scott Atlas resigns from Trump administration, *CNN* (November 30, 2020).

56. "Full Transcript: Dr. Deborah Birx on 'Face the Nation,' January 24, 2021." CBS News, CBS Interactive, 24 Jan. 2021, www.cbsnews.com/news/full-transcript-dr-deborah-birx-on-face-the-nation-january-24-2021/.

| | |
|---|---|
| 57 | ibid. |
| 58 | ibid. |
| 59 | ibid. |
| 60 | "'Ousted' US Vaccine Expert Rick Bright to File Whistleblower Complaint." BBC News, BBC, 24 Apr. 2020, www.bbc.com/news/world-us-canada-52400721. |
| 61 | "Full Transcript: Dr. Deborah Birx on 'Face the Nation,'" January 24, 2021." CBS News, CBS Interactive, 24 Jan. 2021, www.cbsnews.com/news/full-transcript-dr-deborah-birx-on-face-the-nation-january-24-2021/. |
| 62 | "'I Think You Can Trust Me': Fauci Stands Firm as Trump Works to Undermine Him." The Guardian, Guardian News and Media, 15 July 2020, www.theguardian.com/us-news/2020/jul/15/dr-fauci-donald-trump-attacks-covid-19. |
| 63 | Uria, Daniel. "White House Coronavirus Task Force Presents New Guidelines for Reopening." UPI, UPI, 28 Apr. 2020, www.upi.com/Top_News/US/2020/04/27/White-House-Coronavirus-Task-Force-presents-new-guidelines-for-reopening/2711588028682/. |
| 64 | Weiland, Noah, and Maggie Haberman. "For Dr. Deborah Birx, Urging Calm Has Come With Heavy Criticism." The New York Times, The New York Times, 27 Mar. 2020, www.nytimes.com/2020/03/27/us/politics/deborah-birx-coronavirus.html. |
| 65 | DeMarche, Edmund. "Birx Traveled to Delaware Vacation Property with Family after Warning of Holiday Gatherings." Fox News, FOX News Network, 22 Dec. 2020, www.foxnews.com/politics/birx-delaware-property-delaware-coronavirus-thanksgiving-holiday. |
| 66 | "Transcript: Dr. Deborah Birx on 'Face the Nation,'" January 24, 2021." CBS News, CBS Interactive, 24 Jan. 2021, www.cbsnews.com/news/transcript-deborah-birx-on-face-the-nation-january-24-2021/. |
| 67 | https://www.nytimes.com/2021/03/03/us/politics/ronny-jackson-white-house-doctor.html?action=click&algo=bandit-all-sur |
| 68 | Raju, Manu, et al. "First on CNN: Rep. Ronny Jackson Made Sexual Comments, Drank Alcohol and Took Ambien While Working as White House Physician, Pentagon Watchdog Finds." CNN, Cable News Network, 3 Mar. 2021, www.cnn.com/2021/03/02/politics/ronny-jackson-dod-inspector-general-report/index.html. |
| 69 | ibid. |
| 70 | ibid. |
| 71 | Taylor, Jessica, and Brian Naylor. "Ronny Jackson Withdraws As VA Nominee." NPR, NPR, 26 Apr. 2018, www.npr.org/2018/04/26/605471807/dr-ronny-jackson-withdraws-as-va-nominee. |
| 72 | ibid. |
| 73 | Moreno, J. Edward. "Trump Endorses Former White House Physician Ronny Jackson for Congress." TheHill, The Hill, 29 Feb. 2020, thehill.com/homenews/campaign/485261-trump-endorses-former-white-house-physician-ronny-jackson-for-congress. |
| 74 | ibid. |

## Trump's Cabinet

1. "Opinion | Bill Barr's Legacy of Failure." The Washington Post, WP Company, 17 Dec. 2020, www.washingtonpost.com/opinions/letters-to-the-editor/bill-barrs-legacy-of-failure/2020/12/16/e4c9b54c-3f00-11eb-b58b-1623f6267960_story.html.
2. ibid.
3. Lopez, German. "Joe Biden's Long Record Supporting the War on Drugs and Mass Incarceration, Explained." Vox, Vox, 25 Apr. 2019, www.vox.com/policy-and-politics/2019/4/25/18282870/joe-biden-criminal-justice-war-on-drugs-mass-incarceration.
4. Laird, Lorelei (December 7, 2018). "Who is William Barr, Trump's pick to replace Sessions as AG?". ABA Journal.; Gurman, Sadie (May 20, 2019). "Barr, Under Fire, Says He's Fighting for the Presidency, Not Trump". Wall Street Journal. ISSN 0099-9660.
5. Baker, Peter (November 14, 2017). "'Lock Her Up' Becomes More Than a Slogan". The New York Times.
6. Zapotosky, Matt; Barrett, Devlin (January 5, 2018). "FBI has been investigating the Clinton Foundation for months". Washington Post.Blake, Aaron (December 6, 2018). "The red flags on Trump's new attorney general pick". The Washington Post.
7. Barr, William (February 1, 2017). "Former attorney general: Trump was right to fire Sally Yates". The Washington Post.
8. AG Nominee Barr Says It's 'Vitally Important' Mueller Finish Investigation." MarketWatch, MarketWatch, 14 Jan. 2019, www.marketwatch.com/story/ag-nominee-barr-says-its-vitally-important-mueller-finish-investigation-2019-01-14.
9. de Vogue, Ariane (January 15, 2019). "Barr sent or discussed controversial memo with Trump lawyers". CNN.
10. Watkins, Eli (March 26, 2019). "Barr authored memo last year ruling out obstruction of justice". CNN; Gurman, Sadie; Viswanatha, Aruna (December 20, 2018). "Trump's Attorney General Pick Criticized an Aspect of Mueller Probe in Memo to Justice Department". The Wall Street Journal. ^ Blake, Aaron (January 15, 2019). "Barr confirms he shared his Mueller memo with lots of people around Trump". The Washington Post.
11. ibid.
12. Samuelsohn, Darren (April 4, 2019). "Barr's legacy on the line as Mueller team fumes". Politico.
13. Schmidt, Michael S. "Judge Says Barr Misled on How His Justice Dept. Viewed Trump's Actions." The New York Times, The New York Times, 4 May 2021, www.nytimes.com/2021/05/04/us/politics/barr-trump-obstruction-russia-inquiry.html.
14. Schmidt, Michael S. "Judge Says Barr Misled on How His Justice Dept. Viewed Trump's Actions." The New York Times, The New York Times, 4 May 2021, www. nytimes.com/2021/05/04/us/politics/barr-trump-obstruction-russia-inquiry.html.
15. Kimball, Spencer, and Jacob Pramuk. "Trump Did Not Collude with Russia, Says Mueller, and Is Cleared of Obstruction by the Attorney General." CNBC, CNBC, 25 Mar. 2019, www.cnbc.com/2019/03/24/attorney-general-william-barr-to-release-mueller-russia-probe-findings.html.

16 Rocah, Mimi. "William Barr Misled Congress about Mueller's Report. He Must Resign as Attorney General." NBCNews.com, NBCUniversal News Group, 2 Aug. 2019, www.nbcnews.com/think/opinion/william-barr-lied-congress-about-mueller-s-report-he-must-ncna1000881.

17 Yen, Hope; Woodward, Calvin (April 22, 2019). "AP fact check: Trump, AG Barr spread untruths about Mueller report". PBS NewsHour.

18 Kruzel, John (April 22, 2019). "Did Trump 'fully' cooperate with Mueller investigation? No". PolitiFact.

19 ibid.

20 Homan, Timothy R. (April 18, 2019). "Here are the 10 'episodes' Mueller probed for potential obstruction by Trump". TheHill; Lynch, Sarah N.; Sullivan, Andy (April 19, 2019). "In unflattering detail, Mueller report reveals Trump actions to impede inquiry". Reuters.

21 Barr, William P. (March 24, 2019). "Attorney General's Letter to House and Senate Judiciary Committee". Justice.gov. p. 3; Montoya-Galvez, Camilo (March 24, 2019). "The key findings from the Justice Department summary of Mueller's report". www.cbsnews.com; Barr, William (March 24, 2019). "Letter to Lindsey Graham, Jerrold Nadler, Dianne Feinstein, and Doug Collins"

22 Savage, Charlie. "Judge Calls Barr's Handling of Mueller Report 'Distorted' and 'Misleading'." The New York Times, The New York Times, 5 Mar. 2020, www.nytimes.com/2020/03/05/us/politics/mueller-report-barr-judge-walton.html

23 ibid.

24 Lambe, Jerry (September 3, 2020). "Federal Judge Finds Certain Trump Administration Redactions of Mueller Probe Are Lawful". lawandcrime.com.

25 Lambe, Jerry (October 1, 2020). "Judge Finds DOJ Violated Federal Law with Certain Mueller Report Redactions; Orders Pages Released Before Election". lawandcrime.com.

26 Goodin, Emily. "Bill Barr Says Trump Was RIGHT to Accuse FBI and Justice Department of 'Spying' on His Campaign." Daily Mail Online, Associated Newspapers, 31 May 2019, www.dailymail.co.uk/news/article-7090845/amp/Bill-Barr-says-Trump-RIGHT-accuse-FBI-Justice-Department-spying-campaign.html.

27 Morgan, David. "House Approves Authority to Sue Trump Advisers Who Ignore Subpoenas." Reuters, Thomson Reuters, 11 June 2019, www.reuters.com/article/us-usa-trump-congress-idUSKCN1TC2CB.

28 Weiser, Benjamin; Protess, Ben; Benner, Katie; Rashbaum, William (July 1, 2020). "Inside Barr's Effort to Undermine Prosecutors in N.Y." The New York Times. Archived from the original on July 1, 2020.

29 ibid.

30 Balsamo, Michael; Tucker, Eric (May 8, 2020). "Justice Department dropping Flynn's Trump-Russia case". Associated Press; "Attorney General Barr says what Michael Flynn did 'was not a crime'". CBS News. May 8, 2020.

31 Blake, Aaron (February 13, 2020). "Trump just made the DOJ's Roger Stone intervention look even worse". The Washington Post. Sullivan, Eileen; Shear, Michael

(February 12, 2020). "Trump Praises Barr for Rejecting Punishment Recommended for Stone". The New York Times. Archived from the original on February 13, 2020.

32 ibid.

33 ibid.

34 Balsamo, Michael; Lemire, Jonathan (May 17, 2019). "In Barr, Trump has found his champion and advocate". Associated Press.

35 Fandos, Nicholas (May 8, 2019). "House Panel Approves Contempt for Barr After Trump Claims Privilege Over Full Mueller Report". The New York Times.

36 Desiderio, Andrew (June 3, 2019). "House Dems to hold Barr, Ross in contempt over census question; The Oversight Committee wants key documents by Thursday". Politico

37 Foran, Clare, and Ashley Killough. "House Votes to Hold Barr, Ross in Criminal Contempt over Census Dispute." CNN, Cable News Network, 17 July 2019, edition. cnn.com/2019/07/17/politics/house-contempt-vote-barr-ross-census/index.html.

38 Desidero, Andrew (July 17, 2019). "House holds William Barr, Wilbur Ross in criminal contempt of Congress". Politico; Somnez, Felicia (July 18, 2019). "House votes to hold Attorney General Barr, Commerce Secretary Ross in contempt for failing to comply with subpoena on 2020 Census". The Washington Post. Archived from the original on February 16, 2020.

39 Honig, Elie. "Opinion: Bill Barr Can't Erase His Shameful Legacy." CNN, Cable News Network, 15 Dec. 2020, www.cnn.com/2020/12/14/opinions/bill-barr-shameful-legacy-honig/index.html.

40 Zegart, Amy. "The Whistle-Blower Really Knows How to Write." The Atlantic, Atlantic Media Company, 27 Sept. 2019, www.theatlantic.com/ideas/archive/2019/09/what-the-whistle-blowers-memo-taught-me/598939/.

41 Sullivan, Andy. "Explainer: Barr Gives Top Priority to Investigating the Investigators of Russian Meddling." Reuters, Thomson Reuters, 1 Oct. 2019, www.reuters.com/article/us-usa-trump-whistleblower-barr-explaine-idUSKBN1WG4QZ.

42 Prokop, Andrew (September 30, 2019). "Trump and Barr have been urging foreign governments to help them investigate the Mueller probe's origins". Vox; Viswanatha, Aruna; Gurman, Sadie; Legorano, Giovanni (October 6, 2019). "Barr's Requests for Foreign Help Prompt Backlash in Australia, Italy, U.K." The Wall Street Journal; Mazzetti, Mark; Goldman, Adam; Benner, Katie (October 6, 2019). "Barr and a Top Prosecutor Cast a Wide Net in Reviewing the Russia Inquiry". The New York Times.

43 Kutner, Max. "Who Is Joseph Mifsud, the Professor in the George Papadopoulos Russia Investigation?" Newsweek, Newsweek, 2 Nov. 2017, www.newsweek.com/george-papadopoulos-who-joseph-mifsud-professor-697441.

44 Basu, Zachary (December 10, 2019). "Attorney General Bill Barr attacks Russia investigation as "completely baseless"

45 Shortell, David (February 10, 2020). "Barr confirms Justice Department is receiving Giuliani information about Ukraine". CNN; Zapotosky, Matt; Barrett, Devlin (February 11, 2020). "Barr acknowledges Justice Dept. has created 'intake process' to vet Giuliani's information on Bidens". The Washington Post. Archived from the original on February 10, 2020.

46. Shortell, David (February 10, 2020). "Barr confirms Justice Department is receiving Giuliani information about Ukraine". CNN; Zapotosky, Matt; Barrett, Devlin (February 11, 2020). "Barr acknowledges Justice Dept. has created 'intake process' to vet Giuliani's information on Bidens". The Washington Post. Archived from the original on February 10, 2020.
47. https://nypost.com/2019/10/11/rudy-giulianis-relationship-with-associates-subject-of-crimi- nal-investigation-report/
48. Sengupta, Kim (November 1, 2019). "UK intelligence officials shaken by Trump administration's requests for help with counter-impeachment inquiry". The Independent.
49. Johnson, Carrie. "Barr Blasts His Own Prosecutors: 'All Power Is Vested In The Attorney General'." NPR, NPR, 17 Sept. 2020, www.npr.org/2020/09/17/913891515/in-fiery-speech-barr-assails-his-own-prosecutors-for-political-headhunting.
50. Mastrangelo, Dominick. "Barr: DOJ Won't Be Run like Preschool." TheHill, The Hill, 17 Sept. 2020, thehill.com/homenews/administration/516849-barr-doj-wont-be-run-like-preschool.
51. Leonnig, Carol; Zapotosky, Matt; Dawsey, Josh; Tan, Rebecca (June 2, 2020). "Barr personally ordered removal of protesters near White House, leading to use of force against largely peaceful crowd". The Washington Post. ^ Phillips, Morgan (June 2, 2020); "Barr ordered officials to clear area around Lafayette Square before Trump's protest remarks, officials say". Fox News.
52. ibid.
53. Goodin, Emily. "Ivanka Trump Carried the Bible Donald Trump Posed with in Her $1,540 Max Mara Handbag." Daily Mail Online, Associated Newspapers, 3 June 2020, www.dailymail.co.uk/news/article-8381977/Ivanka-Trump-carried-Bible-Donald-Trump-posed-1-540-Max-Mara-handbag.html.
54. Kessler, Glenn (June 9, 2020). "William Barr's Four-Pinocchio claim that pepper balls are 'not chemical'". The Washington Post. Archived from the original on June 9, 2020.
55. ibid.
56. Savage, Charlie (January 14, 2019). "Trump Says He Alone Can Do It. His Attorney General Nominee Usually Agrees". The New York Times. ISSN 0362-4331.
57. Attorney General Barr: BLM and Antifa Are "Essentially Bolsheviks" - The New American
58. https://www.foxnews.com/politics/barr-accuses-media-of-projecting-a-narrative-in-coverage.
59. Peiserc, Jaclyn (August 10, 2020). "'Their tactics are fascistic': Barr slams Black Lives Matter, accuses the left of 'tearing down the system'". Washington Post.
60. Collins, Ben (September 1, 2020). "Trump's 'plane loaded with thugs' conspiracy theory matches months-old rumor". NBC News; Zadrodzny, Brandy; Collins, Ben (June 2, 2020). "False antifa rumors about a suburban invasion take over neighborhood social media apps". NBC News.
61. Wolfe, Jan (September 2, 2020). "U.S. Attorney General Barr says antifa 'flying around' U.S. to incite violence". U.S.News. Reuters.
62. MacFarquhar, Neil; Feuer, Alan; Goldman, Adam (June 11, 2020). "Federal Arrests Show No Sign That Antifa Plotted Protests". The New York Times.

63   Swan, Betsy Woodruff (September 4, 2020). "DHS draft document: White supremacists are greatest terror threat". POLITICO.

64   Gurman, Aruna Viswanatha and Sadie (September 16, 2020). "Barr Tells Prosecutors to Consider Charging Violent Protesters With Sedition". The Wall Street Journal; Benner, Katie (September 16, 2020). "Barr Told Prosecutors to Consider Sedition Charges for Protest Violence". The New York Times. ISSN 0362-4331.

65   Benner, Katie (June 7, 2020). "Barr Says There Is No Systemic Racism in Policing". The New York Times. ISSN 0362-4331.

66   See 18 U.S.C. § 2384.

67   Clark, Dartunorro (September 2, 2020). "Barr denies systemic racism in police shootings of Black men". NBC News.

68   "William Barr: Unbound". The Washington Post. 2020.

69   Cobler, Paul (September 4, 2020). "AG Barr's claim of 1,700 fraudulent ballots in 2017 Dallas City Council race not true, prosecutor says". Dallas News; O'Rourke, Ciara (September 23, 2020). "Fact-checking William Barr on fraudulent ballots in Texas". Austin American-Statesman; Zapotosky, Matt (September 3, 2020). "Barr claims a man collected 1,700 ballots and filled them out as he pleased. Prosecutors say that's not what happened". The Washington Post.

70   ibid.

71   CNN, Daniel Dale, Tara Subramaniam and Holmes Lybrand (September 3, 2020). "Fact- checking Attorney General William Barr's claims on voter fraud, election interference and Jacob Blake". CNN; Gardner, Amy (June 2, 2020). "Election officials contradict Barr's assertion that counterfeit mail ballots produced by a foreign country are a 'real' worry". The Washington Post.

72   Cheney, Kyle; Bertrand, Natasha (September 3, 2020). "Intel officials contradict Trump on voting by mail". Politico.

73   6  Cohen, Zachary (September 4, 2020). "Intelligence bulletin warns Russia amplifying false claims mail-in voting will lead to widespread fraud". CNN.

74   Lambe, Jerry (September 15, 2020). "Bill Barr Pushes 'Wild' and 'Fanciful' Felonious Postman Hypothetical, Says Liberals Are the Ones Projecting 'Bullsh*t'". lawandcrime.com.

75   Kalmbacher, Colin (October 1, 2020). "Nearly 2,000 DOJ Alumni Sign Letter with Dire Warning: Bill Barr Is Working to Rig 2020 Election for Trump". lawandcrime.com.

76   Corasaniti, Nick; Epstein, Reid J.; Rutenberg, Jim (November 11, 2020). "The Times Called Officials in Every State: No Evidence of Voter Fraud". The New York Times.

77   Zapotosky, Matt; Barrett, Devlin (November 10, 2020). "Barr clears Justice Dept. to investigate alleged voting irregularities as Trump makes unfounded fraud claims". The Washington Post.

78   ibid.

79   Zapotosky, Matt; Hamburger, Tom (November 13, 2020). "Federal prosecutors assigned to monitor election malfeasance tell Barr they see no evidence of substantial irregularities". The Washington Post.

80  Balsamo, Michael (December 1, 2020). "Disputing Trump, Barr says no widespread election fraud". apnews.

81  policy by not disclosing during the campaign that Joe Biden's son Hunter had been under criminal investigation since 2018.90

82  Duster, Chandelis (June 23, 2020). "65 faculty members from AG Barr's law school alma mater say he has 'failed to fulfill his oath of office'". CNN.

83  ibid.

84  Reuters (June 24, 2020). "U.S. attorney general Barr blasted by Democrats as 'president's fixer'". CBC News.

85  Boyer, Dave. "Mike Pompeo from Jerusalem Praises Trump Foreign Policy in DNC Convention Speech." The Washington Times, The Washington Times, 25 Aug. 2020, www.washingtontimes.com/news/2020/aug/25/mike-pompeo-jerusalem-praises-trump-foreign-policy/.

86  The Latest: Pompeo was on Trump-Ukraine call, officials say ArchivedOctober 2, 2019, at the Wayback Machine, Wichita Eagle, Associated Press, September 30, 2019.

87  ibid.

88  Wong, Edward; Vogel, Kenneth P. (November 23, 2019). "New Documents Reveal Details of Pompeo's Role in Ukraine Affair". The New York Times.

89  Cohen, Zachary (October 23, 2019). "Judge orders State Department to release Ukraine records in 30 days". CNN.

90  ibid.

91  Panetta, Grace. "Mike Pompeo says US has a 'duty' to investigate the bogus conspiracy the- ory at the center of the Ukraine scandal". Business Insider. Archived from the original on December 5, 2019.

92  Grenoble, Ryan. "Mike Pompeo Looks Ready To Accept Saudi Arabia's Spin On Jamal Khashoggi's Fate." HuffPost, HuffPost, 16 Oct. 2018, www.huffpost.com/entry/mike-pompeo-trump-saudi-arabia-khashoggi_n_5bc60262e4b0a8f17ee65405?ww.

93  Chappell, Bill (November 10, 2020). "Pompeo Promises 'A Smooth Transition To A Second Trump Administration'". NPR.

94  "Pruitt v. EPA: 14 Challenges of EPA Rules by the Oklahoma Attorney General." The New York Times, The New York Times, 15 Jan. 2017, www.nytimes.com/interactive/2017/01/14/us/politics/document-Pruitt-v-EPA-a-Compilation-of-Oklahoma-14.html.

95  Leven, Rachel, et al. "A Behind-the-Scenes Look at Scott Pruitt's Dysfunctional EPA." Center for Public Integrity, 20 Apr. 2018, publicintegrity.org/environment/a-behind-the-scenes-look-at-scott-pruitts-dysfunctional-epa/.

96  Levy, Jonathan, et al. "Opinion: As Pruitt Flies First Class, EPA Barely Gets Off The Ground." HuffPost, HuffPost, 27 Mar. 2018, www.huffpost.com/entry/ opinion-levy-pruitt-first-class_n_5ab70c53e4b054d118e37aa3

97  Benen, Steve. "The Soundproof Phone Booth for the EPA's Pruitt Wasn't Legal." MSNBC, NBCUniversal News Group, 25 Sept. 2020, www.msnbc.com/rachel-maddow-show/the-soundproof-phone-booth-the-epas-pruitt-wasnt-legal-msna1090831.

98    https://www.washingtonpost.com/national/health-science/trump-epa-head-steps-down-after- wave-of-ethics-management-scandal. 07 16 18.

99    ibid.

100   Dennis, Brady, and Juliet Eilperin. "Scott Pruitt Enlisted an EPA Aide to Help His Wife Find a Job - with Chick-Fil-A." The Washington Post, WP Company, 13 June 2018, www.washingtonpost.com/national/health-science/scott-pruitt-enlisted-an-epa-aide-to-help-his-wife-find-a-job--at-chick-fil-a/2018/06/05/b798e4e4-5eac-11e8-9ee3-49d6d4814c4c_story.html.

101   "Scott Pruitt Had EPA Staffer Inquire about Getting His Wife a Chick-Fil-A Franchise." CNBC, CNBC, 8 June 2018, www.cnbc.com/2018/06/05/scott-pruitt-sought-chick-fil-a-franchise-for-wife-had-epa-aide-help.html.

102   ibid.

103   Pruitt spent $3,230 at jewelry store, emails show – ThinkProgress 06 01 18.

104   Trump says EPA is doing 'really, really well' as scandals continue to mount around Scott Pruitt – ThinkProgress

105   ibid.

106   ibid.

107   https://archive.thinkprogress.org/pruitt-scandals-trump-fema-f1746162d6ff/

108   "READ: Scott Pruitt's Resignation Letter | CNN Politics." CNN, Cable News Network, 5 July 2018, www.cnn.com/2018/07/05/politics/scott-pruitt-resignation-letter/index.html.

109   "Carper Statement on Scott Pruitt's Resignation." United States Senator Tom Carper, 5 July 2018, www.carper.senate.gov/public/index.cfm/pressreleases?ID=84261AD2-5585-4655-AD5A-BA114545416D.

110   Kamisar, Ben. "Carson not interested in serving in Trump administration". The Hill.

111   Easley, Jonathan; Hagen, Lisa (November 22, 2016). "Carson: I've been offered job at HUD". The Hill.

112   Warmbrodt, Zachary (January 24, 2017). "Banking Committee approves Ben Carson nomination". Politico.

113   Joe Guillen, Ben Carson won't commit to restoring any Detroit cuts, Detroit Free Press (March 16, 2017).

114   Ben Lane, Here's what Ben Carson thinks about the proposed $6.2 billion HUD budget cut, HousingWire (March 20, 2017).

115   DelReal, Jose A. (April 3, 2017). "Carson assures advocates that White House will include housing funding in infrastructure bill". The Washington Post.

116   Lejeune, Tristan (March 2, 2020). "White House adds VA secretary, CMS chief to coronavirus task force". TheHill.

117   Pramuk, Kevin Breuninger,Jacob (November 9, 2020). "HUD Secretary Ben Carson tests positive for coronavirus". CNBC.

118   Carson says he's 'out of the woods' after battling COVID-19". ABC News.

119   Gross, Elana Lyn. "Ben Carson Says He Took Oleandrin, An FDA-Rejected Supplement Touted By MyPillow Founder, As Coronavirus Treatment". Forbes.

120  Stracqualursi, Veronica (November 20, 2020). "Ben Carson says he was 'desperately ill' from Covid but is now 'out of the woods'". CNN.

121  Glenn Thrush (February 27, 2018). "Ben Carson's HUD, Planning Cuts, Spends $31,000 on Dining Set for His Office". The New York Times.

122  Rene Marsh (February 27, 2018). "HUD staffer files complaint over Ben Carson office redecoration". CNN.

123  Rene Marsh; Gregory Wallace. "Emails show Ben, Candy Carson selected $31,000 dining set". CNN.

124  Glenn Thrush (March 20, 2018). "Ben Carson Defends Buying $31,000 Dining Set to Congress: 'I Left It to My Wife'". The New York Times.

125  Trump's Very Swampy Pardon of a Ben Carson Crony – Mother Jones 12/20.

126  Ben Carson Stands by 'Best Friend' Who Pleaded Guilty to Healthcare Fraud." The Guardian, Guardian News and Media, 13 Nov. 2015, www.theguardian.com/us-news/2015/nov/13/ben-carson-alfonso-costa-healthcare-fraud.

127  ibid.

128  ibid.

129  Wilbur Ross, Trump's Most Corrupt Cabinet Official, Has Got To Go | The Nation 09 10 19, Joan Wash

130  Snyder, Giles (July 13, 2018). "Criticism from Ethics Watchdog Leads Commerce Secretary Ross To Sell Remaining Stocks". NPR.

131  Temple-West, Patrick. "Ross' Financial Disclosure Rejected by Government Ethics Watchdog." POLITICO, 20 Feb. 2019, www.politico.com/story/2019/02/19/wilbur-ross-financial-disclosure-1187524.

132  https://www.salon.com/2020/10/30/wilbur-ross-sat...; Fish, Isaac Stone. "Wilbur Ross Remained on Chinese Joint Venture Board While Running U.S.-China Trade War". Foreign Policy.

133  Alexander, Dan. "Wilbur Ross Still Holds Interest In Shipping Fund He Promised To Divest." Forbes, Forbes Magazine, 7 Oct. 2019, www.forbes.com/sites/danalexander/2019/09/16/wilbur-ross-still-holds-interest-in-shipping-fund-he-promised-to-divest/.

134  ibid

135  Flavelle, Christopher, et al. "Commerce Chief Threatened Firings at NOAA After Trump's Dorian Tweets, Sources Say." The New York Times, The New York Times, 9 Sept. 2019, www.nytimes.com/2019/09/09/climate/hurricane-dorian-trump-tweet.html.

136  Commerce Chief Threatened Firings at NOAA After Trump's Dorian Tweets, Sources Say - The New York Times (nytimes.com)

137  https://www.nbcnews.com/politics/politics-news/leaked-documents-show-commerce-secre-tary-concealed-ties-putin-cronies-11 05 17.

138  ibid.

139  "Russian Businessmen, Officials on New U.S. Sanctions List." Reuters, Thomson Reuters, 6 Apr. 2018, www.reuters.com/article/us-usa-russia-sanctions-factbox-idUSKCN1HD22K

140 "U.S. Department of the Treasury." Announcement Of Additional Treasury Sanctions On Russian Government Officials And Entities, 4 May 2021, www.treasury.gov/press-center/press-releases/Pages/jl2369.aspx

141 Wang, Hansi Lo (July 24, 2018). "Commerce Secretary Grew Impatient Over Census Citizenship Question, Emails Reveal". NPR.

142 Lejeune, Tristan (October 24, 2018). "Administration asks judge to delay trial on census citizenship question". The Hill.

143 "Statement From A.G. Underwood On New Court Order In AG's Lawsuit To Protect The Census." Statement From A.G. Underwood On New Court Order In AG's Lawsuit To Protect The Census | New York State Attorney General, ag.ny.gov/press-release/2018/statement-ag-underwood-new-court-order-ags-lawsuit-protect-census.

144 Honan, Edith; Bahrampour, Tara (October 24, 2018). "Judge declines to grant stay in census citizenship trial". The Washington Post.

145 Wines, Michael (January 15, 2019). "Court Blocks Trump Administration From Asking About Citizenship in Census". The New York Times.

146 Andrew Desiderio, House holds William Barr, Wilbur Ross in criminal contempt of Congress, Politico (July 17, 2019).

147 House Holds Barr and Ross in Contempt Over Census Dispute, New York Times (July 17, 2019).

148 Desiderio, Andrew (June 3, 2019). "House Dems to hold Barr, Ross in contempt over census question; The Oversight Committee wants key documents by Thursday". Politico.

149 ibid.

150 ibid.

151 House Holds Barr and Ross in Contempt Over Census Dispute, New York Times (July 17, 2019).

152 Department of Commerce v. New York, No. 18–966, 588 U.S.(2019).

153 ibid.

154 Haag, Matthew (March 2, 2017). "The Interior Secretary, and the Horse He Rode in On". The New York Times.

155 Rein, Lisa (October 24, 2017). "Where's Zinke? The Interior secretary's special flag offers clues". Washington Post.

156 ibid.

157 Ryan Zinke's Official Portrait Is a Final Slap in the Face for Native American Tribes –Mother Jones 12 20

158 Fears, Darryl; Eilperin, Juliet (June 12, 2017). "Interior secretary recommends Trump consider scaling back Bears Ears National Monument". The Washington Post.

159 Ryan Zinke's Official Portrait Is a Final Slap in the Face for Native American Tribes –Mother Jones 12 20

160 ibid.

161 A Guide to the Ryan Zinke Investigations - The New York Times (nytimes.com)10 31 18

162 Interior IG to scrutinize Zinke's beer-making plans - POLITICO Back ButtonSearch IconFilter Icon08 02 18

163 Grandoni, Dino, and Juliet Eilperin. "Inspector General Will Review Zinke's Involvement in Land Deal Backed by Halliburton's Chairman." The Washington Post, WP Company, 29 Apr. 2019, www.washingtonpost.com/news/energy-environment/wp/2018/06/28/ inspector-general-will-review-zinkes-involvement-in-land-deal-backed-by-hallibur- tons-chairman/.

164 Green, Miranda. "Overnight Energy: Zinke Denies Lying to Investigators: Interior Won't Take FOIA Requests during Shutdown: Ocasio-Cortez Makes Pitch for 'Ambitious' Green New Deal." TheHill, 7 Jan. 2019, thehill.com/policy/energy-environment/overnights/423956-overnight-energy-zinke-says-he-didnt-lie-to.

165 ibid.

166 ibid.

167 Bloomberg.com, Bloomberg, www.bloomberg.com/news/articles/2018-11-07/democrats-vow-probe-of-bid-to-oust-investigator-targeting-zinke.

168 Savransky, Rebecca. "Zinke and His Wife Took Security Detail on Vacation to Turkey, Greece: Report." TheHill, 21 Mar. 2018, thehill.com/homenews/administration/379577-zinke-and-his-wife-took-security-detail-on-vacation-to-turkey-greece.

169 Watson, Kathryn. "Zinke Accuses Democrat Who Wants Him to Resign of Being a Drunk." CBS News, CBS Interactive, 30 Nov. 2018, www.cbsnews.com/news/zinke-accuses-democrat-who-wants-him-to-resign-of-being-a-drunk/.

170 Zapotsky, Matt. "Feds investigating whether former Interior Secretary Zinke lied about East Windsor casino - Hartford Courant". courant.com..

171 Juliano, Nick. "Tribe says 'improper political influence' led Zinke to scuttle casino". POLITICO.

172 Interior chief wants to shed 4,000 employees in department shake-up, Washington Post (June 21, 2017).

173 Joe Davidson, Interior's 'unusual' transfer of senior executives spurs official probe, Washington Post (September 12, 2017).

174 Nathan Rott, Climate Scientist Says He Was Demoted For Speaking Out on Climate Change, NPR (July 19, 2017).

175 Joe Davidson, Interior's 'unusual' transfer of senior executives spurs official probe, Washington Post (September 12, 2017).

176 Darryl Fears & Juliet Eilperin, Zinke says a third of Interior's staff is disloyal to Trump and promises 'huge' changes, Washington Post (September 2, 2017).

177 Darryl Fears & Dino Grandoni, The Trump administration has officially clipped the wings of the Migratory Bird Treaty Act, Washington Post (April 13, 2018).

178 Dawsey, Josh, and Juliet Eilperin. "Interior Secretary Zinke Resigns amid Investigations." The Washington Post, WP Company, 16 Dec. 2018, www.washingtonpost.com/national/health-science/interior-secretary-zinke-resigns-amid-investigations/2018/12/15/481f9104-0077-11e9-ad40-cdfd0e0dd65a_story.html.

179 Shaw, Adam. "Ryan Zinke, Secretary of the Interior, Will Leave His Post at End of Year, Trump Says." Fox News, FOX News Network, 15 Dec. 2018, www.foxnews.

180 Valerie Strauss (December 21, 2016), To Trump's education pick, the U.S. public school system is a 'dead end', The Washington Post,

181 Meet Betsy DeVos, the polarizing charter-school advocate Trump has tapped as education secretary". Business Insider.

182 ibid.

183 Zernike, Kate (November 23, 2016). "Betsy DeVos, Trump's Education Pick, Has Steered Money From Public Schools". The New York Times.

184 Her brother, Erik Prince, a former U.S. Navy SEAL officer, is the founder of Blackwater USA.

185 Ponnuru, Ramesh (November 28, 2016). "DeVos and Detroit's Charter Schools". National Review.

186 Henderson, Stephen (December 3, 2016). "Betsy DeVos and the twilight of public education". Detroit Free Press.

187 Zernike, Kate (November 23, 2016). "Betsy DeVos, Trump's Education Pick, Has Steered Money From Public Schools". The New York Times.

188 Wong, Alia (February 7, 2017). "Education Secretary Betsy DeVos Has Already Affected Public Education". The Atlantic.

189 Elving, Ron (February 7, 2017). "Pence Becomes First VP to Break Senate Tie over Cabinet Nomination". NPR.

190 "Betsy DeVos Is Sabotaging the Education Department's Investigation of for-Profit Colleges." Salon, Salon.com, 15 May 2018, www.salon.com/2018/05/14/betsy-devos-sabatoges-education-department-investigation-into-for-profit-colleges/.

191 Ivory, Danielle; Green, Erica; Eder, Steve. "Education Department Unwinds Unit Investigating Fraud at For-Profits". The New York Times.

192 Cowley, Stacy (July 6, 2017). "18 States Sue Betsy DeVos Over Student Loan Protections". The New York Times.

193 Betsy DeVos Loses Student Loan Lawsuit Brought by 19 States". Time.

194 Green, Erica L. (May 15, 2020). "DeVos Funnels Coronavirus Relief Funds to Favored Private and Religious Schools". The New York Times.

195 Associated Press (July 12, 2020). "DeVos downplays risks of return to schools". Chicago Sun-Times.

196 ibid.

197 Cole, Devan (July 12, 2020). "Betsy DeVos won't say if schools should listen to CDC guidelines on reopening". CNN.

198 Devos, Elisabeth P (September 18, 2018). "Public Financial Disclosure Report (OGE Form 278e)" (PDF)

199 Lerner, Meredith (December 3, 2018). "Betsy DeVos' Financial Disclosure Fails to Account for Divestiture of 24 Assets". Citizens for Responsibility and Ethics in Washington.

200 "DeVos used personal emails for work in 'limited' cases, report finds". NBC News.

201 "DeVos under investigation for potentially violating Hatch Act because of FOX Newsinterview". POLITICO.

202 https://www.nytimes.com/2021/03/03/us/politics/elaine-chao-inspector-general-report.html?action=click&module=Spotlight&pgtype=Ho

203 Lipton, Eric, and Michael Forsythe. "Inspector General's Report Cites Elaine Chao for Using Office to Help Family." The New York Times, The New York Times, 3 Mar. 2021, www.nytimes. com/2021/03/03/us/politics/elaine-chao-inspector-general-report.html.

204 ibid.

205 ibid.

206 Laris, Michael. "Ethics Probe Led to Criminal Referral Involving Elaine Chao, Transportation Dept. Inspector General Says." The Washington Post, WP Company, 4 Mar. 2021, www.washingtonpost.com/local/trafficandcommuting/elaine-chao-ig-report/2021/03/03/169d0e36-7c53-11eb-b3d1-9e5aa3d5220c_story.html.

207 Duncan, Ian, and Michael Laris. "Transportation Secretary Elaine Chao's Office Says No 'Nefarious Motive' for Replacing Acting Inspector General." The Washington Post, WP Company, 22 May 2020, www.washingtonpost.com/nation/2020/05/21/transportation-secretary-elaine-chaos-office-says-no-nefarious-motive-replacing-acting-inspector-general/.

208 LeBlanc, Paul. "Transportation Department Watchdog Asked DOJ to Consider Criminal Probe of Then-Secretary Elaine Chao over Ethics Concerns." CNN, Cable News Network, 4 Mar. 2021, edition.cnn.com/2021/03/03/politics/elaine-chao-inspector-general-transportation-department/index.html.

209 Snyder, Tanya. "DeFazio Calls for IG Probe of Chao." POLITICO, 15 Oct. 2019, www.politico.com/newsletters/morning-transportation/2019/10/15/defazio-calls-for-ig-probe-of-chao-780284.

210 Mintz, Sam, and Tanya Snyder. "Elaine Chao Used DOT Staff to Aid Personal Errands, Father's Business, Inspector Finds." POLITICO, POLITICO, 4 Mar. 2021, www.politico.com/news/2021/03/03/elaine-chao-dot-inspector-general-report-473536.

211 ibid.

212 "U.S. DOJ Declined to Investigate Trump Transport Chief after Inspector General Review." Yahoo! News, Yahoo!, news.yahoo.com/u-declined-prosecute-trump-transport-231813076.html.

213 Transportation Secretary Elaine Chao Sells Stock in Highway Supply Company - The New York Times (nytimes.com) 06 13 19.

# Trump's Senior Advisors

1 Witnesses: Kellyanne Conway Punched Man at Inaugural Ball". *The Daily Beast.* January 24, 2017.

2 Chuck Todd to Kellyanne Conway: "Alternative Facts Are Not Facts" | Video | RealClearPolitics 01 22 17

3 de Freytas-Tamura, Kimiko (January 25, 2017). "George Orwell's '1984' Is Suddenly a Best-Seller". *New York Times.*

4   ibid.
5   Nelson, Louis. "Conway: Judge Trump by What's in His Heart, Not What Comes out of His Mouth." POLITICO, 9 Jan. 2017, www.politico.com/story/2017/01/trump-statements-kellyanne-conway-233344.
6   LoBianco, Tom. "Trump Falsely Claims 'Millions of People Who Voted Illegally' Cost Him Popular Vote | CNN Politics." CNN, Cable News Network, 28 Nov. 2016, www.cnn.com/2016/11/27/politics/donald-trump-voter-fraud-popular-vote/index.html.
7   Post, The Washington. "Kellyanne Conway Asks Reporter's Ethnicity as She Defends Trump's Racist Remarks." Oregonlive, 16 July 2019, www.oregonlive.com/nation/2019/07/kellyanne-conway-asks-reporters-ethnicity-as-she-defends-trumps-racist-remarks.html.
8   ibid.
9   ibid.
10  Byers, Dylan (February 22, 2017). "Kellyanne Conway sidelined from TV after Flynn debacle". *CNN* Money.
11  ibid.
12  Byers, Dylan. "Sean Spicer isn't finished". Retrieved March 10, 2017.
13  Resnick, Gideon (February 2, 2017). "Kellyanne Conway Refers to Fake Bowling Green Massacre". *The Daily Beast*.
14  Schmidt, Samantha (February 3, 2017). "Kellyanne Conway cites 'Bowling Green massacre' that never happened to defend travel ban". *The Washington Post*.
15  Engel, Pamela, "*CNN* fires back at Sean Spicer: We have not 'walked back' comments on Kellyanne Conway's credibility, *Business Insider*, February 7, 2017,
16  Rubin, Jennifer (February 15, 2017). "Can we start ignoring whatever Conway and Spicer say?". *The Washington Post*.
17  Morning Joe" bans Trump aide Kellyanne Conway: She's not credible anymore". *New York Daily News*. February 15, 2017.
18  ibid.
19  Why Kellyanne Conway Hasn't Been on TV Lately"
20  Touchberry, Ramsey. "Republicans Appear to Not Understand the Hatch Act in Defending Kellyanne Conway." Newsweek, Newsweek, 26 June 2019, www.newsweek.com/hatch-act-kellyanne-conway-republican-hearing-1446110.
21  Solender, Andrew. "Here's Why Trump Officials Rarely Face Penalties For Hatch Act Violations." Forbes, Forbes Magazine, 27 Aug. 2020, www.forbes.com/sites/andrewsolender/2020/08/26/heres-why-trump-officials-rarely-face-penalties-for-hatch-act-violations/.
22  "5 CFR 2635.702 - Use of public office for private gain". Retrieved March 10, 2017.
23  Oh, Inae, Did Kellyanne Conway Just Break Federal Ethics Rules by Promoting Ivanka Trump's Clothing Line?, *Mother Jones*, February 9, 2017.
24  Hutzler, Alexandra. "Kellyanne Conway Violated the Hatch Act 60 Times, Ethics Watchdog Claims in New Lawsuit." Newsweek, Newsweek, 27 Dec. 2019, www.newsweek.com/ethics-watchdog-files-lawsuit-over-kellyanne-conway-hatch-act-violations-1479364.

25  Hutzler, Alexandra. "Kellyanne Conway Violated the Hatch Act 60 Times, Ethics Watchdog Claims in New Lawsuit." Newsweek, Newsweek, 27 Dec. 2019, www.newsweek.com/ethics-watchdog-files-lawsuit-over-kellyanne-conway-hatch-act-violations-1479364.

26  *NBC News*, Did Kellyanne Conway's Ivanka Trump Fashion Line Plug Violate Ethics Rules?, February 9, 2017.

27  Pérez-Peña, Richard, and Rachel Abrams, "Kellyanne Conway Promotes Ivanka Trump Brand, Raising Ethics Concerns", *New York Times*, February 9, 2017.

28  ibid.

29  *ABC News*, Legal Experts: Conway Violated Ethics Rules in TV Endorsement of Ivanka Trump Brand. February 9, 2017.

30  Trump counselor Conway violates ethics laws, congressional leaders say,"MarketWatch, February 9, 2017

31  ibid.

32  Freking, Kevin; Superville, Darlene. "Federal Watchdog Agency Says White House Should Fire Kellyanne Conway for Violating the Hatch Act". *Associated Press*.

33  "Federal watchdog agency recommends removal of Kellyanne Conway from federal office for violating the Hatch Act". *Washington Post*.

34  Samuels, Brett. "Kellyanne Conway dismisses Hatch Act violation: 'Let me know when the jail sentence starts'". *The Hill*.

35  Vazquez, Maegan (June 14, 2019). "Trump won't fire Conway despite federal agency recommendation". *CNN*.

36  Kwong, Jessica (June 26, 2019). "Kellyanne Conway had more Hatch Act violation reports filed against her than anyone else in 30 years". *Newsweek*

37  Darby, Luke. "Kellyanne Conway's Kid Is an Anti-Trump Leftist TikTokker". *GQ*.

38  ibid.

39  @claudiamconwayy (July 3, 2020). "imagine mocking a teenage environmentalist who is literally paving the way for climate change efforts. so sad. he really is a horrible person" (Tweet) – via Twitter.

40  "https://twitter.com/claudiamconwayy/status/1295330656151654400". Twitter.

41  @JayShams (June 30, 2020). "Claudia is doing a TikTok live now and taking questions from people. ""Do your parents get along?' Uh, I guess."" (Tweet) – via Twitter.

42  Evans, Greg. "George & Kellyanne Conway Tell Journalists To Stay Away From Daughter Claudia; She Doesn't Take It Well". Deadline.

43  Elliott, Philip; Miller, Zeke (November 18, 2016). "Inside Donald Trump's Chaotic Transition". Time.

44  Colvin, Jill (November 13, 2016). "Trump puts flame-throwing outsider on the inside". *Associated Press*.

45  Mayer, Jane (November 18, 2018) "New Evidence Emerges of Steve Bannon and Cambridge Analytica's Role in Brexit". *The New Yorker*

46  Posner, Sarah (August 22, 2016). "How Donald Trump's New Campaign Chief Created an Online Haven for White Nationalists". *Mother Jones*.

47. Corn, David & Vicens, AJ (November 18, 2016). "Here's Evidence Steve Bannon Joined a Facebook Group That Posts Racist Rants and Obama Death Threats". *Mother Jones*.
48. Jessica Taylor (November 20, 2016). "Energized By Trump's Win, White Nationalists Gather To 'Change The World'". *National Public Radio*.
49. Grynbaum, Michael M. (January 26, 2017). "Trump Strategist Stephen Bannon Says Media Should 'Keep Its Mouth Shut'". *New York Times*.
50. Bennett, Brian (January 29, 2017). "Travel ban is the clearest sign yet of Trump advisors' intent to reshape the country". *Los Angeles Times*.
51. Donald Trump's G20 speech owed a lot to Putin". *The Economist*. July 13, 2017.
52. Concha, Joe (February 2, 2017). "Time cover labels Bannon 'The Great Manipulator'". *The Hill*.
53. Von Drehle, David (February 13, 2017). "The second most powerful man in the world?". Time. pp. 24–31.0.
54. White House Waivers May Have Violated Ethics Rules". *The New York Times*.
55. "Ex-Breitbart employee: There's now a 'concrete paper trail' showing Steve Bannon still runs Breitbart". The Raw Story.
56. "Democrats Accuse Wilbur Ross of Voter Suppression in Hearing on 2020 Census Citizenship Question." Congresswoman Carolyn Maloney, 9 Oct. 2020, maloney.house.gov/media-center/in-the-news/democrats-accuse-wilbur-ross-of-voter-suppression-in-hearing-on-2020-census.
57. ibid.
58. Democrats accuse Wilbur Ross of voter suppression in hearing on 2020 census citizenship question, *CBS News*, Camilo Montoya-Galvez, March 14, 2019.
59. Phippen, J. Weston (January 29, 2017). "Trump Gives Stephen Bannon Access to the National Security Council". *The Atlantic*.
60. Thrush, Glenn; Haberman, Maggie (January 29, 2017). "Bannon Is Given Security Role Usually Held for Generals". *The New York Times*.
61. ibid.
62. "Donald Trump." Washington Examiner, www.washingtonexaminer.com/republicans-dismayed-by-trumps-behavior-in-charlottesville-aftermath.
63. Thrush, Glenn; Haberman, Maggie (August 12, 2017). "Trump's Remarks on Charlottesville Violence Are Criticized as Insufficient". *The New York Times*.
64. Haberman, Maggie; Thrush, Glenn (August 14, 2017). "Bannon in Limbo as Trump Faces Growing Calls for the Strategist's Ouster". *The New York Times*.
65. "NAACP Condemns 'Unite The Right' Hate Rally in Charlottesville, Virginia". NAACP. August 12, 2017.
66. Choi, David (September 2, 2017). "Trump reportedly calls Steve Bannon on his personal phone when John Kelly isn't around". *Business Insider*
67. Parker, Ashley; Rucker, Philip (October 21, 2017). "'The President's Wingman': Absent in the West Wing, Bannon Stays Close to Trump". *The Washington Post*.
68. Chico Harlan (December 25, 2018). "With support from Steve Bannon, a medieval monastery could become a populist training ground". *Washington Post*.

69  ibid.
70  Green, Joshua (December 11, 2017). "How Steve Bannon Rescued Roy Moore's Campaign Against All Odds". *Bloomberg*.
71  Oliphant, James. "Trump Ally Bannon Campaigns for Moore in Alabama." Reuters, Thomson Reuters, 6 Dec. 2017, in.reuters.com/article/usa-election-alabama-bannon-idINKBN1E008Y.
72  Smith, Emily (August 11, 2018). "Steve Bannon trying to get on disgraced Jeffrey Epstein's good side". *Page Six*.
73  WATCH: Embattled Roy Moore loses Alabama Senate race (iheartradio.ca)
74  "Steve Bannon says Ivanka Trump is 'dumb as a brick'". *Business Insider*.
75  Maegan Vazquez. "Bannon: 2016 Trump Tower meeting was 'treasonous'". *CNN*.
76  Higgins, Tucker (January 3, 2018). "Bannon says Trump Tower meeting was 'treasonous,' Russia probe will 'crack Don Junior like an egg'". *CNBC*.
77  Anapol, Avery (January 3, 2018). "Bannon warned Russia probe would focus on money laundering: report". *The Hill*.
78  "Steve Bannon says Ivanka Trump is 'dumb as a brick'". *Business Insider*. Retrieved January 4, 2018.
79  Helmore, Edward (May 29, 2019). "Bannon described Trump Organization as 'criminal enterprise', Michael Wolff book claims". *The Guardian*.
80  Alex Wayne and Jennifer Jacobs (January 3, 2018). "Trump Says Bannon 'Lost His Mind' After Leaving White House". *Bloomberg* L.P.
81  Darren Samuelsohn & Josh Gerstein, Steve Bannon: Roger Stone was our unused WikiLeaks 'access point', *Politico*
82  Mangan, Kevin Breuninger,Dan (November 15, 2019). "Trump ally Roger Stone found guilty of lying to Congress, witness tampering". *CNBC*.
83  Baker, Peter; Haberman, Maggie; LaFraniere, Sharon (July 10, 2020). "Trump Commutes Sentence of Roger Stone in Case He Long Denounced". *The New York Times*.
84  'Karma is a b****': Roger Stone responds to Steve Bannon's arrest, *The Independent*, James Crump.
85  Barone, Vincent (June 3, 2020). "Mysterious 'Federal State of New China' banners seen on planes over NYC". *New York Post*
86  Matt Zapotosky, Josh Dawsey & Rosalind S. Helderman, Steve Bannon charged with defrauding donors in private effort to raise money for Trump's border wall, *Washington Post* (August 20, 2020).
87  Former Trump Campaign Boss Steve Bannon Indicted for Fraud in NY". NBC Boston.
88  Torbati, Yeganeh (August 24, 2020). "In an investigation tied to private border wall, federal prosecutors have Steve Bannon's murky noNPRofit in their sights". The Texas Tribune.
89  Cassidy, John (August 21, 2020). "From Paul Manafort to Steve Bannon, a Brief History of MAGA Money-Grubbing". *The New Yorker*.
90  Alex Horton (August 20, 2020). "The surprising mission of the Postal Service police who arrested Stephen Bannon". *Washington Post*.

91. Zeffman, Henry (August 22, 2020). "Donald Trump Jr builds a wall between himself and Steve Bannon". The Times.
92. Dawsey, Josh; Johnson, Eliana (April 13, 2017). "Trump's got a new favorite Steve". *Politico*.
93. Perez, Evan; Brown, Pamela; Liptak, Kevin (January 30, 2017). "Inside the confusion of the Trump executive order and travel ban". *CNN*.
94. Blitzer, Jonathon (October 13, 2017). "How Stephen Miller Single-Handedly Got the U.S. to Accept Fewer Refugees". *The New Yorker*
95. Shear, Michael D.; Benner, Katie (June 18, 2018). "How Anti-Immigration Passion Was Inflamed From the Fringe". *The New York Times*.
96. Davis, Julie Hirschfeld; Shear, Michael D. (June 16, 2018). "How Trump Came to Enforce a Practice of Separating Migrant Families". *The New York Times*.
97. Sanders, Katie (February 12, 2017). "White House senior adviser repeats baseless claim about busing illegal voters in New Hampshire". *PolitiFact*.
98. Schmidt, Michael S.; Haberman, Maggie (September 1, 2017). "Mueller Has Early Draft of Trump Letter Giving Reasons for Firing Comey". *The New York Times*.
99. chmidt, Michael S.; Haberman, Maggie (September 1, 2017). "Mueller Has Early Draft of Trump Letter Giving Reasons for Firing Comey". *The New York Times*.
100. Brown, Pamela; Borger, Gloria; Perez, Evan (November 9, 2017). "Mueller interviews top White House aide". *CNN*.
101. Global compact for migration". Refugees and Migrants. April 5, 2017.
102. "White House Official Who Advocated for Refugees Sacked and Escorted From Office". Foreign Policy.
103. ibid.
104. Shear, Michael D. (August 13, 2018). "Stephen Miller's Uncle Calls Him a Hypocrite in an Online Essay". *The New York Times*.
105. Glosser, David S. (August 13, 2018). "Stephen Miller Is an Immigration Hypocrite. I Know Because I'm His Uncle". *Politico*.
106. A Familiar Force Nurtures Trump's Instincts on Immigration: Stephen Miller".
107. Trump's immigration push is Stephen Miller's dream come true". *POLITICO*.
108. Lind, Dara (November 7, 2018). "Trumpism doesn't win majorities. And Trump doesn't care". *Vox*.
109. Kullgren, Ian (January 7, 2018). "White House adviser Stephen Miller unloads on *CNN*". *Politico*.
110. Manchester, Julia (January 7, 2018). "Dramatic exchange between White House's Miller, *CNN*'s Tapper debated online". *The Hill*.
111. Hart, Benjamin (January 7, 2018). "Jake Tapper Cuts Off Stephen Miller After Deeply Strange Interview". New York.
112. Stephen Miller And White Nationalism : *NPR* 1 14 19
113. Dickerson, Caitlin; Shear, Michael D. (May 3, 2020). "Before Covid-19, Trump Aide Sought to Use Disease to Close Borders". *The New York Times*.

114  ibid.
115  https://www.mediaite.com/news/im-angry-and...
116  Shear, Michael D.; Haberman, Maggie; Weiland, Noah; LaFraniere, Sharon; Mazzetti, Mark (December 31, 2020). "Trump's Focus as the Pandemic Raged: What Would It Mean for Him?". *The New York Times*.
117  "Stephen Miller reveals Trump's immigration agenda if he's re-elected". *NBC News*.
118  Samuels, Brett (December 14, 2020). "Stephen Miller: 'Alternate' electors will keep Trump election challenge alive". *The Hill*.
119  ibid.
120  WH's Stephen Miller: "An Alternate *Slate* Of Electors" Will Vote Today, Challenges "Not Over" Until January 20 | Video | RealClearPolitics11 14 20
121  ibid.
122  Vladimirov, Nikita (April 15, 2017). "Report: Kushner found Trump advisor Navarro by browsing Amazon". *The Hill*.
123  "New White Paper on Donald J. Trump's Economic Plan". www.donaldjtrump.com.
124  Vladimirov, Nikita (April 15, 2017). "Report: Kushner found Trump advisor Navarro by browsing Amazon". *The Hill*.
125  Trump's attack dog on trade". *Politico*.
126  Trump's Muse on U.S. Trade with China". *The New Yorker*. October 12, 2016.
127  "Cooking up an economic policy". *The Economist*.
128  Johnson, Simon (September 30, 2016). "Trump's Magical Economic Thinking". Project Syndicate.
129  Watkins, Eli. "Peter Navarro says 'there's a special place in hell' for Justin Trudeau". *CNN*.
130  Higgins, Kayla Tausche,Tucker (May 31, 2019). "Mnuchin and Lighthizer opposed Trump tariffs on Mexico, source says". *CNBC*.
131  "Infrastructure report" (PDF). peternavarro.com.
132  Mufson, Steven (January 17, 2017). "Economists pan infrastructure plan championed by Trump nominees". *The Washington Post*
133  Shelbourne, Mallory (February 12, 2018). "White House releases 55-page, $1.5 trillion infrastructure plan". *The Hill*.
134  Weaver, Dustin (March 10, 2018). "Trump's infrastructure push hits wall in Congress". *The Hill*.
135  Haberman, Maggie (April 6, 2020). "Trade Adviser Warned White House in January of Risks of a Pandemic". *The New York Times*.
136  Swan, Jonathan; Talev, Margaret (April 7, 2020). "Navarro memos warning of mass coronavirus death circulated in January". *Axios*.
137  Steck, Em; Kaczynski, Andrew. "Navarro publicly said Americans had 'nothing to worry about' while privately warning coronavirus could cost lives and dollars". *CNN*.

138  Swan, Jonathan. "Inside the epic White House blowup over "game-changer" hydroxychloroquine". *Axios*.

139  ibid.

140  McDonald, Jessica (July 9, 2020). "Navarro Doesn't Give Full Picture On Hydroxychloroquine". FactCheck.org.

141  https://www.foxnews.com/politics/trade-adviser-peter-navarro-tears-into-fauci-in-blistering-op-ed-wrong-about-everything. 07 15 20.

142  ibid.

143  Knutson, Jacob. "White House economic adviser claims lockdowns will kill "many more" Americans than coronavirus". *Axios*.

144  Callahan, Patricia; Rotella, Sebastian (September 1, 2020). "The Trump Administration Is Backing Out of a $647 Million Ventilator Deal After *ProPublica* Investigated the Price". *ProPublica*.

145  Lynch, David J.; Leonnig, Carol D.; Stein, Jeff; Dawsey, Josh (September 2, 2020). "Tactics of fiery White House trade adviser draw new scrutiny as some of his pandemic moves unravel". *Washington Post*.

146  Walsh, Joe. "White House Advisor Peter Navarro Releases Dubious Voter Fraud Report". *Forbes*.

147  "This might be the most embarrassing document created by a White House staffer". Philip Bump, *The Washington Post*. 12 18 2020.

148  ibid.

149  Bump, Philip (December 18, 2020). "This might be the most embarrassing document created by a White House staffer". *The Washington Post*.

150  Argento, Mike, and Dylan Segelbaum. "Witness in Pa. Election Fraud Suit from York Is a Ghost Hunter with a Long Criminal Record." York Daily Record, York Daily Record, 10 Dec. 2020, www.ydr.com/story/news/2020/12/08/witness-pa-election-fraud-suit-ghost-hunter-long-criminal-record/6496500002/.

151  Shuham, Matt. "Peter Navarro Puts Out 'Immaculate Deception' Report Rehashing Debunked Trump Complaints." Talking Points Memo, 17 Dec. 2020, talkingpointsmemo.com/news/peter-navarro-puts-out-immaculate-deception-report-rehashing-debunked-trump-complaints.

152  Dunn, Adrienne. "Fact Check: Hugo Chávez's Family Does Not Own Dominion Voting Systems." USA Today, Gannett Satellite Information Network, 18 Dec. 2020, www.usatoday.com/story/news/factcheck/2020/12/18/fact-check-hugo-chavezs-family-does-not-own-part-dominion-voting-systems/3926344001/.

153  Bump, Philip. "Analysis | This Might Be the Most Embarrassing Document Created by a White House Staffer." The Washington Post, WP Company, 19 Jan. 2021, www.washingtonpost.com/politics/2020/12/18/this-might-be-most-embarrassing-document-created-by-white-house-staffer/.

## All the President's Liars

1  Spicer promises honesty as Trump's spokesman | TheHill

2   Nguyen, Tina. "Sean Spicer's Agony Will Never End – to His Boss's Delight". *Vanity Fair*.
3   Donald Trump's inaugural crowds don't quite measure up to Barack Obama's - *The Washington Post*
4   ibid.
5   "Trump's Inauguration Crowd: Sean Spicer's Claims versus the Evidence." The Guardian, Guardian News and Media, 22 Jan. 2017, www.theguardian.com/us-news/2017/jan/22/trump-inauguration-crowd-sean-spicers-claims-versus-the-evidence.
6   Alderman, Julie. "The Lies of Sean Spicer." Media Matters for America, www.mediamatters.org/new-york-times/lies-sean-spicer.
7   Collinson, Stephen. "Analysis: New US Intel Report Shows Russia, Trump and GOP Acolytes Have Same Goals." CNN, Cable News Network, 17 Mar. 2021, www.cnn.com/2021/03/17/politics/trump-russia-elections/index.html.
8   Swoyer, Alex. "James Comey: Trump Briefed on Dossier Salacious Parts Only." AP NEWS, Associated Press, 19 Dec. 2018, apnews.com/bdb6fde269f59430cf-b8a03dd846e092.
9   Williams, Katie Bo. "Trump Compares Intel Leaks to Nazi Germany." TheHill, 11 Jan. 2017, thehill.com/policy/national-security/313796-trump-compares-intel-leaks-to-nazi-germany.
10  ibid.
11  Stelter, Brian (January 21, 2017). "White House press secretary attacks media for accurately reporting inauguration crowds". *CNN*.
12  Makarechi, Kia. "Trump Spokesman's Lecture on Media Accuracy Is Peppered With Lies". *Vanity Fair*.
13  Graham, David A. "'Alternative Facts': The Needless Lies of the Trump Administration". *The Atlantic*.
14  Feldman, Josh (January 22, 2017). "Chris Wallace Grills Priebus: 'How Does Arguing About Crowd Size' Help the American People?". Mediaite.
15  Jaffe, Alexandra (January 22, 2017). "Kellyanne Conway: Spicer 'gave alternative facts' on inauguration crowd". *NBC News*.
16  "AP FACT CHECK: White House Spokesman Sean Spicer Gets Election Facts Wrong." Talking Points Memo, 25 Jan. 2017, talkingpointsmemo.com/news/fact-check-seanspicer-election-claims.
17  Wines, Michael. "All This Talk of Voter Fraud? Across U.S., Officials Found Next to None." The New York Times, The New York Times, 18 Dec. 2016, www.nytimes.com/2016/12/18/us/voter-fraud.html.
18  White House defends refugee ban, Steve Bannon's spot on National Security Council - *New York Daily News* (nydailynews.com)1/31/17
19  Montanaro, Domenico. "FACT CHECK: Spin Aside, Trump's National Security Council Has A Very Big Change." NPR, NPR, 30 Jan. 2017, www.npr.org/2017/01/30/512489785/fact-check-spin-aside-trumps-national-security-council-has-a-very-big-change.

20. Flores, Reena. "Trump Adds Steve Bannon to National Security Team." CBS News, CBS Interactive, 30 Jan. 2017, www.cbsnews.com/news/donald-trump-adds-steve-bannon-to-nsc-national-security-team/.
21. "White House and CNN Clash over Kellyanne Conway's 'Credibility'." Yahoo! News, Yahoo!, news.yahoo.com/white-house-and-cnn-clash-over-kellyanne-conways-credibility-205252820.html.
22. White House Briefing 2/7/17
23. CNN Twitter 2/7/17
24. Savransky, Rebecca. "Spicer: 'Wrong and Misleading' to Say Gorsuch Called Trump's Attacks on Judges 'Disheartening'." TheHill, 21 Mar. 2017, thehill.com/homenews/administration/325112-spicer-wrong-and-misleading-to-say-gorsuch-called-trumps-attacks-on.
25. White House Briefing 2/9/17
26. *The Washington Post*, 2/9/17.
27. Alderman, Julie. "The Lies of Sean Spicer." Media Matters for America, www.mediamatters.org/new-york-times/lies-sean-spicer.
28. ibid.
29. White House press briefing, 2/21/17.
30. *The Washington Post*, 2/23/17.
31. "'Not about Religion': How Trump Officials Have Attempted a Travel Ban Rebrand." The Guardian, Guardian News and Media, 15 Mar. 2017, www.theguardian.com/us-news/2017/mar/15/trump-administration-travel-ban-muslim-religion.
32. White House press briefing, 2/22/17.
33. See Statement entitled "DONALD J. TRUMP STATEMENT ON PREVENTING MUSLIM IMMIGRATION," website DonaldJTrump.com
34. Donald Trump Wants "Complete Shutdown" Of Muslim Entry to US | Time 12/7/15
35. Media Matters, 2/13/17
36. White House Press Briefing, 3/8/17.
37. "Sean Spicer Wrongly Claims Fox Reporter's Phones Were 'Tapped'." CNNMoney, Cable News Network, money.cnn.com/2017/03/08/media/sean-spicer-james-rosen-claim/index.html.
38. Goldman, Adam. "Justice Dept. Seizes Washington Post's Phone Records." *The New York Times*, The New York Times, 8 May 2021, www.nytimes.com/2021/05/07/us/politics/justice-department-washington-post-phone-records.html.
39. ibid.
40. Martosko, David. "Spicer: Most of Bush's Gitmo Releases Were 'Court-Ordered'." Daily Mail Online, Associated Newspapers, 8 Mar. 2017, www.dailymail.co.uk/news/article-4295246/Spicer-Bush-s-Gitmo-releases-court-ordered.html.
41. White House Press Briefing, 3/8/17.
42. FactCheck.org, March 9, 2017.
43. White House Press Briefing, 3/10/17.

44  "Journalists Outraged by Tillerson's Plan to Travel without Press." *CNNMoney*, Cable News Network, money.cnn.com/2017/03/10/media/rex-tillerson-state-department-no-press/index.html.

45  White House Press Briefing, 3/20/17.

46  Wagner, John. "Spicer: Just the 'Beginning Phase' of Investigating Whether Trump Tower Was Surveilled." The Washington Post, WP Company, 28 Apr. 2019, www.washingtonpost.com/news/post-politics/wp/2017/03/20/spicer-just-the-beginning-phase-of-whether-trump-tower-was-surveilled/.

47  White House Press briefing, 3/28/17.

48  Alderman, Julie. "The Lies of Sean Spicer." Media Matters for America, www.mediamatters.org/new-york-times/lies-sean-spicer.

49  ibid.

50  AP Fact Check, 3/29/17.

51  ibid.

52  Sean Spicer resigns as White House press secretary". *CBS News*. July 21, 2017.

53  Karni, Annie (September 17, 2019). "For Sean Spicer, the Revolving Door Led to a Dance Routine in a Lime Green Shirt". *The New York Times*.

54  https://www.cbsnews.com/news/comey-lost-the-confidence-of-rank-and-file-fbi-employees-says-sara; Shabab, Rebecca (February 5, 2018). "Emails indicate James Comey was well-liked by FBI staffers". *CBS News*.

55  White House spokeswoman Sarah Huckabee Sanders admitted to the special counsel's investigators that she misled the media about why President Trump canned top G-man James Comey 4/18/19

56  ibid.

57  Palmeri, Tara. "Sarah Sanders: 'The president is not a liar'". *Politico*.

58  Blake, Aaron (June 27, 2017). "Sarah Huckabee Sanders lambastes fake news — and then promotes a journalist accused of deceptive videos". *The Washington Post*.

59  Russo, Amy. "Sarah Huckabee Sanders Falsely Claims Trump Has Always Condemned Violence Against Journalists." HuffPost, HuffPost, 22 Feb. 2019, www.huffpost.com/entry/sarah-huckabee-sanders-trump-violence-media_n_5c701de1e-4b00eed08339ca9.

60  "The Latest: Sanders attacks *CNN*, media in briefing". *Associated Press*. June 27, 2017.

61  White House: Women who accused Trump of sexual harassment are lying; Trump to announce Fed pick next week". *CBS News*.

62  "Washington Insider: White House Story On Porter 'Doesn't Add Up'." HuffPost, HuffPost, 14 Feb. 2018, www.huffpost.com/entry/insider-white-house-story-porter_n_5a83bc64e4b0cf06751faa09.

63  Mangan, Dan; Breuninger, Kevin. "FBI director contradicts White House timeline on Rob Porter abuse probe, says agency finished background check last summer". *CNBC*.

64  Coaston, Jane (February 8, 2018). "The White House press office changed its story on Rob Porter 3 times in one day". *Vox*.

65  Liptak, Kevin. "Sarah Sanders Says -- as Far as She Knows -- Trump Didn't Know of Porn Star Payment | CNN Politics." CNN, Cable News Network, 7 Mar. 2018, www.cnn.com/2018/03/07/politics/stormy-daniels-donald-trump-payment/index.html.

66  Fredericks, Bob (May 3, 2018). "Sanders: I didn't know about Trump's 'hush money' payment". *New York Post*.

67  ibid.

68  Cummings, William. "'I'm an honest person,' defensive Sarah Sanders says when grilled about credibility". *USA Today*.

69  Higgins, Tucker. "White House on separating migrant children from parents: 'It's very biblical to enforce the law'". *CNBC*.

70  Sarah Sanders refuses to say press is not 'enemy of the people'". *The Independent*. Retrieved August 2, 2018.

71  "White House drafts more clearance cancellations demanded by Trump". *Washington Post*. Retrieved August 18, 2018.

72  Wise, Justin (August 17, 2018). "Trump aides discussed using security clearance revocations to distract from negative stories: report". TheHill.

73  Stelter, Brian (November 8, 2018). "Reporters condemn White House decision to bar *CNN*'s Acosta". *CNN* Business.

74  White House shares doctored video to support punishment of journalist Jim Acosta". *The Washington Post*.

75  Anapol, Avery. "Reporters Accuse Sanders of Sharing Edited Video of Acosta-Aide Exchange." TheHill, 9 Nov. 2018, thehill.com/homenews/administration/415673-reporters-accuse-sarah-sanders-of-sharing-edited-video-of-acosta-aide.

76  Harwell, Drew (November 9, 2018). "White House shares doctored video to support punishment of journalist Jim Acosta". MSN.

77  Rosenkrantz, Holly. "Sanders Repeats Claim on Terrorists at the Border Refuted by Administration's Own Data." CBS News, CBS Interactive, 7 Jan. 2019, www.cbsnews.com/news/sanders-repeats-claim-on-terrorists-at-the-border-refuted-by-administrations-own-data-chris-wallace-fox-news-sunday/.

78  "Only six immigrants in terrorism database stopped by CBP at southern border from October to March". *NBC News*.

79  Wilstein, Matt (January 6, 2019). "Chris Wallace Shuts Down Sanders' Claim About Terrorists Crossing Border". *The Daily Beast*.

80  Baker, Peter; Rogers, Katie (June 13, 2019). "Sarah Huckabee Sanders Leaving White House at the End of the Month". *The New York Times*.

81  Fabian, Jordan, and Brett Samuels. "Trump: I Told Sanders to Stop Briefings Because Press Covers Her 'Rudely'." TheHill, 22 Jan. 2019, thehill.com/homenews/administration/426394-trump-i-told-sanders-to-stop-briefings-because-press-covers-her.

82  ttps://www.washingtonpost.com/opinions/2018/12/11/sarah-sanders-her-legacy-wish-transparent-honest/

83  Singman, Brooke (April 8, 2020). "Trump names campaign spokeswoman Kayleigh McEnany as new White House press secretary". *Fox News*.

84  Smith, David; Holden, Emily (April 8, 2020). "'We won't see coronavirus here'... and other gems from Trump's new press secretary". *The Guardian*.

85  Panetta, Grace (April 7, 2020). "New White House press secretary Kayleigh McEnany claimed in February that 'we will not see diseases like the coronavirus' come to America". *Business Insider*.

86  Wu, Nicholas (April 8, 2020). "New White House press secretary Kayleigh McEnany takes heat for past comments on Obama, coronavirus". *USA Today*.

87  Nashrulla, Tasneem (March 28, 2017). "This Trump Surrogate Accused Obama Of Golfing After Daniel Pearl's Murder – 6 Years Before He Was Elected President". BuzzFeed News

88  ibid.

89  Farley, Robert; Kiely, Eugene (April 24, 2020). "The White House Spins Trump's Disinfectant Remarks". FactCheck.org

90  Dale, Daniel; Cohen, Marshall; Subramaniam, Tara (May 2, 2020). "Fact check: New White House press secretary makes false claims in first briefing". *CNN*. Atlanta, Georgia: Turner Broadcasting Company.

91  Bump, Philip. "Analysis | McEnany Has Mastered the 'All of the Credit, None of the Blame' Approach to the Pandemic." The Washington Post, WP Company, 2 Dec. 2020, www.washingtonpost.com/politics/2020/12/02/mcenany-has-mastered-all-credit-none-blame-approach-pandemic/.

92  Smith, David (May 1, 2020). "Trump 'cannot tell a lie' – but can Kayleigh McEnany, his new press secretary?". *The Guardian*.

93  Blake, Aaron. "Analysis | Kayleigh McEnany Makes a Thoroughly Trump-Ian Debut." The Washington Post, WP Company, 3 May 2020, www.washingtonpost.com/politics/2020/05/01/kayleigh-mcenany-just-made-thoroughly-trump-ian-debut/.

94  iely, Eugene (May 1, 2020). "White House Press Secretary Repeats Russia Talking Point". FactCheck.

95  Dearen, Jason. "AP Report: Top White House Officials Buried CDC Report, Emails Show." PBS, Public Broadcasting Service, 8 May 2020, www.pbs.org/newshour/politics/ap-report-top-white-house-officials-buried-cdc-report-emails-show.

96  ibid.

97  Dearen, Jason (May 8, 2020). "AP Exclusive: Docs show top WH officials buried CDC report". *Associated Press*.

98  ibid.

99  Baker, Peter; Astor, Maggie (May 26, 2020). "Trump Pushes a Conspiracy Theory That Falsely Accuses a TV Host of Murder". *The New York Times*.

100  Moye, David. "Report: Kayleigh McEnany Voted By Mail 11 Times In Last 10 Years." HuffPost, HuffPost, 27 May 2020, www.huffpost.com/entry/kayleigh-mcenany-mail-voting_n_5eced5dec5b6cce3ddf0ba65.

101  Contorno, Steve (May 27, 2020). "Trump press secretary Kayleigh McEnany has voted by mail 11 times in 10 years". Tampa Bay Times.

102  "McEnany's mission: Stand by, defend, punch back for Trump". *AP News*. June 8, 2020.

103 Watson, Kathryn (June 3, 2020). "White House press secretary compares Trump's church visit to Churchill surveying WWII damage". CBS New

104 ibid.

105 John Greenberg (September 9, 2020). "McEnany says Trump never downplayed the virus. He did, and Woodward's tape explains why". *PolitiFact*.

106 John Greenberg (September 9, 2020). "McEnany says Trump never downplayed the virus. He did, and Woodward's tape explains why". *PolitiFact*.

107 ibid.

108 ibid.

109 Wemple, Erik (September 9, 2020). "Kayleigh McEnany just one-upped Sean Spicer."

110 Lockhart, Joe (September 11, 2020). "Kayleigh McEnany has crossed a line". *CNN*.

111 Kelly, Makena (November 4, 2020). "Trump declares premature victories in battle- ground states on Twitter". The Verge.

112 *FOX News*Cuts Away From Trump News Conference After Kayleigh McEnany Repeats Baseless Fraud Allegations (msn.com)11/09/20

113 ibid.

114 https://www.realclearpolitics.com/video/2020/12/15/*CNN*s_acosta_to_mcenany_isnt_it_hypocritical_for_y

115 Fact checking McEnany's first White House press briefing since Trump's election loss - *CNN*Politics 11/20/20

116 ibid.

117 ibid.

## Trump's Lawyers

1 Hettena, Seth. "What Happened to America's Mayor?" Rolling Stone, Rolling Stone, 6 Nov. 2020, www.rollingstone.com/politics/politics-features/rudy-giuliani-new-york-trump-997712/.

2 Bradner, Eric. "Giuliani on Trump Tape: 'Men at Times Talk like That'." CNN, Cable News Network, 9 Oct. 2016, edition.cnn.com/2016/10/09/politics/rudy-giuliani-donald-trump-state-of-the-union-debate/.

3 "Rudy Giuliani's Claims about Stormy Daniels Payment Conflict with Trump's Past Statements." PBS, Public Broadcasting Service, 3 May 2018, www.pbs.org/newshour/show/rudy-giulianis-claims-about-stormy-daniels-payment-conflict-with-trumps-past-statements.

4 Wise, Justin. "Ex-Trump Homeland Security Adviser Rips Giuliani, Calls Claim Ukraine Hacked DNC a 'Conspiracy Theory'." TheHill, The Hill, 29 Sept. 2019, thehill.com/homenews/administration/463541-ex-trump-homeland-security-adviser-calls-claim-russia-did-not-hack.

5 "Trump Defends Giuliani and Renews Call for the DNC Server." MSNBC, NBCUniversal News Group, 26 May 2021, www.msnbc.com/msnbc/watch/trump-defends-giuliani-and-renews-call-for-the-dnc-server-71375941834.

6. "Text of the Memo of Trump's Conversation with Zelensky." KLAS, KLAS, 25 Sept. 2019, www.8newsnow.com/news/memo-trump-prodded-ukraine-leader-on-biden-claims/.

7. Protess, Ben, and William K. Rashbaum. "Lev Parnas, Giuliani Associate, Faces New Fraud Accusations." The New York Times, The New York Times, 4 Feb. 2021, www.nytimes.com/2021/02/04/nyregion/lev-parnas-fraud-sec.html.

8. Vogel, Kenneth P., et al. "Prosecutors Subpoena Trump Fund-Raisers Linked to Giuliani Associates." The New York Times, The New York Times, 21 Nov. 2019, www.nytimes.com/2019/11/20/us/politics/trump-fund-raisers-subpoenaed.html.

9. Shuster, Simon. "Ukrainian Oligarch Dmitry Firtash Linked to Trump's Circle." Time, Time, 15 Oct. 2019, time.com/5699201/exclusive-how-a-ukrainian-oligarch-wanted-by-u-s-authorities-helped-giuliani-attack-biden/.

10. Bump, Philip. "Analysis | The Complex Network Pushing for Ukraine Dirt - with Rudy Giuliani at Its Center." The Washington Post, WP Company, 16 Jan. 2020, www.washingtonpost.com/politics/2020/01/16/complex-network-pushing-ukraine-dirt-with-rudy-giuliani-its-center/.

11. Giuliani interview goes off the rails (yahoo.com)09 20 19.

12. ibid.

13. Bufkin, Ellie. "Bolton: Rudy Giuliani Is 'a Hand Grenade Who's Going to Blow Everybody up'." Washington Examiner, 15 Oct. 2019, www.washingtonexaminer.com/news/bolton-rudy-giuliani-is-a-hand-grenade-whos-going-to-blow-everybody-up.

14. Burris, Sarah. "Rudy Giuliani's Bizarre COVID-19 Conspiracy Theory: Obama Granted NIH Funds to Wuhan Lab - in 2017." Salon, Salon.com, 27 Apr. 2020, www.salon.com/2020/04/26/rudy-giulianis-bizarre-covid-19-conspiracy-theory-obama-granted-nih-grant-to-wuhan-lab--in-2017_partner/.

15. Rowles, Dustin. "The 'Borat' Sequel Captures Rudy Giuliani In A Compromising Position." UPROXX, UPROXX, 21 Oct. 2020, uproxx.com/viral/rudy-giuliani-captured-compromisiong-borat-sequel/.

16. ibid.

17. Darrah, Nicole. "Trump Lawyer Giuliani Says 'I Was Tucking in My Shirt' in Borat 'Honey Trap'." The Sun, The Sun, 22 Oct. 2020, www.thesun.co.uk/news/12990958/rudy-giuliani-response-borat-seduce-sacha-baron-cohen/.

18. Tomasky, Michael (12/1/2020) "'They Stole that Eletoin from Me' Rudy Giuliani Said Decades Ago." *The New York Times*

19. Bryan, Miles. "From Obscure To Sold Out: The Story Of Four Seasons Total Landscaping In Just 4 Days." NPR, NPR, 11 Nov. 2020, www.npr.org/2020/11/11/933635970/from-obscure-to-sold-out-the-story-of-four-seasons-total-landscaping-in-just-4-d.

20. Hennigan, W.J., and Vera Bergengruen. "Why Trump's Recruitment of Poll Watchers Is Stoking Fears." Time, Time, 22 Oct. 2020, time.com/5902731/trump-poll-watchers/.

21. Man featured at Giuliani press conference is a convicted sex offender (*Politico*.com)11 09 20

22. Friedman, Matt. "Man Featured at Giuliani Press Conference Is a Convicted Sex Offender." Politico PRO, 9 Nov. 2020, www.politico.com/states/new-jersey/story/2020/11/09/man-featured-at-giuliani-press-conference-is-a-sex-offender-1335241.

23  https://www.independent.co.uk/news/world/amerias/...11 20 20

24  Allassan, Fadel. "Giuliani Says He's 'More of a Jew than Soros Is' in Bizarre, Conspiracy-Laden Interview." Axios, 23 Dec. 2019, www.axios.com/giuliani-soros-conspiracy-theories-new-york-magazine-f952e25c-e85a-4de6-bfb2-b2751382a414.html.

25  Durkee, Alison. "Dominion Demands Sidney Powell Retract 'Knowingly Baseless' Voting Machine Conspiracy Theory." Forbes, Forbes Magazine, 17 Dec. 2020, www.forbes.com/sites/alisondurkee/2020/12/17/dominion-demands-sidney-powell-retract-knowingly-baseless-voting-machine-conspiracy-theory/.

26  "Giuliani Claims 'Chavez Approved' Venezuelan Election Technology Was Used to Rig Election." The Independent, Independent Digital News and Media, 19 Nov. 2020, www.independent.co.uk/news/world/americas/us-election-2020/giuliani-trump-election-fraud-venezuela-b1749911.html.

27  Swenson, Ali. "Smartmatic Does Not Own Dominion Voting Systems." AP NEWS, Associated Press, 17 Nov. 2020, apnews.com/article/fact-checking-afs:Content:9740535009?aff_id=1262.

28  Ng, Alfred. "Why Trump's Claims of Massive Voting Machine Fraud Don't Have Merit." CNET, CNET, 17 Nov. 2020, www.cnet.com/news/why-trumps-claims-of-massive-voting-machine-fraud-dont-have-merit/.

29  ibid.

30  ibid.

31  ibid.

32  ibid.

33  ibid.

34  The legal threats and headaches fueling pardon appeals from Trump's family and friends CNN - Breaking News, Latest News and Videos 12 03 20.

35  ibid.

36  Johnson, Glen, and Margaret Talev. "Republicans Discuss Extreme Electoral College Play to Cling to Power." Axios, 11 Nov. 2020, www.axios.com/trump-electoral-college-biden-68d94e27-ace7-4da8-9e22-af7a62fe5149.html.

37  "Giuliani Calls for 'Trial by Combat' at D.C. Rally." Yahoo! News, Yahoo!, news.yahoo.com/giuliani-calls-trial-combat-d-180408746.html.

38  Manegold, Catherine (Sept. 27, 1992) "Rally Puts Police Under New Scrutiny". *The New York Times*

39  In the midst of the Capitol siege, Trump tried calling Tommy Tuberville but got the wrong senator (msn.com) 01 08 21

40  Giuliani calls wrong senator in last-ditch effort to delay certification of Biden's win (msn.com)

41  Honig, Elie. "Opinion: Trump's Bizarro-World 'Elite Strike Force' Legal Challenge Is about to Implode." CNN, Cable News Network, 23 Nov. 2020, www.cnn.com/2020/11/23/opinions/trump-legal-challenge-election-honig/index.html.

42  ibid.

43  A., Andrea. "Sidney Powell Files Lawsuit vs Gretchen Whitmer, One Other for Fabrication of Ballots." HNGN, 30 Nov. 2020, www.hngn.com/articles/233317/20201129/sidney-powell-files-new-michigan-lawsuit.htm.

44  ibid.

45  Haberman, Maggie, and Alan Feuer. "Trump Team Disavows Lawyer Who Peddled Conspiracy Theories on Voting." The New York Times, The New York Times, 23 Nov. 2020, www.nytimes.com/2020/11/22/us/politics/sidney-powell-trump.html.

46  ibid.

47  Levin, Bess, and Kenzie Bryant. "Trump Fires Sidney Powell for Election Conspiracies as Though He's Not About to Claim China Paid Poll Workers to Change All the Ballots to Biden." Vanity Fair, www.vanityfair.com/news/2020/11/donald-trump-sidney-powell.

48  "Sidney Powell Accused Of Raiding Nonprofit To Pay Personal Legal Expenses." HuffPost, HuffPost, 13 May 2021, www.huffpost.com/entry/sidney-powell-raiding-defending-the-republic_n_609d7f8ae4b03e1dd387607d.

49  Lambe, J. "Sidney Powell's 'Military Intelligence Expert' Witness Was Actually an Army Mechanic Who Never Worked in Military Intelligence: Report." Law & Crime, Law & Crime, 12 Dec. 2020, lawandcrime.com/2020-election/sydney-powells-military-intelligence-expert-witness-was-actually-an-army-mechanic-who-never-worked-in-military-intelligence-report/.

50  "Sidney Powell's 'Kraken' Suits Fail in Michigan and Georgia (3)." Bloomberg Law, news.bloomberglaw.com/business-and-practice/sidney-powells-kraken-suits-fail-in-michigan-and-georgia-3.

51  ibid.

52  ibid.

53  Levy, Pema. "The Legal Assault on Democracy Is Clearly Unethical. But the Lawyers Will Probably Get Away with It." Mother Jones, 14 Dec. 2020, www.motherjones.com/2020-elections/2020/12/trump-lawyers-ethics-sanctions/.

54  UNITED STATES DISTRICT COURT SOUTHERN DIVISION TIMOTHY ... reason.com/wp-content/uploads/2020/12/King-v-Whitmer-ruling-12-7-20.pdf.

55  Zitser, Joshua. "Pro-Trump Lawyer Lin Wood Insists He Is Not Insane after Tweeting That Mike Pence Should Face Execution by Firing Squad." Business Insider, Business Insider, 2 Jan. 2021, www.businessinsider.com/pro-trump-lawyer-l-lin-wood-tweets-that-pence-executed-2021-1.

56  Pro-Trump lawyer Lin Wood insists he is not insane after tweeting that Mike Pence should face execution by firing squad (msn.com) 01 02 21

57  ibid.

58  Twitter. twitter.com/LLinWood/status/1344448775692177409?s=20.

59  Sullum, Jacob. "Treating Lin Wood's Wild Conspiracy Theories As a Psychiatric Symptom Invites Him to Play Free Speech Martyr." Reason.com, Reason, 1 Feb. 2021, reason.com/2021/01/31/treating-lin-woods-wild-conspiracy-theories-as-a-psychiatric-symptom-invites-him-to-play-free-speech-martyr/.

60  Moye, David. "Pro-Trump Lawyer Mocked For Claiming Mike Pence Guilty Of Treason." HuffPost, HuffPost, 1 Jan. 2021, www.huffpost.com/entry/l-lin-wood-pence-execution-treason_n_5fef9625c5b6fd33110de8de.

## Trump's Felons

1. Haberman, Maggie (March 21, 2017). "Roger Stone, the 'Trickster' on Trump's Side, Is Under F.B.I. Scrutiny". *The New York Times*
2. Hillyer, Quin (January 25, 2019). "The FBI's ridiculous riot gear and pre-dawn raid on Roger Stone was excessive and unnecessary". Washington Examiner.
3. Elfrink, Tim (May 26, 2017). "Roger Stone Keeps Pushing Seth Rich Conspiracy Theories Despite Family Pleas". Miami New Times.
4. Toobin, Jeffrey (June 2, 2008). "The Dirty Trickster". *The New Yorker*.
5. Duffy, Michael; Cooper, Matthew (September 20, 1999). "Take my party, please". *CNN*.
6. Tucker, Eric; Long, Colleen; Balsamo, Michael (April 28, 2020). "FBI documents reveal communication between Stone, Assange". *AP News*.
7. Harris, Andrew M.; Kocieniewski, David; Voreacos, David (January 25, 2019). "Trump Associate Roger Stone Arrested in Florida as Part of Special Counsel Probe". *Bloomberg*.
8. Lafraniere, Sharon, and Zach Montague. "Roger Stone Is Convicted of Impeding Investigators in a Bid to Protect Trump." The New York Times, The New York Times, 15 Nov. 2019, www.nytimes.com/2019/11/15/us/politics/roger-stone-trial-guilty.html.
9. Dilanian, Ken, et al. "Prosecutor Says Roger Stone Lied Because 'the Truth Looked Bad for Donald Trump'." NBCNews.com, NBCUniversal News Group, 7 Nov. 2019, www.nbcnews.com/politics/donald-trump/prosecutor-says-roger-stone-lied-under-oath-because-truth-looked-n1077641.
10. Benen, Steve. "Why Trump's Written Answers to Mueller Were Deemed 'Inadequate'." MSNBC, NBCUniversal News Group, 25 Sept. 2020, www.msnbc.com/rachel-maddow-show/why-trumps-written-answers-mueller-were-deemed-inadequate-msna1221061.
11. Mangan, Dan. "Trump Talked to Roger Stone about WikiLeaks, Rick Gates Says in Testimony Contradicting the President." CNBC, CNBC, 12 Nov. 2019, www.cnbc.com/2019/11/12/trump-had-call-with-roger-stone-about-wikileaks-rick-gates-says.html.
12. Gillette, Sam. "Former Trump Aide Convicted of Interfering in Russia Investigation, Faces Decades in Prison." PEOPLE.com, 17 Nov. 2019, people.com/politics/former-trump-aide-roger-stone-convicted-lying-wikileaks/.
13. Khalil, Ashraf. "Trial Reveals Roger Stone Quoted Nixon as He Urged Witness to Stonewall Congress." PBS, Public Broadcasting Service, 7 Nov. 2019, www.pbs.org/newshour/nation/trial-reveals-roger-stone-quoted-nixon-as-he-urged-witness-to-stonewall-congress.

14  Neidig, Harper. "Prosecutors Reveal Extensive Record of Stone's Communications." TheHill, The Hill, 7 Nov. 2019, thehill.com/regulation/court-battles/469456-prosecutors-reveal-extensive-record-of-stones-communications.

15  ibid.

16  Lafraniere, Sharon, and Zach Montague. "Roger Stone Is Convicted of Impeding Investigators in a Bid to Protect Trump." The New York Times, The New York Times, 15 Nov. 2019, www.nytimes.com/2019/11/15/us/politics/roger-stone-trial-guilty.html.

17  LaFraniere, Sharon (February 10, 2020). "Prosecutors Recommend Roger Stone Receive 7- to 9-Year Sentence". *The New York Times*. ISSN 0362-4331

18  Benner, Katie; LaFraniere, Sharon; Goldman, Adam (February 11, 2020). "Prosecutors Quit Roger Stone Case After Justice Dept. Intervenes on Sentencing". *The New York Times*.

19  Balsamo, Michael (February 11, 2020). "All 4 prosecutors in Roger Stone case quit after Justice Department says it will seek shorter prison term for Trump ally". *Chicago Tribune*.

20  "DOJ Files New Sentencing Memo in Roger Stone Case." MSNBC, NBCUniversal News Group, 26 May 2021, www.msnbc.com/mtp-daily/watch/doj-files-new-sentencing-memo-in-roger-stone-case-78577221986.

21  ibid.

22  Basu, Zachary (February 12, 2020). "Prosecutors resign from Stone case after DOJ overrules sentencing memo". *Axios*.

23  Smith, David (February 12, 2020). "Barr agrees to testify to Congress amid growing outrage over Roger Stone case". *The Guardian*. ISSN 0261-3077.

24  ibid.

25  Hsu, Spencer S.; Weiner, Rachel; Olorunnipa, Toluse (July 10, 2020). "Trump commutes sentence of confidant Roger Stone who was convicted of lying to Congress and witness tampering". *The Washington Post*.

26  Breuninger, Kevin (June 24, 2020). "Ex-Roger Stone prosecutor tells Congress of pressure from 'highest levels' to give Trump ally 'a break'". *CNBC*.

27  ibid.

28  ibid.

29  Johnson, Carrier (June 23, 2020). "Politics Influenced Justice Department In Roger Stone Case, DOJ Lawyer Tells Hill". *NPR*.

30  ibid.

31  "History of Roger Stone in Timeline - Popular Timelines." Populartimelines.com, populartimelines.com/timeline/Roger-Stone.

32  Sullivan, Eileen; Shear, Michael D. (February 12, 2020). "Trump Praises Barr for Rejecting Punishment Recommended for Stone". *The New York Times*.

33  Jarrett, Laura; Collins, Kaitlin; Polantz, Katelyn; LeBlanc, Paul (February 11, 2020). "Trump withdraws Treasury nomination of ex-US attorney who oversaw Stone prosecution". *CNN*.

34. Polantz, Katelyn (February 12, 2020). "Judge denies Roger Stone's request for a new trial". *CNN*.
35. Polantz, Katelyn (February 14, 2020). "Roger Stone makes another request for a new trial after tumultuous week". *CNN*.
36. Stahl, Jeremy (February 20, 2020). "Roger Stone Sentenced to More than Three Years for "Covering Up" for Trump". *Slate*.
37. ibid.
38. ibid.
39. ibid.
40. Johnson, Katanga (February 24, 2020). "U.S. judge rejects Roger Stone's request she be kicked off his case". *Reuters*.
41. Martin, Jeffrey (March 16, 2020). "Roger Stone's Motion for New Trial Denied, Must Report to Prison in 14 Days". *Newsweek*.
42. Dukakis, Ali (April 30, 2020). "30-day delay in Roger Stone beginning prison sentence due to COVID-19". *ABC News*.
43. Polantz, Katelyn (May 29, 2020). "Roger Stone ordered to report to prison by June 30". *CNN*.
44. Gerstein, Josh; Cheney, Kyle (June 24, 2020). "Roger Stone seeks to delay prison, citing virus concerns". *Politico*.
45. Cheney, Kyle; Gerstein, Josh (June 26, 2020). "Judge sets July 14 surrender date, immediate home confinement for Roger Stone". *Politico*.
46. McCurdy, Christen (June 27, 2020). "Federal judge delays Roger Stone's sentence by 2 weeks". United Press International.
47. Baker, Peter; Haberman, Maggie; LaFraniere, Sharon (July 10, 2020). "Trump Commutes Sentence of Roger Stone in Case He Long Denounced". *The New York Times*. ISSN 0362-4331.
48. https://nypost.com/2020/12/23/trump-pardons-paul-manafort-roger-stone-and-charles-kushner/
49. The background of both Trump and Manafort with Russian and Ukrainian oligarchs is fully discussed in the author's prior book, Treason and Betrayal.
50. "Trump's New Right-Hand Man Has History of Controversial Clients and Deals." The Guardian, Guardian News and Media, 27 Apr. 2016, www.theguardian.com/us-news/2016/apr/27/paul-manafort-donald-trump-campaign-past-clients.
51. Swan, Betsy. "Indicted Oligarch Dmytro Firtash Praises Paul Manafort, Says Trump Has Third-Grade Smarts." The Daily Beast, The Daily Beast Company, 19 Mar. 2019, www.thedailybeast.com/indicted-oligarch-dmytro-firtash-praises-paul-manafort-says-trump-has-third-grade-smarts.
52. "Spain Seeks Extradition for Ukrainian Oligarch Linked to Senior Tories." The Independent, Independent Digital News and Media, 25 Nov. 2016, www.independent.co.uk/news/uk/crime/dmitry-firtash-spain-seeks-extradition-ukrainian-oligarch-linked-senior-tories-alleged-money-laundering-a7439621.html.
53. The author is the principal attorney with this New York-based law firm.

54  Ortiz, Erik, and Marianna Sotomayor. "Paul Manafort Once Worked to 'Benefit the Putin Government': Report." NBCNews.com, NBCUniversal News Group, 22 Mar. 2017, www.nbcnews.com/politics/donald-trump/paul-manafort-once-worked-benefit-putin-government-report-n736881.

55  "Russian Oligarch Loaned $10 Million to Manafort Business, Documents Show." NBCNews.com, NBCUniversal News Group, 24 July 2018, www.nbcnews.com/news/us-news/russian-oligarch-loaned-10-million-manafort-business-documents-show-n887196.

56  McCallion, Kenneth F. "A Real Estate Empire Built on Corruption: The Trouble with Trump's Foreign-Cash Connection." Nydailynews.com, New York Daily News, 8 Apr. 2018, www.nydailynews.com/opinion/kenneth-f-mccallion-trump-real-estate-built-corruption-article-1.2856797.

57  Foer, Franklin, and Julia Loffe. "Did Manafort Use Trump to Curry Favor With a Putin Ally?" The Atlantic, Atlantic Media Company, 2 Oct. 2017, www.theatlantic.com/politics/archive/2017/10/emails-suggest-manafort-sought-approval-from-putin-ally-deripaska/541677/.

58  Schindler, John R. "Mueller Finally Unmasked the Trump Campaign's Secret Russian Operative." Observer, Observer, 2 Apr. 2018, observer.com/2018/04/russia-gru-agent-in-mueller-probe-is-konstantin-kilimnik/.

59  Saletan, William. "A New Report Adds Evidence That Trump Was a Russian Asset." Slate Magazine, Slate, 18 Mar. 2021, slate.com/news-and-politics/2021/03/trump-russian-asset-election-intelligence-community-report.html.

60  "Konstantin Kilimnik: Elusive Russian with Ties to Manafort Faces Fresh Mueller Scrutiny." The Guardian, Guardian News and Media, 9 Nov. 2018, www.theguardian.com/us-news/2018/nov/09/konstantin-kilimnik-russia-trump-manafort-mueller.

61  Tucker, Eric. "Trump Pardons Former Campaign Chairman Paul Manafort." PBS, Public Broadcasting Service, 23 Dec. 2020, www.pbs.org/newshour/politics/trump-pardons-former-campaign-chairman-paul-manafort.

62  "Publications." Publications | Intelligence Committee, www.intelligence.senate.gov/publications/report-select-committee-intelligence-united-states-senate-russian-active-measures.

63  Papenfuss, Mary. "Paul Manafort Lied To Investigators About Feeding U.S. Polling Data To Russian Spy: Court Files." HuffPost, HuffPost, 25 May 2021, www.huffpost.com/entry/paul-manafort-donald-trump-russian-spy-polling-kilimnik_n_60ac457fe-4b0a24c4f7fb62e.

64  Klar, Rebecca. "Giuliani Consulted with Manafort on Ukraine Info: Report." TheHill, The Hill, 3 Oct. 2019, thehill.com/homenews/administration/464151-giuliani-consulted-with-manafort-on-ukraine-info-report.

65  ibid.

66  Dilanian, Ken. "Manafort Convicted on 8 Counts; Mistrial Declared on 10 Other Charges." NBCNews.com, NBCUniversal News Group, 22 Aug. 2018, www.nbcnews.com/news/all/manafort-convicted-8-counts-n901231.

67  Perez, Evan. "Former Trump Campaign Chairman Paul Manafort Released from Prison." CNN, Cable News Network, 13 May 2020, www.cnn.com/2020/05/13/politics/paul-manafort-release-prison-coronavirus/index.html.

68   "Flynn Initially Failed to Disclose Russia-Linked Payments on Ethics Form." Fox News, FOX News Network, 2 Apr. 2017, www.foxnews.com/politics/flynn-initially-failed-to-disclose-russia-linked-payments-on-ethics-form.

69   ibid.

70   "Trump Says He Fired Flynn Because He Lied to Pence, FBI, Insists There's 'Nothing to Hide.'" CBS News, CBS Interactive, 3 Dec. 2017, www.cbsnews.com/news/michael-flynn-trump-fired-flynn-because-he-lied-to-fbi-pence/.

71   Swan, Betsy Woodruff, and Kyle Cheney. "Flynn Urged Russian Ambassador to Take 'Reciprocal' Actions, Transcripts Show." POLITICO, POLITICO, 29 May 2020, www.politico.com/news/2020/05/29/trump-flynn-russia-ambassador-289905.

72   ibid.

73   Prokop, Andrew, et al. "Michael Flynn Has Signed a Plea Deal with Robert Mueller. Trump Should Be Very Worried." Vox, Vox, 1 Dec. 2017, www.vox.com/2017/12/1/16706534/michael-flynn-fbi-charged-deal.

74   Pappas, Alex. "Flynn Hires Vocal Mueller Team Critic, after Mysteriously Firing Attorneys." Fox News, FOX News Network, 12 June 2019, www.foxnews.com/politics/flynn-hires-vocal-mueller-team-critic-after-mysteriously-firing-attorneys.

75   ibid.

76   Winter, Tom. "Michael Flynn Moves to Withdraw Guilty Plea after Justice Department Flips on Prison Time." NBCNews.com, NBCUniversal News Group, 15 Jan. 2020, www.nbcnews.com/politics/justice-department/michael-flynn-moves-withdraw-guilty-plea-after-doj-flips-prison-n1115761.

77   Savage, Charlie. "Court Denies Flynn's Bid to End Case and Renews Fight Over McGahn Subpoena." The New York Times, The New York Times, 31 Aug. 2020, www.nytimes.com/2020/08/31/us/politics/michael-flynn-appeals-court.html.

78   Mogensen, Jackie Flynn. "To celebrate the Fourth, Michael Flynn posts a pledge to conspiracy group QAnon". *Mother Jones*.

79   Michael Flynn calls for Trump to suspend the constitution and declare martial law to re-run election". *The Independent*. December 3, 2020. Archived from the original on December 8, 2020

80   "Trump Will 100% Be next President, Says Michael Flynn." The Independent, Independent Digital News and Media, 14 Dec. 2020, www.independent.co.uk/news/world/americas/us-election-2020/michael-flynn-trump-president-b1773087.html.

81   "Violence Flares in Washington as Far-Right Trump Supporters Clash with Counter-Protesters." The Guardian, Guardian News and Media, 13 Dec. 2020, www.theguardian.com/us-news/2020/dec/13/trump-supporters-rally-against-election-outcome-as-proud-boys-and-antifa-face-off.

82   "Heated Oval Office Meeting Included Talk of Special Counsel and Martial Law - CNN Video." CNN, Cable News Network, 19 Dec. 2020, www.cnn.com/videos/politics/2020/12/19/oval-office-meeting-trump-martial-law-powell-flynn-diamond-sot-nr-vpx.cnn.

83   "Twitter Permanently Bans Michael Flynn, Sidney Powell in QAnon Purge." Yahoo! News, Yahoo!, news.yahoo.com/twitter-permanently-bans-michael-flynn-215552379.html.

84. "Former Trump Campaign Official Rick Gates Pleads Guilty in Special Counsel Investigation." CBS News, CBS Interactive, 23 Feb. 2018, www.cbsnews.com/news/rick-gates-expected-to-plead-live-updates/.

85. Blake, Aaron. "Analysis | Trump's Swampiest Pardons, Ranked." The Washington Post, WP Company, 20 Jan. 2021, www.washingtonpost.com/politics/2021/01/20/trumps-swampiest-pardons-ranked/.

86. Winter, Tom, et al. "Ex-Trump Adviser George Papadopoulos Pleads Guilty in Mueller's Russia Probe." NBCNews.com, NBCUniversal News Group, 31 Oct. 2017, www.nbcnews.com/news/us-news/trump-campaign-adviser-george-papadopoulos-pleads-guilty-lying-n815596.

87. Weiner, Rachel. "George Nader Sentenced to 10 Years in Prison for Child Sex Charges." The Washington Post, WP Company, 26 June 2020, www.washingtonpost.com/local/legal-issues/george-nader-sentenced-to-10-years-in-prison-for-child-sex-charges/2020/06/26/d8b2c2e4-b6f7-11ea-a8da-693df3d7674a_story.html.

88. ibid.

89. Singman, Brooke, and Jake Gibson. "Alex Van Der Zwaan Sentenced to 30 Days in Prison for Lying to Federal Investigators in Special Counsel Probe." Fox News, FOX News Network, 16 May 2018, www.foxnews.com/politics/alex-van-der-zwaan-sentenced-to-30-days-in-prison-for-lying-to-federal-investigators-in-special-counsel-probe.

90. Samuels, Brett. "Michael Cohen Pleads Guilty to Eight Counts." TheHill, 21 Aug. 2018, thehill.com/regulation/administration/402906-cohen-pleads-guilty-to-federal-charges.

91. "Michael Cohen Pleads Guilty, Says He Coordinated Hush Money with Trump to Influence Election." Los Angeles Times, Los Angeles Times, 22 Aug. 2018, www.latimes.com/politics/la-na-pol-cohen-plea-deal-20180821-story.html.

92. Solis, Marie. "Did the FBI Seize Michael Cohen's Taped Conversations with the President? Trump's Inner Circle Worries Yes: Report." Newsweek, Newsweek, 13 Apr. 2018, www.newsweek.com/michael-cohen-tapes-trump-fbi-885181.

93. Dowd, Katie. "Are These the Checks Donald Trump Gave Michael Cohen for the Stormy Daniels Payment?" SFGATE, San Francisco Chronicle, 27 Feb. 2019, www.sfgate.com/politics/article/cohen-testimony-campaign-finance-violation-check-13649011.php.

94. Sciutto, Jim, et al. "Cohen Claims Trump Knew in Advance of 2016 Trump Tower Meeting | CNN Politics." CNN, Cable News Network, 27 July 2018, www.cnn.com/2018/07/26/politics/michael-cohen-donald-trump-june-2016-meeting-knowledge/index.html.

## Trump's Corporate Boosters

1. McCausland, Phil, and Anna Schecter. "Cambridge Analytica Harvested Data from Millions of Unsuspecting Facebook Users." NBCNews.com, NBCUniversal News Group, 20 Mar. 2018, www.nbcnews.com/news/us-news/cambridge-analytica-harvested-data-millions-unsuspecting-facebook-users-n857591.

2. Lapowsky, Issie. "What Did Cambridge Analytica Really Do for Trump's Campaign?" Wired, Conde Nast, www.wired.com/story/what-did-cambridge-analytica-really-do-for-trumps-campaign/.

3. Molina, Brett. "FTC Makes It Official: Cambridge Analytica Deceived Facebook Users with Data Collection." USA Today, Gannett Satellite Information Network, 6 Dec. 2019, www.usatoday.com/story/tech/2019/12/06/facebook-ftc-cambridge-analytica-deceptive-data-collection/4356531002/.

4. "Cambridge Analytica Director 'Met Assange to Discuss US Election'." The Guardian, Guardian News and Media, 7 June 2018, www.theguardian.com/uk-news/2018/jun/06/cambridge-analytica-brittany-kaiser-julian-assange-wikileaks.

5. Sharkov, Damien. "Cambridge Analytica's Facebook Data Accessed from Russia, British Lawmaker Says." Newsweek, Newsweek, 18 July 2018, www.newsweek.com/russia-had-access-cambridge-analytica-facebook-leaks-and-might-have-used-them-1029601.

6. "To Use Trello, Please Enable JavaScript." Trello, trello.com/c/HwoIT2z8/203-what-did-cambridge-analytica-really-do-for-trumps-campaign.

7. "Cambridge Analytica Parent Firm SCL Elections Fined over Data Refusal." BBC News, BBC, 10 Jan. 2019, www.bbc.com/news/technology-46822439.

8. Resnick, Brian. "Cambridge Analytica's 'Psychographic Microtargeting': What's Bullshit and What's Legit." Vox, Vox, 23 Mar. 2018, www.vox.com/science-and-health/2018/3/23/17152564/cambridge-analytica-psychographic-microtargeting-what.

9. "PolitiFact - Trump Campaign Used Cambridge Analytica in Final Months of Campaign." @Politifact, 21 Mar. 2018, www.politifact.com/factchecks/2018/mar/21/jack-posopiec/trump-campaign-used-cambridge-analytica-final-mont/.

10. Cambridge Analytica CEO 'admits to dirty tricks'". The Week. 20 March 2018.

11. "Cambridge Analytica sends 'girls' to entrap politicians". The Times. 20 March 2018.

12. Tau, Byron; Ballhaus, Rebecca (23 May 2018). "Israeli Intelligence Company Formed Venture With Trump Campaign Firm Cambridge Analytica". *Wall Street Journal*.

13. Basu, Zachary. "Cambridge Analytica: We Ran All of Trump's Digital Campaign." Axios, 20 Mar. 2018, www.axios.com/cambridge-analytica-we-ran-all-of-trumps-digital-fa46cf30-5be6-4851-8978-e60b15681d2b.html.

14. "Fresh Cambridge Analytica Leak 'Shows Global Manipulation Is out of Control'." The Guardian, Guardian News and Media, 4 Jan. 2020, www.theguardian.com/uk-news/2020/jan/04/cambridge-analytica-data-leak-global-election-manipulation.

15. Channel 4 News investigation reveals a huge Trump campaign data leak, exposing how 3.5 million Black Americans were listed as 'Deterrence' - to try to stop them voting in 2016. #DeterringDemocracy https://t.co/wkxKfbynu6" / Twitter.

16. ibid.

17. Bowden, John. "MyPillow CEO Says Trump Was 'Chosen by God' to Run for President." TheHill, 1 Mar. 2019, thehill.com/blogs/blog-briefing-room/news/432233-mypillow-ceo-says-trump-was-chosen-by-god-to-run-for-president.

18  Karni, Annie. "Who Is Mike Lindell, One of Trump's Last Remaining Supporters from Corporate America?" The New York Times, The New York Times, 16 Jan. 2021, www.nytimes.com/2021/01/16/us/politics/mypillow-notes-lindell-trump.html.

19  Karni, Annie. "Who Is Mike Lindell, One of Trump's Last Remaining Supporters from Corporate America?" The New York Times, The New York Times, 16 Jan. 2021, www.nytimes.com/2021/01/16/us/politics/mypillow-notes-lindell-trump.html.

20  Musto, Julia. "Mike Lindell Says MyPillow Making Masks to Fight COVID-19, Calls on Other Manufacturers to Help." Fox News, FOX News Network, 27 Mar. 2020, www.foxnews.com/media/mypillow-making-masks-amid-covid-pandemic.

21  Casiano, Louis. "MyPillow Founder Mike Lindell, at White House Coronavirus Briefing, Tells People to Pray during Crisis." Fox News, FOX News Network, 30 Mar. 2020, www.foxnews.com/politics/mypillow-founder-mike-lindell-at-white-house-coronavirus-briefing-tells-people-to-pray-during-crisis.

22  Parks, Brad, and Artemis Moshtaghian. "MyPillow CEO Helped Pay for Suspected Kenosha Shooter Kyle Rittenhouse's $2M Bail, Attorney Says." ABC7 San Francisco, KGO-TV, 22 Nov. 2020, abc7news.com/kyle-rittenhouse-rittenouse-shooting-mypillow-ceo-mike-lindell/8153234/.

23  Dicker, Ron. "MyPillow Guy Mike Lindell Shouts Out Unproven COVID-19 'Cure' To Trump." HuffPost, HuffPost, 2 Oct. 2020, www.huffpost.com/entry/my-pillow-guy-mike-lindell-donald-trump-oleandrin_n_5f76ff71c5b6dd94f1e91938.

24  Ellefson, Lindsey. "Anderson Cooper Confronts My Pillow's Mike Lindell on Unproven Coronavirus Claims: 'You're Not a Scientist' (Video)." TheWrap, TheWrap, 18 Aug. 2020, www.thewrap.com/anderson-cooper-mike-lindell-coronavirus/.

25  "Carson Took Oleander Extract, Promoted by My Pillow CEO, to Treat COVID Infection." Yahoo! News, Yahoo!, news.yahoo.com/ben-carson-took-oleander-extract-promoted-by-the-my-pillow-ceo-to-treat-his-covid-19-201219623.html.

26  "Trump Says 'We'll Look at' Treating COVID with an Untested, Toxic Plant Extract Touted by MyPillow CEO." CBS News, CBS Interactive, 19 Aug. 2020, www.cbsnews.com/news/trump-oleandrin-covid-treatment-toxic-plant/.

27  Kirkpatrick, David D., and Mike McIntire. "Before the Capitol Riot, Calls for Cash and Talk of Revolution." The New York Times, The New York Times, 16 Jan. 2021, www.nytimes.com/2021/01/16/us/capitol-riot-funding.html.

28  "MyPillow CEO Brings Notes to White House Calling for 'Martial Law If Necessary'." The Independent, Independent Digital News and Media, 16 Jan. 2021, www.independent.co.uk/news/world/americas/us-election-2020/mypillow-lindell-white-house-martial-law-b1788176.html.

29  Brown, Emma, and Hannah Knowles. "Dominion Threatens MyPillow CEO Mike Lindell with Lawsuit over 'False and Conspiratorial' Claims." The Washington Post, WP Company, 19 Jan. 2021, www.washingtonpost.com/politics/2021/01/18/dominion-mike-lindell-mypillow/.

30  Corse, Alexa. "Dominion Sues MyPillow, CEO Mike Lindell Over Election Claims." The Wall Street Journal, Dow Jones & Company, 22 Feb. 2021, www.wsj.com/articles/dominion-sues-mypillow-ceo-mike-lindell-over-election-claims-11613996104.

31  ibid.

32. "Goya Foods Chief Calls Trump 'Real, Legitimate, and Still Actual President'." The US Sun, The US Sun, 28 Feb. 2021, www.the-sun.com/news/2424103/cpac-goyafoods-ceo-trump-real-president/.

33. "Goya Foods CEO Is Back to His Shenanigans after Being Censured for Spreading Election Lies." Daily Kos, www.dailykos.com/stories/2021/3/2/2018944/--Clearly-not-learned-his-lesson-Latino-groups-slam-censured-Goya-CEO-for-more-election-lies.

34. Ramirez, Sonia. "Goya Foods CEO Facing Backlash after Stating U.S. Is 'Blessed' to Have Trump." Chron, Houston Chronicle, 10 July 2020, www.chron.com/houston/article/Goya-Foods-CEO-facing-backlash-after-stating-15399525.php.

35. "Trumps Tweet Support for Goya Foods amid Boycott Campaign | Pictures." Reuters, Thomson Reuters, 16 July 2020, www.reuters.com/news/picture/trumps-tweet-support-for-goya-foods-amid-idUSKCN24G0L6.

36. "Trumps Tweet Support for Goya Foods amid Boycott Campaign | Pictures." Reuters, Thomson Reuters, 16 July 2020, www.reuters.com/news/picture/trumps-tweet-support-for-goya-foods-amid-idUSKCN24G0L6.

37. ibid.

38. ibid.

39. Salcedo, Andrea. "Goya's CEO Falsely Claims Trump Is the 'Real,' 'Legitimate' President. Critics Call for a Boycott." The Washington Post, WP Company, 1 Mar. 2021, www.washingtonpost.com/nation/2021/03/01/goya-ceo-cpac-trump-boycott/.

40. ibid.

# ABOUT THE AUTHOR

Attorney and Author Kenneth Foard McCallion is a graduate of Yale University and Fordham Law School. These two companion books - *Profiles in Courage* (and *Profiles in Cowardice*) *in the Trump Era* - are his fifth and sixth books. As a practicing attorney for several decades, he began his career as a prosecutor for the U.S. Department of Justice and the New York State Attorney General's Office, specializing in high-profile organized crime, racketeering and counter-intelligence cases. Since entering private practice, the author has specialized in international human rights, environmental law, and complex litigation. He is an Adjunct Professor at Cardozo Law School in New York City and has lectured at Fairfield University. An avid sailor, he spends as much time as possible with his family sailing the eastern seaboard. He is also the author of *Shoreham and the Rise and Fall of the Nuclear Power Industry*, *The Essential Guide to Donald Trump*, *Treason & Betrayal: The Rise and Fall of Individual*-1, and *COVID-19: The Virus That Changed America and the World*.

www.ingramcontent.com/pod-product-compliance
Lightning Source LLC
LaVergne TN
LVHW021659060526
838200LV00050B/2419